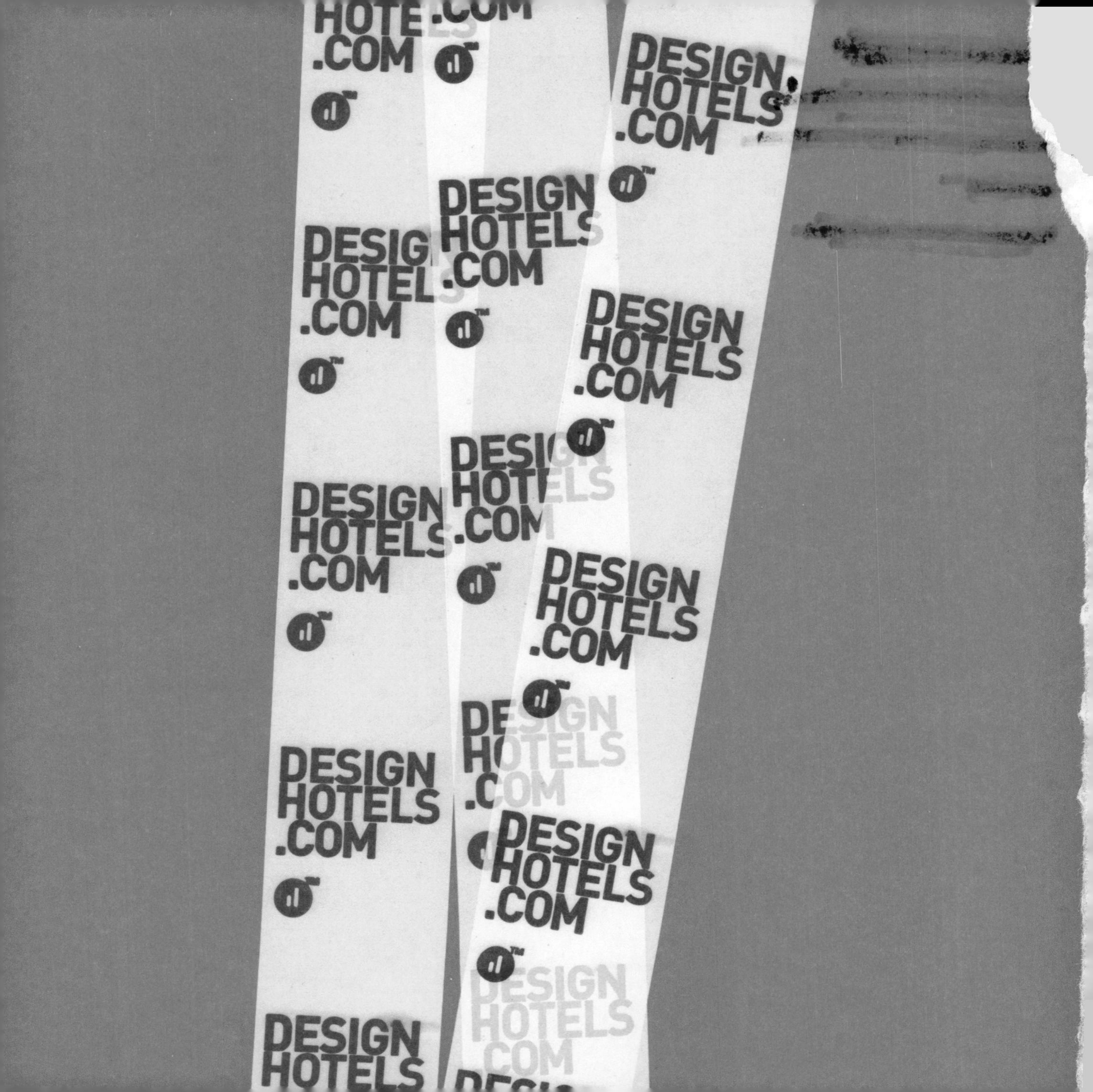
DESIGN
HOTELS
.COM

DESIGN HOTELS™ YEAR BOOK 08™

LOOKING FORWARD

In 2008, Design Hotels™ celebrates its 15th year of existence: but to celebrate we've chosen to focus on the future instead of looking back at what we've accomplished. As hotel design becomes simultaneously more specific and more diverse, we are looking ahead to what's coming over the next 15 years in an almost philosophical sense. This is why we've asked designers and hoteliers from a selection of our member hotels – each representing a different approach and from a different part of the world – to describe their thoughts and visions on future hotel design in words, images or both.

Back to the present: This year Design Hotels™ has added 38 new properties – all exemplary in some way – to our portfolio, bringing our total membership to 162 hotels in 40 countries. We are honing in on the best ideas floating in the ether, concepts that represent the kernels of new movements that will unfold into innovative environments, amenities and services that do not yet exist but are just around the corner. Heightened emotions, consciously sustainable buildings and operations, new possibilities opened up by high technology as well as individualised service and a focus on the local: all of these emphases are just the beginning of a new era in travel, the hospitality industry and the very core of hotel design.

The most successful hotels of the future will be a number of things – they will be luxurious, but perhaps not in the way we know luxury today. They will be visually inspiring, evoke emotions and perhaps even automatically interact with us. They will make our entrances and exits easy and seamless. Some of them will be just as comfortable as home, but better, because someone else is doing the work. They may very well tell a story we never knew, or offer us the opportunity to learn something. The exact attributes of most successful future hotels will vary widely, but the best will certainly combine all or a few of the above suggestions into a holistic experience for an increasingly discerning guest. What the hotel of the future will look like also depends upon how responsibly and aesthetically we develop as a global society.

The thoughts and ideas you'll see in this book's introductory section are those of the architects and designers whose work we respect and whose visions make our company the multifaceted enterprise that it is. Their philosophies are not necessarily, or not always, ours, but it is their range that helps us to become an authority in what we do – which is essentially to curate, care for and present a collection of properties (whose stunning images and descriptions follow) that you can trust embodies the visions that match yours. And those of the coming era.

Claus Sendlinger
CEO & President, Design Hotels AG

KARIM RASHID [01]
CARLOS COUTURIER [02]
BUHRO & DREHER [03]
ARMIN FISCHER [04]
PRIYA PAUL [05]
COLIN SEAH [06]
VINCENZO DE COTIIS [07]
FG STIJL [08]
RICHARD HASSELL [09]

WHERE DO WE GO FROM HERE?

Take a look around you. Perhaps you are paging through this book in the lobby of a Design Hotels™ member hotel, in a book-store for architecture and the arts, on a transcontinental flight or even at home. What objects or spaces do you see, how are they designed, how do they make you feel? Do they tell a story? Are they high-tech or natural? Environmentally friendly? Do they reflect who or where you are in any way?

Whatever they are and however you feel, your surroundings likely contain clues to the dramatic changes in design that will occur in the coming years. Some of these changes are already palpable, as buildings and objects in general – and hospitality properties in particular – are increasingly designed to be more sustainable.

These developments are more focused on the individual or the local atmosphere, are "softer" and embody a new definition of luxury that radically departs from the ostentation of the past. And these shifts are only the beginning, set to amplify and morph into true movements. Some of the movements may turn out to be on divergent paths, but all will have a relevance to and a connection with humankind's evolution.

The world that is now taking shape is much different from the unemotional, high-tech world of cyborgs and hyperspeed that cyberpunk author William Gibson por-trayed in his early 1980s novel *Neuromancer*. In many ways, in fact, things appear to be heading in the opposite direction. In his 2006 book, *A Whole New Mind*, American author Daniel Pink heralds this period as the outset of the "Conceptual Age," a time in which the industrial era's left-brained, linear and logical thinking will shift into the more abstract right-brain experience, placing more value on "high-touch, high-concept" approaches. Says Pink: "High concept involves the capacity to detect patterns and opportunities, to create artistic and emotional beauty, to craft a satisfying narrative, and to combine seemingly unrelated ideas into something new. High touch involves the ability to empathise with others, to understand the subtleties of human interaction, to find joy in one's self and elicit it in others, and to stretch beyond the quotidian in pursuit of purpose and meaning."

In commemoration of the company's 15th year, the staff for this edition of the Design Hotels™ Yearbook asked some of the most interesting and innovative designers, architects and hoteliers in the Design Hotels™ community to share their thoughts on what the upcoming 15 years will hold in terms of design, hotels, design in hotels and, of course, design hotels. As Finnish industrial designer Harri Koskinen posits, "The fundamental purpose of design is to either answer or formulate essential questions." And *Where do we go from here?* is just one of them. _«

EMOTIONAL EVOLUTION

The ability to feel and express emotion is one of our most human characteristics, and, according to more than a few of the world's top designers, the spaces we live in and objects we use are set to appeal even more to our inner states of mind in the coming years.

"Soft qualities" like empathy, understanding and compassion are steadily gaining value in Western society. Corporate marketing has long known this, with successful companies paying heed to Saatchi & Saatchi CEO Kevin Roberts's idea that there is something beyond brands. His "lovemarks" – products that command respect, passion, commitment, loyalty, sensuality and a host of other attributes that are strongly tied to the user – represent a revolution in understanding the emotional side of why people buy (and show why Apple has done so well in recent years). Design plays no small role here. As the movement's manifesto states, "A poorly designed object cannot be a lovemark".

The relevance of emotion is even entering the sciences. According to German biologist Andreas Weber, author of *Alles Fühlt* (Everything Feels), even the field of biology is about to undergo a paradigm shift, as it considers growing proof that evolution has had far more to do with an organism's emotional states than with the Darwinian idea that beings are essentially small machines that evolve only for efficiency's sake.

So – mechanism or mood? The cool, superfunctional "modern hotel" aesthetic is already falling by the wayside and is set to continue doing so. As recently as ten years ago, many would have scoffed at the idea of ambient music, programmed, indirect lighting or the soft whiff of an aromatherapy-based scent in a hotel or public space. (Or they at least preferred the ubiquitous minimalism and utter efficiency of the 1990s to such "esoteric" stimuli.) Now, however, it is far more common to engineer spaces not only to appeal to all senses and create ambience but also (or even) to generate deeper mood shifts. What is more, soon spaces not only will create well-being, but will react, and consequently interact, with the people occupying them.

Berlin-based architect Jürgen Mayer H.'s heat-sensitive chairs and chaises, which hilariously display an exact imprint of the sitter's body in a lighter colour (the material turns lightest where the body is hottest), are just the beginning, as are Dutch industrial designer Bas Kools's chairs that twist around their sitters in a kind of hug, or the popular small home appliances and kitchen tools that sport faces and feet to appear as if they have funny personalities.

"Design, stripped to its essence, can de defined as the human nature to shape and make our environment in ways without precedence in nature, to serve our needs and give meaning to our lives."

JOHN HESKETT

In the not-so-distant future, extrapolations on these technologies will create interiors that can "perceive" and personally interact with their users' states of mind – not on command but by measuring heartbeats, breathing rates or brainwave frequency, and consequently dimming or brightening the lights or infusing the air with a calming or invigorating fragrance.

And what emotions will future travellers look to experience? It could be the heady euphoria of an innovative, almost sculptural space such as Ron Arad's Duomo in Rimini, Italy (see page 290), taken to another level, or the lusty dusk of Vincenzo de Cotiis's Hotel Straf in Milan (see page 270) times ten. Says Gerard Glintmeijer of Amsterdam-based design team FG stijl: "Sometimes you go into an environment and you seem to smell things better, your glass of wine is nicer, your senses become more alive. It's about senses." Heightened, even extreme, emotions will always be desirable when people travel, for release or escape.

But the predominant mood of the future in hotel design will likely be calmer, kinder and more tactile. High touch meets high concept indeed. New interiors might represent even more of a respite from an accelerating world than they do now, dominated by an increased sensitivity and concern for our fellow man and the earth itself, along with the everlasting search for meaning.

Design scholar John Heskett claims that "design, stripped to its essence, can be defined as the human nature to shape and make our environment in ways without precedence in nature, to serve our needs and give meaning to our lives." In an age of great prosperity coupled with the world-as-we-know-it on the edge, looking for that meaning becomes more important, even if it means finding it in a kitchen appliance or a resort space whose space is perfectly in sync with both its surroundings and the feelings of the people in it. _«

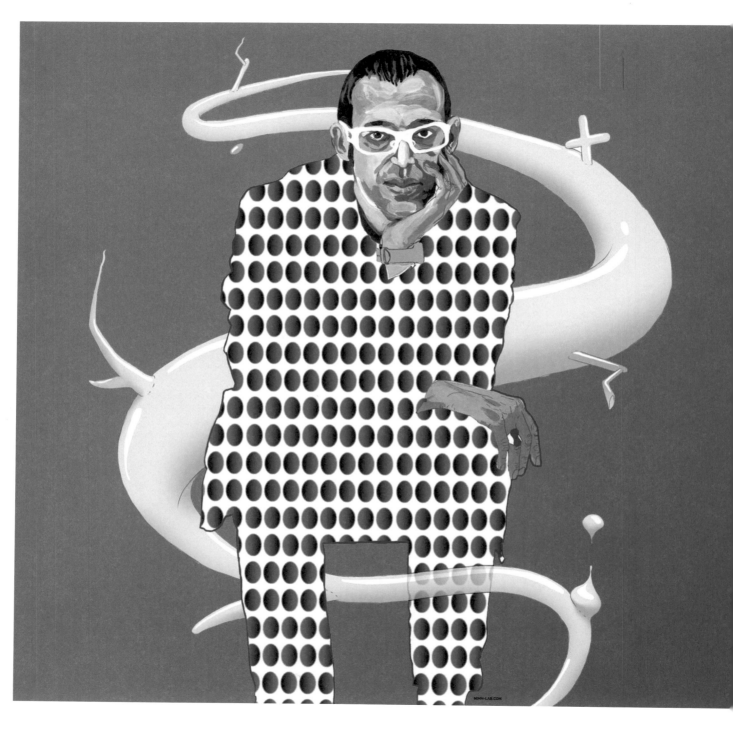

KARIM RASHID

*New York-based, Egyptian-born
Karim Rashid is one of the most prolific
and eloquent designers of the modern era.
His design oeuvre ranges from quirky small
appliances to mind-bogglingly flashy hotels, like
the Semiramis in Athens, Greece. The Semiramis
(see page 238) is a prime example of Rashid's
exuberant signature style.*

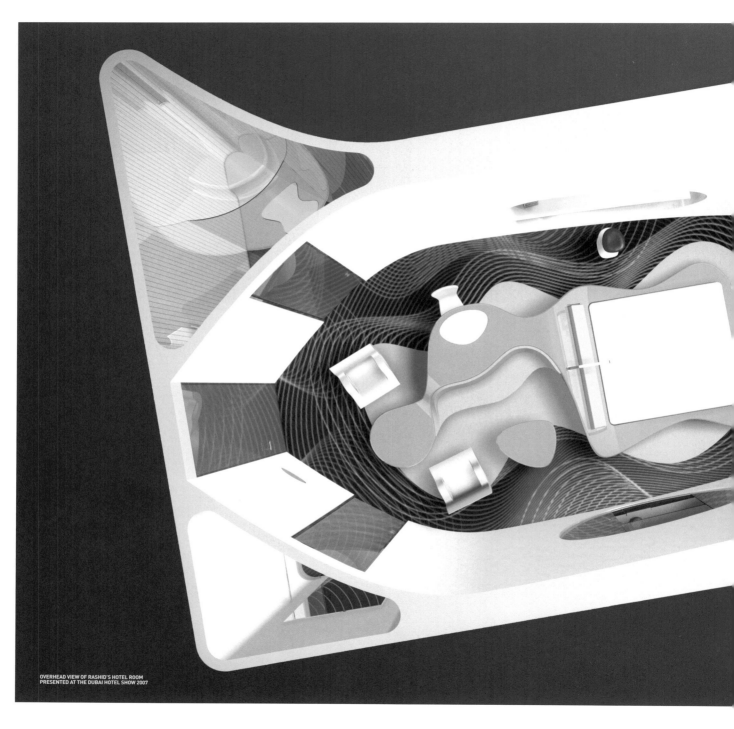

OVERHEAD VIEW OF RASHID'S HOTEL ROOM
PRESENTED AT THE DUBAI HOTEL SHOW 2007

"RIGHT NOW GROWTH IS BASED ON CAPITALISM AND ANSWERING VERY WILD DREAMS IN THE SENSE OF MEGA STRUCTURES, BUT VERY FEW HUMAN AND CULTURAL ASPECTS ARE BEING EMBRACED."

We are building amazing things in Dubai, for example: islands, shopping malls, hotels, huge buildings, indoor ski hills. But almost nothing has to do with real human interaction, and there is a lack of a contemporary aesthetic that addresses the societal and behavioural issues of this new global citizen. Twenty-three percent of the cranes in the world are in Dubai. We need to talk about the future that these cranes are shaping. We have to shape culture; design is the essence of the evolution of our society. Design shapes our present and our future. Design is not style; it is a way of life.

KARIM RASHID

CARLOS COUTURIER

*Carlos Couturier is one of the four founding members
(the others are brothers Jaime, Moises and Rafael
Micha) of Mexico's groundbreaking hotel group
Grupo Habita. The group's madly innovative
properties Condesa df, Habita, Básico, Azúcar
and La Purificadora have seismically shifted
Mexican hospitality's landscape.
(See hotels on pages 066–092.)*

NIMH-LAB.COM

MANKIND WILL BE MORE SENSIBLE AND SENSITIVE ABOUT ITS SURROUNDINGS IN THE NEXT 15 YEARS. RESPECT, TOLERANCE AND SOLIDARITY WILL INFLUENCE THE WAY OBJECTS, SPACES AND TECHNOLOGY ARE DESIGNED.

PEOPLE WILL WANT COMFORT BUT PEACE OF MIND AS WELL. WEALTH, LUXURY BUT BASIC EXPERIENCES. INDEPENDENCE. HUBS FOR SOCIAL INTERACTION. ISOLATION. THE INDEPENDENT, ISOLATED INDIVIDUAL WILL DEMAND BEAUTY. DESIGN WILL HAVE TO PROVIDE THIS BEAUTY. SEARCH FOR PERFECTION WILL RULE THE NEXT 15 YEARS.

AS LONG AS THERE IS WORLD PEACE, THE COMING 15 YEARS WILL BE THE MOST CREA-TIVE AND INNOVATIVE IN HUMAN HISTORY.

THE NARRATIVE IMPERATIVE

For centuries, most world cultures have been built around or defined by stories – tales like Homer's Odyssey, parables found in the Torah, the Bible, the Koran and other scriptures, Greek and Roman mythology, and epics like Beowulf – by means of oral tradition and the written word. Why?

Because the human brain responds far better to narrative than to a cold, hard fact. A story, a connection to history, or an explanation within a context will always be easier to understand or recall than a simple statistic or purely logical train of thought. "Story" is one of Daniel Pink's main concepts in *A Whole New Mind*, and, he says, the place in which high concept and high touch – the hallmarks of his "Conceptual Age," intersect. Pink cites the thoughts of cognitive scientist Mark Turner: "Narrative imagining – story – is the fundamental instrument of thought. Rational capacities depend on it. It is our chief means of looking into the future, of predicting, of planning and of explaining. Most of our ... thinking is organised as stories."

"You cannot change reality but you can change the eyes that see it, the nose that smells it and the hand that feels it."

LINZI COPPICK, LONDON *

The visual side to storytelling may date all the way back to cave paintings. Today, many top hotel designers already use narrative – either inherent in the hotel's context or new tales that come from the outside – to add another dimension to their creations. Exemplary properties include the New Majestic in Singapore, which is located on a Chinatown street in which Chinese men once met with their mistresses. Its design elements, such as mirrors over beds, provocative art and free-standing antique bathtubs, hearken back to this era. In Frankfurt's Goldman 25hours Hotel (see page 198), each room is designed around a local personality. The Other Side in the upper reaches of Norway (see page 326)

was built around the shape of a shamanic drum used by the region's indigenous cultures and takes its narrative cues from nature; the décor of Helsinki's Klaus K (see page 154) is based on the *Kalevala*, Finland's national epic. Although guests in such hotels might not become aware of the stories until a second or third visit, these visually transmitted narratives add depth to the property and an emotional as well as intellectual starting point.

Today's designers see the use of narrative signals and symbols being taken to a higher level in the future, with more abstraction or constantly rotating scenarios within a space. A space can blatantly express reinterpretations of old tales or tell new stories, or simply act as a backdrop for them. Surfaces can change, furnishings can be replaced or rearranged, layouts shifted to create new flows through a space, and an entirely new narrative can surprise the guest each time he or she checks in.

Perhaps a little further into the future, hotel guests will be able to create their own stories and environments in hyper-real holographic surroundings. Here, all the senses could come fully into play as they enter entire worlds, in a virtual reality that feels no different from "reality." How distant are fully sensual interactive environments like the amazing holodeck used by the space-travellers on the *Star Trek* television series? Not nearly as far away as we might think.

Such developments are perhaps a three-dimensional extension of the human need to identify with a narrative thread. "The story, from *Rumpelstiltskin* to *War and Peace*, is one of the basic tools invented by the human mind for the purpose of understanding. There have been great societies that did not use the wheel, but there have been no societies that did not use stories," explains Ursula K. Le Guin, a science-fiction

author. As the oral traditions of indigenous peoples are now being recorded for fear of their loss, an entirely visual language continues to evolve around us.

And as stories have shaped our cultures, we all have our own personal narratives. As mentioned above, given the present developments in biotechnology that can react to human systems, perhaps someday soon a hotel room will be able to not only present us with a historically or otherwise interesting narrative but also learn about each of ours, and create an interior space that reflects the many facets of who each of us really is. Or present to us with stories we had never thought of, which happen to show us a version of what each of us really wants to be. «

* Linzi Coppick has spent the past 20 years designing interiors for hotels, restaurants and retail outlets. With Keith Hobbs, she designed the interior of The Metropolitan Hotel (see page 496) in London and many other projects as part of United Designers. Now a partner in Forme UK, she carried out a solo soft refurbishment of the hotel last year.

03

BUHRO
&
DREHER

*Frankfurt-based interior design duo Delphine Buhro
and Michael Dreher – both of whom come from the
fine-art world – created the interiors for Goldman
25hours Hotel (see page 198) in Frankfurt using a
different well-known personality as the inspiration
for each room.*

NIMH-LAB.COM

How do we see hotels in 15 years? Well, the cocoon of the hotel will go in a modern direction and represent something we desire, maybe with the exterior having nothing to do with reality. But the interior will be like a pleasant home. Guests will become more isolated and need places where they can feel at home. The hotel will represent two worlds that straddle the line between freedom and what is foreign.

We also think that the hotel will represent one concept – the businessman, for example, doesn't talk about the nice bed, but he talks about the public space, the service. Public spaces will become more and more important, and the hotel will become a place where people who live in the city will go. It will be a trip at home, because resources will become scarcer and only certain people can travel, and like the components in a mobile phone, the components in a hotel will become more and more compact. Hotels will become places to which you can escape every day.

We tell stories beyond a certain standard, with a lot of details and content. In our representation, we want to say that the bird is an animal that adjusts to the environment. The pigeon is an urban creature – pigeons always find places in which they can survive. **If you want to be free, be free. If you want to feel at home, feel at home.**

04

ARMIN FISCHER

Armin Fischer is the founder and director of Augsburg, Germany-based 3meta, an interior design firm whose vision has come to fruition in private residences, restaurants, public spaces and hotels like Hamburg's 25hours Hotel (see page 208).

RAPID ASSOCIATION WITH ARMIN FISCHER

FUTURE HOTEL DESIGN: Everything will become more individual. It doesn't necessarily have to be done in local materials or have local atmosphere; it's more about personal style. At the moment some hotels and lobbies feel impersonal. One is green, the other's blue, but they are ultimately interchangeable. Hoteliers or designers will have more influence on very unique design.

INDIVIDUALITY: In some hotels, there's a fireplace room or lounge and guests can mix their own drinks and write down what they drank in a notebook. This is trust. When there's something intimate like a kitchen in a hotel, you get something personal. In hotels where there is no 24-hour service, why shouldn't there be a small kitchen? This might become more widespread.

TECHNOLOGY: Technology will disappear. It's something I don't want to be confronted with. But it was to be there and work without any problems. What I'd most like is something with two buttons for loud/quiet, dark/light.

LUXURY: I was once in a super-luxurious hotel, and we were greeted by butlers, cooks … it was like an army. It was too much for me. I think people want a simpler kind of luxury. For me, luxury is when it's quiet. When I hear the neighbours and elevator in a hotel, it's not luxury.

EMOTION: It's emotional if you make a stool out of an Afri-Cola bottle case and put a really high-quality leather cushion on it. This is something the guest has direct contact with and can touch. It has to be qualitatively good and tactile, like good bedding. It's a subliminal emotional evocation when you leave the hotel room and you don't know why you like it so much. Materials play a huge role in how you feel. Maybe in 15 years, travellers will be more discerning about what they want to touch and live in. For a certain look and feel they might pay a little more. In the end it's about quality.

SUSTAINABILITY: You have to watch out for installing fashionable stuff that's out in ten years. But some materials increasingly used within the eco-movement – stone, leather or wood – become more beautiful the older they are.
Other recyclables, like Tetra-Paks, are now being made into pressed material with which you can build furniture but, well, they're still ugly.
At some point with new technology, however, we will be able to use them. I like taking an object and making something else out of it.

"An interior designer will have to imagine himself as an actor who can play and produce every design role. The story will have to be exciting and varied; hotels will have to constantly renew themselves – It's all moving. Who wants to always watch the same film?"

ARMIN FISCHER

IT'S ALL ABOUT YOU

——

(wherever you are, whatever you bring with you)

Individual on the inside

One essential aspect of the hotel of the future will be a more highly developed response to each visitor's individuality in terms of bespoke materials, highly custom-ised services and "we already know who you are and what your preferences are."

Services such as the ultimate concierge, in-house guides leading unusual tours, personal assistants and fitness trainers already exist in the world's best hotels. But what may be the decisive factor in the future are these things along with how familiar a hotel feels to a visitor – meaning, in part, how much the property seems like ... home. Such environments can spring from both sensitive design and extremely individualised service, in which, perhaps, a guest's consumer, aesthetic and even dining preferences are known before his or her arrival, with amenities, interiors and menus adjusted accordingly.

"We would like hotels in the future to be more singular. To flee from the global aesthetic."
SANDRA TARRUELLA & ISABEL LÓPEZ *

This trend is going the other way as well, and is only set to continue, as a vanguard within the population installs what once were purely hotel-based services or acces-sories – concierges, high-tech features such as plasma-screen walls, and oversize, well-equipped bathrooms that look like hotel spas – in their homes. According to Ilse Crawford, hotel consultant and author of *Home Is Where the Heart Is*, "[People] want to combine art with living, and living with the kind of home and interiors that celebrate all aspects of their lives."

The difference is that in a hotel, the guest doesn't have to work for what he or she wants. Comfort, even in the smallest, simplest details (like the perfect pillow, measured to fit a guest's neck and head, as in the Park Hotel, Tokyo; see page 606), experiences that a guest couldn't have at home and even the opportunity to learn something new are all taken care of by someone – or something – else.

Comprehensive customised service may even shape a redefinition of what luxury is. That luxury is only about conspicuous consumption is long passé; futurologists, like the UK's The Future Laboratory, find that intangibles like time, experience, emotion and rarity are what are considered modern luxury in many sectors of society, and that these concepts will only grow in the future. According to luxury-sector experts, including Italian fashion guru Giorgio Armani, the old ideas of luxe have become too democratic and easily acces-sible to the masses. The new concepts attached to luxury, however, appeal to a sense of the rare, unique and indefinable.

That "rare" and "unique" are gaining in value might be one explanation for the current fine-arts market boom. While most people can afford to purchase a bottle of Christian Dior perfume, artworks are usually one-of-a-kind and represent an emotional connection between owner and creator ... as well as something someone else simply cannot have.

Seeing this genuine exclusivity as a state-ment, some hotels are now taking on a double role and hanging unique artworks as if corridors and lobbies were art galleries. The Chambers in both Minneapolis and New York (see pages 104 and 108, respec-tively), Iceland's 101 Hotel (see page 252) and the Condesa *df* (see page 066) have built identities in part around curated, high-concept art collections.

In 15 years, hotel guests may be able to commission their own art, fashion or one-off furnishings before checking in; or, in in-room replicators, use their own creativity to make what they like when they arrive. Perhaps properties in the future will have not only a concierge for help and a sommelier for fine wines, but also a resident artist, fashion designer or architect on call to create whatever inspiration a guest needs.

* Sandra Tarruella and Isabel López are co-creative directors of the renowned Barcelona-based firm Tarruella & López Interioristas, which has created innovative, sleek interiors for hotels like Hotel Omm (see page 366) and Grand Hotel Central (see page 356), both in Barcelona, as well as many restaurants in Spain and throughout the European continent.

Local focus

Another aspect of what is individual is the local. Globalisation has been in high gear since the early 1980s, and developments in hotel design have largely followed suit. Yet despite a pervasive homogenisation of international urban space, many in the industry see the design pendulum swinging in the other direction. Again, the clean-lined global aesthetic prevalent in hotels over the past two decades is giving way to a sensibility that incorporates tiny details that offer visitors a taste of the local culture, both visually and in other ways, before these elements disappear entirely. Examples are Kit Kemp's "modern English" interiors in London, Uma Paro's use of indigenous décor in Bhutan (see page 549) and reindeer antlers and moss insets in the Grims Grenka in Oslo (see page 328).

Local detailing is even moving beyond design into the realm of small but important reflections of local customs or behaviours. Says Colin Seah, the Singapore-based lead designer for the New Majestic Hotel and director of the Ministry of Design: "What is local might not even be in the country's history – it's more about digging your teeth into what exists and finding the zeitgeist, rather than assuming a global answer to what a hotel needs to be."

In the New Majestic, for example, the twelve top-floor rooms are arranged with connecting doors in groups of four, so guests can rent three sets of mega-large rooms. Why? "In Singapore lots of people my age love to throw parties, but most of us don't live in large apartments. Instead we book a hotel room – or two rooms. For me that's local," says Seah. "It's not about an aesthetic; it's just understanding of local habits. It trickles down to designing rooms."

Architect Chan Soo Khian's Alila Villas Lonudhua and Hadahaa in the Maldives and Tanah Lot in Bali also use local influences but give them a sustainable twist: Thatch and shingles are replaced by sloped timber trellis roofs combined with waterproof membranes underneath, providing weather and solar protection at the same time as holistically integrating and engaging architecture, landscape and interiors. "Craft, culture and climate drive the designs to embrace the essence of the destination and achieve a spiritual sense of place," says Soo Khian.

"As people focus more on themselves the hotel will have to provide authentic experiences that allow the customer to be indulgent and escape into another world. These authentic experiences could range from super elite small hotels that are highly customized to hotels that offer pared-down experiences that are almost anti-luxury. Hotels will still be spaces that mirror our homes and lifestyle but are yet an escape from the ordinary."

SIR TERENCE CONRAN

It is the combination of high-level service and the guest feeling as if his or her personal needs and indeed very personality are not only taken care of but reflected in the space's surroundings, along with a sensitivity to what makes a specific location unique, that will mark the most successful future properties. _«

*Sir Terence Conran is one of the design world's most revered figures, in terms of his activities as a restaurateur, product, textile, furniture and interior designer, founder of the interior retailer Habitat and general style guru – innovatively mixing the mid-century moderns with a contemporary vision – for 50 years. He is also a writer and heads The Conran Foundation.

05

PRIYA PAUL

Priya Paul is president of the India-based Park Hotel group, which has collaborated with Sir Terence Conran for many of their properties, including the Park Hotels Bangalore, Chennai, New Delhi and Kolkata. See pages 560-568.

HOW WILL SERVICES CHANGE IN THE HOTELS OF THE FUTURE?
I think that some bits of it are already creeping into the hotel – like customised or mood lighting, or things guests select before they arrive. But I think when people travel, they want what they have at home without having to work for it. You're outsourcing all that care, so I think certainly there will be more customisation in terms of what you can choose: your art, fun things to do, food and itineraries.

WHAT DOES THIS MEAN FOR THE HOTEL?
It's about recognising that people are individual. Customisation entails a higher staff-to-guest ratio. If you're going to be customised and create different experiences, you need more people – it's especially important in a small, intimate hotel. You can't just focus on something beautiful and let people wander aimlessly.

WHAT IS AN "AUTHENTIC EXPERIENCE"?
It means not plastic. You want to discover a place, go down deep into the layers of a city, veer off the beaten track to suss out what a place is. I think authenticity also means being in touch with the city and engaging with what is local. Guests now and in the future want to learn much more about what they're doing and where they are. The hotel is an important provider of local knowledge. The story of the city is an interesting thing: in our hotels we integrate aspects of the city, whether it's the art, or looking at design references and things like that.

DO YOU THINK HOTELS ARE BECOMING MORE LIKE HOMES AND HOMES MORE LIKE HOTELS?
If you have a 4,000-square-metre home it has to run like a hotel! You have to use hotel services to run your lifestyle if you live like that. But the lines are definitely blurring. In a hotel you want the comfort of what you have in your home, but you also want more. People look for different personalities in hotels, subject to what personality they want to project or what lifestyle they want to enjoy for that particular moment, and hotels are innovating much more in terms of design.
So in the future I think you'll have everything. While there is a backlash of people who want simple, cut and dried, others will seek to be excited every time, stimulated. I think it depends on how you're travelling and what you're travelling for.

WHAT DO YOU THINK LUXURY – OR ANTI-LUXURY – WILL MEAN IN THE FUTURE? The sky's the limit. There might be people who want to live in a cave-like atmosphere and be eco-warriors. But then, you can have caves that are well lit and fantastic – or caves that have authentic experiences of living in a cave. And quiet luxury will be at the very high end, in my opinion: smaller hotels that have a discreet luxury that's not in your face, but have the attributes of privacy.

WHAT'S THE FUTURE FOR YOU? I think in 15 years we'll be more visible in region, not just in India. We see ourselves continuing on the luxury trend and building upon our foundations.

06

COLIN SEAH

Architect and designer Colin Seah is founder and design director of the Singapore-based Ministry of Design, which was instrumental in creating the interiors for Singapore's New Majestic Hotel (see page 630), an eclectic property whose look and experience relies heavily on local influences and back-stories. The multi-award-winning Ministry's mission is to "disturb, question and redefine the fundamental elements of Space, Ritual and Perception."

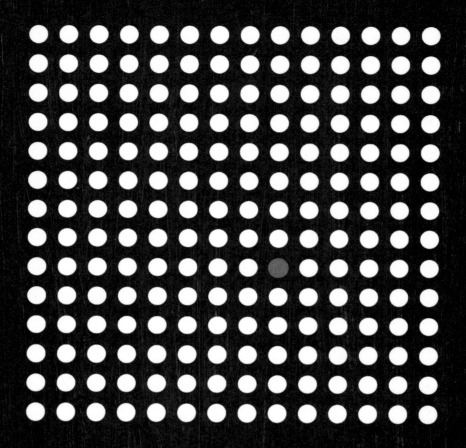

IN THE MODEL OF THE FUTURE
GLOBALISATION WILL BE REVERSED!
LOCALISATION WILL BE REVERED!

YOU WILL KNOW WHERE YOU ARE IN THE WORLD.

YOU ARE HERE

WHAT ARE YOUR THOUGHTS ON NARRATIVE?

Narrative is a valid and powerful entry point for any designer. Sometimes, with older buildings or a context you're sensitive to, you can start with a nugget of a narrative and not be exactly certain where it's going to end. In our case (with the New Majestic), it was open-ended. By going back to the drawing boards countless times, the narrative became richer and more fleshed out. I don't think one can see the end result when starting on a narrative. In this respect, the designer cannot be god – in fact, the role of the architect or designer as a godlike figure is over.

IS THE WORLD BECOMING MORE LOCAL?

There has been a disturbing convergence, like an invisible hand, in the choice of what's acceptable and what's not in every aspect of design, especially in non-Western countries. But now there's a movement against this with projects that are locally grounded and designed by local architects and designers. From my point of view, hotels are both destinations for people who are not from a certain place as well as ambassadors for the location. It's part of a need to rediscover what we're losing. And what is local might not even be in the country's history: it's about digging your teeth into what exists, finding what is local now, the zeitgeist, rather than

assuming a global and irrelevant answer to what a hotel needs to be. The scary flip side is that the desire to preserve something local can be taken to the level of kitsch, almost parody. Most of us live in cities in which modernisation is erasing much of the past, but if a building or design tries to conserve what used to be there without any sensitivity, it becomes a lifeless and banal memorial as opposed to a vibrant piece of conservation. The more sophisticated traveller will be able to tell the difference.

WHAT MIGHT BE THE BIGGEST SHIFTS IN HOTEL DESIGN IN THE NEXT 15 YEARS?

The use of the world's limited resources will impact the way we think about things dramatically. Certain issues will be global, but how we respond to them on a local level will be different in every corner of the world. And anything that has an impact on the economy will impact design. The future of hotels is very much attached to how the economy rises and falls.

WHAT DO THE DOTS ON YOUR DESIGN SIGNIFY?

I'm quite inspired by the dot that you find on any generic map: "You are here". Here, the dot takes on a three-dimensional quality, you see the red dot and you know where you are in the world. Any given dot will, however, be very different from the dot beside it.

07

VINCENZO DE COTIIS

Vincenzo de Cotiis is not only an architect but a
multifaceted designer (he does products, interiors
and even a unique line of fa shion) with a deconst-
ructivist, very material-focussed aesthetic.
The Milan-based artist created the industrial
interiors for Hotel Straf (see page 270).

NIMH-LAB.COM

*the future for me is an attitude ...
more and more to contact with "the Art"..*

"Contact with art will grow increasingly important for architecture and design unlinked from static disciplines. The speed of artistic expression stimulates cu just an inspiring lifestyle." VINCENZO DE COTIIS

e future. For many years the "object" has become a clear artistic expression
ral creativity and links to society without contamination or restriction ...

SYNTHESIS & SUSTAINABILITY

▬▬▬

What about the places in hotel design where emotion, narrative, customisation, localisation, technology, beauty and pressing global issues intersect? Can all of these things be reconciled and synthesised? Ideally, yes. The best future hotels will likely incorporate many or all of the above points in their construction, concept and operations.

Future travellers will want to know that where they're staying has values as well as value. These clients will be savvier and better able to assemble the various pieces of the travel and hospitality puzzle than people today. But they will expect the architects, designers, hoteliers and even staff of any property to be able to do this as well.

In the next 15 years, hotel design simply for design's sake – design that becomes too complex in its self-reference, or that self-righteously ignores its context – will no longer fly. A well-designed hotel will need to not only carefully consider the many aspects of its authenticity, but also take universal issues like its resource use and carbon footprint into account, perhaps even giving back to the region it serves, and at the same time staying abreast of technological developments, like Elizabeth Redmond's POWERleap, which generates energy from nightclub dancers or sidewalk pedestrians, or even providing new, energy-efficient forms of entertainment.

Hotel designers will also need to become very good at seeing the bigger picture, and maintain a high degree of flexibility in the face of great economic, environmental and social changes. "Using resources will impact the way we think about things dramatically. And anything that has an impact on the economy will impact design," says Seah. "Certain issues will be global, but how we respond to them on a local level will be different in every corner of the world."

As alternative, more energy-conscious modes of travel are forced to develop – ships, wind-powered flight, maybe even beaming – slower-motion docks for travellers will evolve, as will the accompanying design. As definitions of abstract concepts like luxury change, the most luxurious travel experience might embrace simplicity most. Or, in a more homogeneous world, it might offer fantastic escapes that appeal entirely to experience and heightened senses.

"The future person is a global citizen, working freely to shape our planet. The hotel room embraces the global village, and emphasises that a stay is pleasurable. We should live in a soft, engaging and inspiring place." KARIM RASHID

The designers and architects of future hotels will very much have to think on their feet, responding to society's needs and requirements in a cohesive way at the same time as staying true to what it's all really for. The best in future hotel design will rely on designers' ability to synthesise information, create relationships between seemingly disparate elements, appeal to the emotional, take a multilateral approach and not be afraid to cross boundaries and come up with innovative solutions. Hopefully the results will take into deep consideration just what kind of future we're creating.

What you will see around you in 15 years, perhaps reading the 2023 edition of this book, will likely vary widely; ideally, the next evolution of hotel design will embody the high-touch, high-concept values of Pink's Conceptual Age. Where we go from here lies in the hands of ourselves as a society, our sense of responsibility and aesthetics as individuals, and the ever-evolving visions of hotel designers now and tomorrow. _«

08

FG STIJL

FG stijl is an Amsterdam-based design studio
headed by Colin Finnegan and Gerard
Glintmeijer. For the past 12 years, the duo
has created innovative interiors for shops,
offices, restaurants and hotels such as
Do & Co in Vienna (see page 126) and The
Dominican in Brussels (see page 138).

WHAT KIND OF STORIES DO YOU THINK FUTURE DESIGN WILL TELL?

That of individuality and a sense of space. We are all individuals. I like the idea of walking into a room and being able to simply say "could you change this colour to purple for me?" Technology will give us a lot of great benefits – but technology has to stay human. When you're a guest in a hotel you don't want to have to be taught to use everything!

HOW WILL TECHNOLOGY CHANGE DESIGN?

Design has to be open to technological advances. It's through computers that amazing forms of architecture are possible; with them, you can build dreams and fluid forms. It's even possible to use natural materials in a different way.

WHAT DOES THE FUTURE MEAN TO YOU, AS DESIGNERS?

You have to be flexible: to go into the future and keep the concept, but change with time. When you open a restaurant or hotel, techniques change, entertainment changes, ideas of comfort change. We always try design an interior that you can add on to – there's a degree of flexibility. In design you have to be ready for the future.

WILL PEOPLE STILL TRAVEL AT ALL?

The travel issue will be solved within 15 to 20 years – people will travel more and more. Mankind has always solved its greatest problems so far!

WHAT WILL THE WORLD LOOK LIKE THEN?

We foresee fluid cities. Like in the Middle Ages, with small alleyways and everything curving in a naturalistic way. Things were never in a straight line. The environment let people walk. The future will perhaps return to the speed of walking. We recently saw a model for an amazing Chinese city for three million people, but everything was within a 15-minute walk. Hopefully people would build new cities, anyway! We keep making the mistake of thinking we have the best, greatest ideas and tearing down parts of old cities. Or we build our greatest ideas next door to the old ones. We've made this mistake very often.

"In the next 15 years we will continue to design individual spaces for individual p
will become less uniform, and sustainability will be achieved through the use o
strength and longevity." GERARD GLINTMEIJER, FG STIJL

e. Luxury is found in bespoke service and in details. In this way the world
ity. Our visions are shaped around people, and a design concept must radiate

09

RICHARD HASSELL

Richard Hassell, along with his partner Wong
Mun Summ, leads the Singapore-based
multidisciplinary architecture firm WOHA,
which has won many awards for its innovative
design and environmental sensitivity.
The firm has completed a multitude of structures, including high-rise buildings in Bangkok
and Singapore and Alila's new properties in
Bali (see page 582) and the Maldives
(see pages 622 and 626).

SEVEN THOUGHTS ON FUTURE HOTEL DESIGN

❶ IS GREEN THE NEW BLACK?

There is a sudden scramble to appear green, taking up the lead of Hollywood celebrities following Al Gore. This question asks whether this is a real commitment and change in mindset, or just this season's attitude.

❷ WILL TRAVEL BE THE FUR OF THE NEXT DECADE?

If environmental issues become increasingly serious, as predicted, then jet travel, as a highly visible greenhouse-gas activity, may become socially unacceptable. We can expect to see picketing of airports, maybe even attacks on airlines or frequent flyers, by people frustrated with the poor progress on environmental issues.
Jet travel may move from glamorous to offensive, as happened to fur. Maybe we will see a return of low-energy travel, such as airships, or even wind-powered mega yachts in the environmental future. These slower but more glamorous forms of travel might even be more enjoyable, with no jet-lag! Maybe the journey will once again be more important than the destination.

❸ DO WE NOW VISIT INTERIORS LIKE WE USED TO TOUR COUNTRIES?

We now have design destinations that we read about, discuss and visit, just like tourists or pilgrims. Although we can run out of countries, run out of traditional cultures, and what remains is like a tired theme park, contemporary cultural attractions are endlessly renewable, fresh and authentic.
Another aspect is the way a hotel interior that you would hate in your own home can be quite fun in a hotel for one night – it's a holiday from taste, a chance to experience an alien lifestyle.

❹ IS THE RESORT URBAN OR THE CITY A RESORT?

There's a rapid cross-fertilisation between the lifestyle services offered by the city and the resort, and rapid travel has meant that we keep the same mindset and frenzied lifestyle wherever we go. But the end result seems to be an unbearable surfeit of everything we demand and are bored with wherever we go.

❺ IS DESIGN FIDDLING WHILE ROME BURNS?

The orchestra kept playing while the Titanic sank. I think everyone pretends that the big problems of the world don't exist, but they are there – poverty, environmental destruction, mass extinctions, epidemics, famine – just waiting for the right moment to overwhelm us. Meanwhile, we address the little things, and hope that our little moments of beauty or innovation have some cumulative value.

❻ IS DIFFERENCE THE NEW BRAND STANDARD?

We notice that all brands now want to be different in every way, and in this aim, they are all the same.

❼ IS MY HOME LIKE A HOTEL OR A HOTEL LIKE MY HOME?

Just as hotels try to be more simplified and residential, people are building garden bathrooms and massage tables into their homes, and signing up for more and more elaborate concierge services.

"Maybe the journey will once again be more important than the destination."

RICHARD HASSELL

Americas

Europe

Europe

Africa

Asia/Pacific

Americas

HOTEL UNIQUE

Architecture / Interior Design
Ruy Ohtake / João Armentano

→ Brazil
São Paulo

HOTEL UNIQUE → Brazil
São Paulo

→ Open
01/2003

→ Rates
USD 400 –
USD 5500

→ Rooms
95

Dark glass and a desert garden of small sandy-coloured cubes of rock, palms and agaves are the first impressions that the hotel offers. A kind of urban artwork, the sculptural modern architecture and overall originality designed by Ruy Ohtake and João Armentano certainly make the Unique one of a kind.

A prodigy of craftsmanship, the spacey, green-weathered copper that adorns the façade stretches across the building's unusual shape, which is created by a large inverted arch with circular windows. Located in the tony residential area of Jardins in São Paulo, the dazzling building rises like a gracious ocean-liner. The reception area and adjacent bar The Wall are both lit by a huge wall of transparent glass during the day and otherwise indirectly illuminated by walls of beige marble. Sharp geometric forms throughout give the spectacle an even grander sense of clarity. Dramatic 24-metre hollows and corridors in the interior define the curved design that is continued inside the rooms.

This curvilinear theme finds expression in a massive bed stitched from dozens of velvet tubes that shimmers in purple, dark blue and green and is placed right in the middle of the guestroom. A carefully choreographed spectrum of circles and squares, ellipses and sine curves flow in and out of each other, creating a design language that is softened by wooden flooring, sleek white furnishings and transparent glass tables and fittings. Unusual accessories picked up from around the globe underline the concept even further. The rooms, a blend of high-tech details and natural elements, are a study in ultra cool modernism. Furthermore, the architectural design is complemented by a futuristic concept of "aerial landscaping," – which involves filling voids and space with plants hanging from cables as opposed to being in pots on the ground or even outside. The Unique definitely makes for a singular experience in São Paolo, a unique city in its own right.

→ Address
Avenida Brigadeiro Luis Antonio
4700 – Jardim Paulista
São Paulo 01402-002
Brazil

HOTEL ST. PAUL → Canada
Montreal

→ Open
06/2001

→ Rates
USD 179 –
USD 489

→ Rooms
120

HOTEL ST. PAUL

Architecture / Interior Design
Ana Borrallo / Acanto Interiors

HOTEL ST. PAUL → Canada
Montreal

Given that this ten-storey high-rise is often described as "muscular Beaux Arts," it comes as a surprise that the Hotel St. Paul's interior is so soft and ethereal.

Located in one of Montreal's hippest quarters, the St. Paul has been attracting the attention of design and architecture aficionados since it opened in 2001. One of the city's first high-rises when it was built in 1900, the architects and designers Ana Borrallo and Acanto Interiors have chosen to blend the new with the old. Some of the majestic details that reveal the hotel's rich history, such as a massive lobby fireplace now covered in a layer of translucent alabaster, have been retained; the rest is charged with contemporary design flair. The design team was inspired by the Canadian landscape in the guestrooms, where fire, ice, earth and sky have been used as abstract metaphors. Floors featuring different colour schemes and interior characteristics complete this philosophy.

Earth rooms are solid, grounded and more tactile in their choice of colours, materials and furnishings. The sky rooms are atmospheric spaces, obviously focusing on light and air. Overall, the furnishings are understated, combining materials such as silk, stone and metal to create a comfortable setting without being too prominent. Windows on each of the hotel's nine floors of guestrooms face outwards, affording beautiful views of the skyline and Montreal's historic Old Port.

FLORIS SUITE
HOTEL

→ Curaçao
Dutch Caribbean

→ Open
08/2001

→ Rates
USD 260 –
USD 395

→ Rooms
72

FLORIS SUITE HOTEL
Architecture / Interior Design
Jan des Bouvrie

A reflection of Curaçao's unique cultural heritage, renowned Dutch designer Jan des Bouvrie's mix of Dutch colonial design with a Caribbean temperament magnificently befits the location's history as the most important of the Dutch Antilles islands.

Clean lines and open spaces combine with exotic touches and Art Deco highlights. Since opening in 2001, the Floris Suite Hotel has wooed the international clientele setting foot on this island.

Bouvrie's modern translation of classic comfort is on full display throughout the property's suites, painted in cool, subtle tones and featuring dark wood furniture. Each suite features stone floors, mahogany doors and custom-made Neo colonial furniture, including pieces from the designer's Treco/Castelijn and Young collections. Refuge from the glaring sun can be found on each room's private patio, where guests can chill out in the shade of elegantly arched roofs. The splendid tropical garden was carefully landscaped by Diana Henriquez de Fernandez and creates the perfect setting for meandering along the shady pathways to the beautifully shaped pool area. The swimming pool itself is like a Caribbean version of a Roman bath, comprised of several interconnecting squares of Bisazza glass mosaics in various colours. If you are after the kind of refreshing experience only the open sea can offer, then head to the hotel's private beach, which, incidentally, is also one of the most sought-after on Curaçao.

→ **Address**
Piscadera Bay
Curaçao
Dutch Caribbean

LALUNA

→ Grenada
West Indies

→ Open
2000

→ Rates
USD 360 –
USD 990

→ Rooms
16

LALUNA

Architecture / Interior Design
Gabriella Giuntoli / Carmelina Santoro

Trickling down a picturesque hillside of Grenada, Laluna stirs a tasty melange of Caribbean, Balinese and Italian design elements to create a smart and utterly tropical hotel overlooking Portici Beach.

Designer Gabriella Giuntoli, who built villas for Giorgio Armani and Sting, has teamed with Carmelina Santoro to create a masterpiece on ten acres of untouched land in the West Indies. The bougainvillea-filled grounds of the Laluna begin at the end of a narrow dirt road and offer a westward panorama of the turquoise bay. For the look of the 16 traditionally thatched-roof cottages, Giuntoli and Santoro opted for a contrast of walls painted in bold primary colours and warm natural tones to create an intimate, luxurious Caribbean setting. An artful fusion of Asian elements, such as Vietnamese thatch and Indonesian teak furniture, is paired with West Indian details, including carved coconut shells and paintings by world-renowned 80-year-old Grenada artist Canute Calliste.

Inside the cottages, the design team has gone for a West Indian take on "concrete chic" with dappled amber, mauve and russet walls, built-in counters and couches, and swirling floor designs covered by simple straw rugs. Teak furnishings on polished concrete floors, simple baseline lamps and generous, handcrafted Balinese four-poster beds swathed in white fabric and piled with soft pillows add to the creation of a clean yet utterly relaxed setting. Seating areas are painted in spicy colours of cinnamon, sienna and yellow, which contrast with the surrounding landscape's natural blues and greens. As the sun sets, you can relax on plush silk-covered daybeds on the deck and watch the silver moon rising in the cobalt sky, which is how Laluna got its name.

→ **Address**
P.O. Box 1500
Morne Rouge, Grenada
West Indies

ROCKHOUSE
HOTEL

→ Jamaica
Negril

→ Open
11/1994

→ Rates
USD 95 –
USD 395

→ Rooms
35

ROCKHOUSE HOTEL
Architecture / Interior Design
Jean-Henri Morin / Cornerstone Design

The hexagonal bungalows hovering over deep turquoise Caribbean waters along Jamaica's volcanic coastline give the Rockhouse Hotel a look and feel straight out of a Robinson Crusoe fantasy.

Topped with thatched roofs and made of local timber and cut stone, the bungalows act as the centrepiece of this island getaway on the sunset-rich tip of Jamaica. In planning the hotel's layout and design, Australia-based architect Jean-Henri Morin aimed for the same seamless transition between the forces of nature and man's existence as that beautifully exemplified by life in African villages. The bar and restaurant are the meeting point of Morin's "village" and offer an exquisite dining area on a deck suspended above Pristine Cove. A stunning infinity pool set in a modern take on a rock garden – along with a new temple-like spa pavilion – perfects this back-to-nature experience.

The Rockhouse's design concept borrows extensively from its surroundings, with clear references made to the sea and abundant nature – including the boat-shaped terraces on the edge of the cliff, which might have been the inspiration for the hotel's name. In addition to the cosy bungalows and generous villas, the hotel also features studios, which all have distinctly Caribbean breezy linen curtains and nostalgic yet highly functional overhead ceiling fans. The simple lines and nautical forms of the custom-made furniture constructed of local wood are further evidence that Morin's design is in tune with its environment.

→ **Address**
West End Road
Negril
Jamaica

ROCKHOUSE
HOTEL

→ Jamaica
Negril

CONDESA DF

→ **Mexico**
Mexico City

→ **Open**
01/2005

→ **Rates**
USD 165 –
USD 395

→ **Rooms**
40

→ **Address**
Avenida Veracruz 102
Mexico City, DF 06700
Mexico

CONDESA DF

Architecture / Interior Design
Javier Sánchez / India Mahdavi

CONDESA DF   → **Mexico**
Mexico City

CONDESA DF → **Mexico**
Mexico City

Tucked between historic façades on a tree-lined road, the Condesa *df* hotel fuses the name and spirit of its bohemian surroundings with architect Javier Sánchez and interior design guru India Mahdavi's inventive, playful simplicity.

From rooms to rooftop, the hotel's 1928 French Neoclassical building encompasses functional originality and incorporates local elements like custom-made furniture and stone tile flooring. Its most prominent interior characteristic is the inner courtyard – for Sánchez, the most important part of the hotel: "The patio is where people can see and be seen," he says. Indeed, its restaurant has become one of Mexico City's prime locations for people-watching.

The remainder of the hotel is imbued with Mahdavi's fluid modernity. Her idea was to re-interpret the work of Mexican architect Luis Barragán and design tranquil lodgings in the style of monks' rooms, some of which open onto the patio. Forty airy bedrooms in moss green, cream and chocolate brown tones are spiced up with retro lamps and indigenous touches such as hand-woven rugs; suites open to a wooden terrace amidst treetops, standing in mild contrast to the pure white of the shutters, walls and curtains. In the charmingly titled Myself area, a hammam, wet areas and a gym invite guests to indulge in relaxation. A floral theme persists throughout the property, from the cushion covers down to the chopstick wrappers accompanying sushi served at the rooftop La Terazza bar, which affords views over the adjacent Parque de España and the Castillo de Chapultepec. The basement bar features weightless furniture design and the ground-floor El Patio restaurant promotes a constant flux between in- and outdoors. Simple and glamorous, Condesa *df* welcomes guests to a perfect representation of the city's new hip culture.

HABITA

→ Mexico
Mexico City

→ Open
10/2000

→ Rates
USD 205 –
USD 325

→ Rooms
36

HABITA

Architecture / Interior Design
TEN Arquitectos / Enrique Norten, Bernardo Gómez-Pimienta

Like a cool ice cube standing on a hot street corner, Mexico City's HABITA signalled a new advent in hotel design when it opened in 2000 in one of the world's most populous cities.

Initiated by Carlos Couturier, Jaime Micha, Moisés Micha and Rafael Micha of the adventurous hotelier group Grupo Habita, the hotel broke new ground in hotel design with its modern interiors sensationally wrapped in frosted glass panels. The complete makeover of the 1950s building by Mexican architects TEN Arquitectos, led by Enrique Norten and Bernardo Gómez-Pimienta, has the effect of encapsulating the 36-room hotel in a floating glass box suspended from the façade of the five-storey structure. The glass sheath serves as an "air-filled buffer," an ingenious idea in terms of climatie and acoustics that also mediates views while providing privacy. Sandwiched between the new and old façades are the original balconies and newly designed corridors. B+B Italia furniture dots the lobby, and contemporary art is freshly served with the inclusion of a metal Jan Hendrix mural hanging in the reception area.

→ **Address**
Av. Presidente Masaryk 201
Col. Polanco C.P. 11560
Mexico City
Mexico

HABITA   → **Mexico**
            Mexico City

In line with the austerity of the exterior look, only a bed, Eames chairs and a cantilevered plane of glass serving as both desk and table occupy the space of the guestrooms. Everything else is concealed behind a polished panelled wall. This reduced aesthetic visibly expands the experience of the otherwise compact rooms. The daylight afforded by the large floor-to-ceiling glass window and door onto the balconies is aesthetically matched by Artemide's Ptolomeo and Flos' Parenthesis lamps in every room. The two sheets of glass create an out-of-this-world atmosphere in the middle of the tree-lined Polanco district – which is transformed every night into a dazzling light show for everyone outside to enjoy at the push of a button. Guests simply create the golden glow by turning on their interior lights.

BÁSICO

→ **Mexico**
Playa
del Carmen

→ **Open**
06/2003

→ **Rates**
USD 168 –
USD 238

→ **Rooms**
15

→ **Address**
Playa del Carmen
Quintana Roo, C.P. 77710
Mexico

BÁSICO

Architecture / Interior Design
Moisés Isón and José Antonio Sánchez

BÁSICO

→ **Mexico**
Playa
del Carmen

BÁSICO

→ **Mexico**
Playa
del Carmen

Located just steps from the ocean in the bustling centre of Playa del Carmen, the Básico attracts a style-savvy young crowd with 15 quirky rooms distributed over four floors. Here, traditional ideas of everyday Mexico are brought to life: References to public schools, "cantinas" and the petroleum industry permeate the property, and most aspects of Héctor Galván's design are made of recycled materials such as plumbing pipes, woods, cotton, rubber tires, plastic, glass and even latex. Made from a mixture of concrete and Caribbean sand, the building fits perfectly with the local beach atmosphere. Inside, lush plants, colourful details and rich textures remind guests of the country's popular culture.

The ground level features a 15-metre ceiling and multipurpose bar that also serves as the reception. Doorless and windowless, the entrance area's feel is that of a public market opening towards the street. The first two storeys house air-conditioned guestrooms with white concrete walls, tile floors and intentionally exposed plumbing and electrical ducts. Along with the pink neon lamps and subdued lighting, this creates an almost sexual tension, punctuated with surprises like floating beds and fun objects such as autographed footballs, magazine drawers, floating tires for swimming and even beach club passes. Each room has a tub and a large mirror in front of the bed. In the top floor's Azotea Bar and pool area, two petroleum water tanks act as pools, offering superb views of the Caribbean Sea. On steamy evenings, guests can enjoy the sea breeze, accompanied by the sounds of local DJs, in customised truck fronts that serve as cabanas with built-in mattresses.

Admittedly basic, yet speckled with popular accents to amuse and entertain, the design and architecture team behind Básico has updated Mexican nationalism and made it something for the world to enjoy.

DESEO

→ Mexico
Playa del Carmen

→ Open
10/2001

→ Rates
USD 168 –
USD 248

→ Rooms
15

DESEO

Architecture / Interior Design
Central de Arquitectura / Omelette

A glowing white two-storey structure in the mellow fishing village of Playa del Carmen, the Deseo has become one of the hottest spots on the Yucatán Peninsula.

Created by the groundbreaking Mexican Grupo Habita's four partners – Carlos Couturier, Jaime Micha, Moisés Micha and Rafael Micha – the hotel lives up to that certain charm of the Caribbean coast while creating a level of design sophistication aimed directly at the discerning international style connoisseur. Designed by the young architectural firm Central de Arquitectura, the layout creates a strong focal point on the pool and lounge area. Distinct elements with a relaxed Caribbean flavour, such as the comfortable Belize chairs around the poolside, are joined by generous, inviting daybeds made of Chechen wood and casually hung with breezy linen curtains. Horizontal slats of light wood along the arcades surrounding the inner courtyard and pool lend the Deseo a geometric clarity. These reveal their true beauty when the sun sets and the shadows create an inspiring, sultry night atmosphere.

Each of the 15 rooms and suites represents a literally and emotionally cool retreat from the heat with their ivory cream marble floors and natural colour palette designed to soothe both the eye and the mind. Using the creative directives of the Grupo Habita, the architectural mission was to create a total comfort zone – to feel cared for and to fully replenish energy reserves in luxury – without being overbearing. This is accomplished by means of deliciously cool interiors cleverly warmed up by a lighting concept that seems to prolong the sunset's glory with variable filters in shades of blue, orange and magenta. More traditional style elements, like the imposing stone entrance modelled on a Mayan temple or the mangle-wood balcony railings, manage to ground the design concept with local tastes.

→ Address
5th Ave. & 12th St.
Playa del Carmen
Quintana Roo, C.P. 77710
Mexico

LA PURIFICADORA → Mexico
Puebla

→ Open
03/2007

→ Rates
USD 145 –
USD 325

→ Rooms
26

→ **Address**
Callejón de la 10 Norte 802
Paseo San Francisco, Barrio el Alto
72000 Puebla
Mexico

LA PURIFICADORA
Architecture / Interior Design
Legorreta + Legorreta, Serrano Monjaraz Architects

LA PURIFICADORA → **Mexico**
Puebla

Located in the historic centre of Puebla, a colonial city on the road between Mexico City and Veracruz, is the new incarnation of a late 19th-century factory long used to purify water for the production of ice.

The building's tradition of purity is still the guiding leitmotif at the simple and minimalist yet modern and edgy La Purificadora. Famous for his use of bright colours, natural light and thick walls, renowned Mexican architect Ricardo Legorreta took on the project as a challenge. Limiting himself entirely to the colours of black and white, he used materials like stone from the original construction, old wood, onyx and specially fabricated floor tile in creating the hotel's public spaces, which include a roof terrace with an artist-rendered 30-metre pool as well as ground-floor patio, restaurant, library and wine cellar. Elements found by an on-site archaeologist, such as bottles and glass fragments, are also incorporated into the hotel's construction and graphic design.

Most of the hotel's 26 guestrooms – including three suites – offer spectacular views of the city, which has been named a UNESCO World Heritage Site. As would be expected from the innovative hoteliers at the Grupo Habita hotel group, La Purificadora offers travellers and locals alike a comforting yet always stimulating experience – a mix of tradition and contemporary flavour in its purest form.

LA PURIFICADORA → Mexico
Puebla

LA PURIFICADORA → **Mexico**
Puebla

AZÚCAR

→ Mexico
Veracruz

→ Open
12/2005

→ Rates
USD 120 –
USD 420

→ Rooms
20

AZÚCAR

Architecture / Interior Design

Elias Adam and Jose Robredo / Carlos Couturier

The founders of the ultrahip Mexican hotels Condesa *df* and Habita have now created the hotel Azúcar, named for the sugar cane grown in the Gulf state of Veracruz, where their latest hideaway is located. The sweet brainchild of hotelier Carlos Couturier, the resort focuses on effortless elegance and a fusion with nature. Step in and step back in time to a place of breathtaking natural beauty as you saunter through the twenty low-lying whitewashed (bungalows), each topped with a thatched roof and having a private, intimate terrace overlooking the stunning Gulf of Mexico. Just one look at the blues of sky and sea, and guests are overcome by an atmosphere that is airy, breezy and easy.

Shaped by curved walls, the spare white-on-white interiors are simple to the extreme, but possess a kind of authentic style that both hearkens to the past and fulfils the modern traveller's style demands. "I see my hotel as an ecological, organic project. It is a design hotel yet it is somehow anti-design. I wanted to recuperate a lifestyle gone by – that of my grandparents – and give guests the pleasures of simple things," says Couturier, mentioning that the chairs found in each bungalow are reproductions of those his grandparents – who came to Veracruz from France in the 1930s to grow vanilla – had at their ranch.

Other elements, some with interesting backstories, also meld a contemporary feel with oftenhandmade, local flavour. The red-cedar woodwork in the private spaces comes, in fact, from driftwood that Couturier collected from the beach with his tractor after a major flood in Veracruz in 1999. It is a quirky display of hands-on design with a new-historical twist: "I stored the wood away for years until I founded Azúcar. I decided to use much of it as supports for the beds or as beams and door frames," says the hotelier. In the bathrooms, sinks and shower doors are in the same fibreglass that local fishermen's boats are made of, giving them a translucent, modern look when the light shines through them. Each bungalow is named after a Veracruz sugar mill, and a locally made hammock stretches across every private patio, inviting guests to swing away as the Gulf breezes blow.

Public spaces are largely open-air, like the relaxing *biblioteca* (library), where guests can lounge in wicker chairs or on pink pillows under jug lamps hanging from an open thatched ceiling, or an outdoor spa that features a yoga space and a wide array of holistic spa services. Visitors can take a dip in a funky pool whose deck is bedecked with sunbleached pink beanbags, and, after exploring the nearby archaeological ruins 30 minutes to the north or the charming fishing village of San Rafael, they can dine on catch-of-the-day seafood on almost cartoon-like colourless furniture in the hotel's sugar-white restaurant.

Azúcar's simplicity offsets its luscious surroundings, but it's all a treat that keeps you coming back for more. "The hotel is about going back to basics, to one's roots," says Couturier, summing up both the hotel's attributes and its, well, tributes: it claims to be a "tribute to the sugar industry, forgotten talents; a tribute to what is ours; the smell of a humid field, the *sombrero* (Mexican hat), *huarache* (Mexican sandal), and *machete* (Mexican knife)." It is also a tribute to Celia Cruz – the Cuban salsa diva who sang a song dedicated to the sweet white stuff – and peppered many others – with the simple word *Azúcar!* It is a word that implies the exquisite energy and enthusiasm emanating from this hotel.

→ **Address**
Km 83.5 Carretera Poza Rica – Nautla
Loocalidad Montegordo Veracruz
Mexico C.P. 93588

AZÚCAR

→ **Mexico**
Veracruz

biblioteca

AZÚCAR

→ Mexico
Veracruz

| HOTEL
HEALDSBURG | → United States
Healdsburg | → Open
11/2001 | → Rates
USD 275 –
USD 820 | → Rooms
55 |

HOTEL HEALDSBURG

Architecture / Interior Design
Frost Tsuji Architects, David Baker & Associates

This three-way collaboration between California architects David Baker and Wendy Tsuji and landscape architect Andrea Cochran authentically fits into an old town square and the healthy lifestyle of California wine country.

For Baker, it was vital for the three-storey stucco building to have high ceilings and ground-floor windows in order to create an inviting presence to the hotel and as its famous Dry Creek Kitchen restaurant. Light is an important element of the overall design, flooding through French doors leading onto private balconies, under trellised walkways, or through a glass-encased, free-standing stairwell surrounded by bamboo shoots. Artfully landscaped areas embrace the garden pool and spa and

→ Address
25 Matheson Street
Healdsburg, CA 95448
United States

HOTEL
HEALDSBURG

→ United States
Healdsburg

spill onto public alleyways that cut across the well-kept grounds, over which steel and glass corridors are suspended, connecting different parts of the hotel.

Guestrooms display a bountiful mix of materials and creature comforts: teak furniture, hickory-pecan wood floors, Tibetan rugs, goose-down duvets and six-foot soaking tubs. Adding to the country-retreat feel are Adirondack chairs, the lobby's bar and fireplace and a screened-in porch. Reminiscent of an American summer camp, films are shown on the lawn under the stars. The obvious value placed on design is further underlined by the hotel's own Hand Fan Museum, which exhibits fans from around the world.

TOWNHOUSE → United States → Open → Rates → Rooms
Miami Beach 09/2000 USD 115 – 70
USD 450

TOWNHOUSE
Architecture / Interior Design
India Mahdavi

After only three days of planning on location in Miami, Paris-based architect and designer India Mahdavi knew the Townhouse simply had to reflect "sea, sex and sun." Which is precisely what it does so well.

The celebrated former art director of interior design impresario Christian Liaigre's studio emphasised both strong light and places inviting improvised social interaction in this fun, flirtatious and affordable South Beach setting. The Townhouse's rooftop terrace overlooking the infamous beach ranks among the most original in Miami, which, given the local penchant for extravagance, is definitely not a title to be sniffed at. Bronzed bodies lounge about on queen-sized waterbeds, drawing further attention by being placed under the shade of cardinal-red parasols. A giant water tower sprays a cooling mist over the terrace and even features an integrated sound system. Music plays a vital role in the hotel's overall concept and resounds in each floor's wide corridor. Taking the idea of encouraging communal spaces even one step further, the hallways are dotted with benches, comics and magazines are laid out, and even a gym machine stands ready for action.

Space is maximised in the minimalist guestrooms by Mahdavi's chosen furnishings, which represent simple volumes rather than distinct designs. An inviting L-shaped sofa even provides an impromptu spot for an extra overnight guest to stretch out on for free. Stark white-on-white furnishings are softened by puffy sky-blue scatter cushions on the beds and accentuated by playful patches of fire-engine red, such as the old-fashioned phone, which is also a nod to the building's 1939 origins and Art Deco surroundings. The effects of the sea's weathering are initially mirrored in the roughly sanded pinewoods, but then lacquered to a glossy white finish.

→ **Address**
150 20th Street
Miami Beach, FL 33139
United States

CHAMBERS
MINNEAPOLIS

→ United States
  Minneapolis

→ Open
  09/2006

→ Rates
  USD 225 –
  USD 3500

→ Rooms
  60

CHAMBERS MINNEAPOLIS

Architecture / Interior Design
The Rockwell Group

In the new Chambers, the American Midwest's Twin Cities have at last acquired their first boutique hotel – and it is one that meets the calibre of its more modern twin, Minneapolis, which often takes daring risks when it comes to creativity. The Chambers Minneapolis is near the renowned Walker Art Center, the first American museum to feature the edgy Young British Artist (YBA) movement.

New York-based architect David Rockwell has now given those artists a second home in two early 20th-century buildings, connected by a four-storey glass corridor, that have been forged into a minimalist hotel-cum-gallery. Nearly 250 original works adorn the five-storey hotel, with installations by YBA artists Damien Hirst, Gary Hume, Angus Fairhurst and Sam Taylor-Wood dominating the lobby, courtyard and rooftop lounge. This sister hotel to Rockwell's Chambers New York shares a minimalist aesthetic, signature woven-wood front doors, and Rockwell's own furniture designs, but the façade of this Chambers is wrapped with specially weathered Korten steel that gives its exterior a warm, rusty brown texture that weathers, ages and responds to Minnesota's ever-changing climate.

The driving force behind the Chambers Minneapolis is local developer, art collector and Walker Art Center board member Ralph Burnet, and the hotel's rotating exhibits showcase exemplary pieces from Burnet's own extensive art collection. To ensure that the art stays centre stage, the design is kept discreet. White walls, gleaming terrazzo floors and the occasional onyx-stained wood floor provide a perfect backdrop, while rust brown fixtures by lighting design firm L'Observatoire International artfully shape light and shadow to add drama and character to the spaces.

The 60-room hotel has 15 suites, but there are also plenty of venues for non-sleepers to enjoy. Rockwell added a penthouse level with an outdoor terrace and bar to the building, a cellar restaurant whose café and bar rest in the lobby and three meeting room areas, each with a fresh-air valve onto an interior courtyard. Super-chef

→ **Address**
901 Hennepin Avenue
Minneapolis, MN 55403
United States

Jean-Georges Vongerichten's dining menus and the artworks of stainless steel, painted aluminum, a life-sized gorilla sculpture and real dead bull's head (by Hirst, of course) demonstrate this is not meant to be a home away from home but a stimulating experience. Most unique is the incorporation of flat-screen monitors and video installation art into the hotel. In most properties simply a bland pause, the corridors are now galleries. Visitors don't have to idle outside their rooms to view the video works, however: they're available on in-room television as well.

Guestrooms are modern and minimalist, yet are lavish with detail and quality. Oversize bathrooms feature rain showers, heated floors, LCD televisions and Italian glass tiles. All suites have "rain-sky" showers – three curtains of illuminated rain – in addition to deep soaking tubs. Several of the rooms have their own private balconies, and each, of course, has its own original art. An exception to Rockwell's minimalist design is hidden inside the hotel's central staircase. Here, a vivid, five-story, graffiti arts mural winds up the stairway and depicts the four elements of earth, wind, air and water. Perhaps a fitting motif in a city whose people are notoriously open and earthy, and, as the meaning of its name – "city of lakes" – reveals, has more than 20 lakes within its boundaries.

CHAMBERS
MINNEAPOLIS

→ United States
Minneapolis

CHAMBERS

→ United States
New York

→ Open
03/2001

→ Rates
USD 425 –
USD 2000

→ Rooms
77

→ Address
15 West 56th Street
New York, NY 10019
United States

CHAMBERS
Architecture / Interior Design
The Rockwell Group

While this urban Manhattan hotel's luxury of height and spaciousness never fails to impress, the details of handicraft and original artworks are even more visually inspirational.

Seen from the pavement, the townhouse façade appears to have only five storeys, but a recessed tower rises up 14 floors, providing two suites with panoramic terrace views over Manhattan. Within the modern, soaring two-storey lobby, attention is drawn to details selected by designer/architect David Rockwell, such as latticework and the woven walnut wood that make up the entrance's extraordinary giant doors. Rockwell's stunning Town restaurant has a 24-foot ceiling, and strands of Swarovski crystal beads trim its golden panelled walls. A mezzanine over the main floor serves as an exhilarating yet relaxing place to people-watch or sip a cocktail. Rich walnut floors, a reception desk made of ebony and parchment and more than 500 original artworks throughout the hotel offer a real feast for sore eyes. A site-specific work has been created for each floor, which might be a mural or a photographic work that spans the entrance to a room and beyond. The permanent collection includes works by John Waters, Do-Ho Suh, and Bob and Roberta Smith.

Iridescent glass tiles, cashmere throws and felt-covered ottomans are uptown luxuries, yet a downtown vibe is created through adding un-finished surfaces, canvas-covered night tables, desks made out of glass and sawhorses, and colouring pencils and paper – a thoughtful offering for those wishing to go sketching at the nearby Museum of Modern Art.

CHAMBERS   → United States
             New York

Europe

AUGARTEN HOTEL
Architecture / Interior Design
Günther Domenig and Andreas Thaler

→ Austria
Graz

AUGARTEN HOTEL → Austria
Graz

→ Open
2000

→ Rates
EUR 115 –
EUR 230

→ Rooms
56

Günther Domenig has created a unique statement for modernity with the Augarten Hotel's unusual glass and metal structure in Graz – a city of Gothic, Renaissance and Baroque architecture, which was also Europe's Cultural City in 2003.

To Domenig, good architecture is all about capacity, economy and stature. At the same time, the hotel calls Domenig the "architect of the game," meaning that here is a place in which guests are invited to play. In the guestrooms and apartments, straightforward streamlined furnishings by Cappellini and Ligne Roset are well arranged in sitting areas, workspaces and balconies or terraces and also feature original artwork. It all comes together to make space for work, contemplation and, yes, play. In one particularly remarkable example, the 21st-century, red aluminium "Rosso" desk by Austrian designer Gunter Damisch is perfectly paired with Verner Panton's 1960s cantilevered plastic chair.

No space is overlooked as a creative venue or place to exchange ideas: examples being a 24-hour bar or indoor pool ringed by rainbow-coloured "Supra sofas" that Damisch designed using high-density, high-tech foam. Vibrant works from 30 different contemporary painters and sculptors are displayed like museum pieces throughout the hotel. To soak in the sights of the old city, take a seat on the rooftop terrace where Gustav Troger's elongated figure *Jochen Rindt* contemplates the view and Marianne Maderna's abstract sculpture *Faltung 3* lengthens the hotel's general verticality.

→ **Address**
Schönaugasse 53
8010 Graz
Austria

HOTEL DANIEL → **Austria**
Graz

→ **Open**
06/2005

→ **Rates**
EUR 59 –
EUR 99

→ **Rooms**
101

HOTEL DANIEL

Architecture / Interior Design
Oliver Massabni / Studio Aisslinger

Berlin's famed Studio Aisslinger has created a fully forward-looking hotel in downtown Graz, minutes from the Old Town. Winner of many architectural prizes, including multiple red dot awards, Werner Aisslinger is the design force behind Berlin's Loftcube and other notable projects.

In the Daniel, he extends his modular vision to both the façade and the interiors. A basic recessed cube set in a grid-work pattern, the exterior plays on multiplicity with echoes of I.M. Pei and Le Corbusier's large-scale projects. Public spaces on the first floor have been designed as a loft divided into three major parts: black and green 1950s-style terrazzo floors in the entrance area are elegantly combined with Aisslinger's Flori chairs. Two bars sit on the grey plaster floor, one of which doubles as the reception in oak wood covered in a white Corian surface. A varnished teak floor in the lounge is surrounded by a grey broken natural stone wall – with an open fireplace set into it – and features a black Eames chair and an Arco lamp by Flos.

In the guestrooms, maximising space is the foremost operating principle, as is creating an enduring, non-trendy design. Multifunctional panels and surfaces create work and storage areas, with the whole forming an integrated living room rather than a collection of afterthoughts. The oak-framed bed melds seamlessly with the wall, a motif that finds itself repeated elsewhere, including the windowsill, which doubles as a desk/work surface. Felt in hues of grey and green and large coloured panels lend simplicity and elegance to the design; stone separates bed and bath areas and an abundance of oak wood emphasises comfort. A cosy feeling has been prioritised over the search for cool design, reflecting Aisslinger's desire to create projects that have lasting design appeal.

→ **Address**
Europaplatz 1
8020 Graz
Austria

WINE & SPA
RESORT
LOISIUM HOTEL

→ Austria
Langenlois

→ Open
10/2005

→ Rates
EUR 120 –
EUR 280

→ Rooms
82

WINE & SPA RESORT LOISIUM HOTEL

Architecture / Interior Design
Steven Holl / Furniture hand made by the Wittmann Carpentry Workshop

Wine may have long been an old-boy world full of hand-picked vines and châteaux owned by aristocrats, but Austria's ascent to the world wine scene has helped change all that. New techniques and architecture are making wine lovers take note and journey to Langenlois, in Kamptal Valley, 45 minutes from Vienna. And now there is an architectural spot worthy of their visual attention – the Wine & Spa Resort Loisium Hotel.

Designed by noted American architect Steven Holl, this wine-world centre is already attracting its own pilgrims, drawn not only to its spectacular look but also to its unique concept as a spa for oenophiles. From an original visitor's centre and cellar exposition, the idea evolved to this luxury hotel, based on a trinity motif consisting of the underground cellars, the ground-level centre and a "floating" hotel. The ground floor is almost entirely transparent, consisting of pillars surrounded by glass, which creates a hover-

ing, suspended effect for the building that sits above. The visitor's centre is a textured metal cube. Another cube, this time in bright yellow, ushers guests to the underground labyrinth of the Nidetzky family's extensive wine cellars.

Set amidst lush vineyards, panoramic views constantly remind guests that they are in wine country. Featuring Holl's trademark interplay of space and light, the hotel's public and private spaces are dominated by a few design elements: abundant glass and lattice-work, as well as a repetition of similarly proportioned rectangular forms in windowpanes, doorframes, counters, even mirrors. Cork as a material, form and texture is woven into the hotel's space from the lighting fixtures in the restaurant dining room to the texture of the lobby staircase and concrete walls. This emphasis on cork echoes, of course, the hotel's *raison d'être* – to celebrate wine in a spa atmosphere. But it is more than that – the lobby rejoices in

→ **Address**
Loisium Allee 2
3550 Langenlois
Austria

WINE & SPA
RESORT
LOISIUM HOTEL

→ **Austria**
Langenlois

design itself in the "Kiesler Eck," a display of furnishings created for art maven Peggy Guggenheim in 1942 and available as reproductions by the modern Wittmann Carpentry Workshop. Coloured concrete in a unique hue (a combination of ochre and adobe red) sets off the greenery that surrounds the glassed-in lobby.

Past the lobby complex, guests' eyes are directed over a stone pool, lined with rocks from the local Kamp River, then over a swimming pool and to the vines themselves. The two pools interact as grounding spaces, bringing an aquatic touch to the airy architecture and reflecting the sky and surrounding landscape to bring the elements of water, earth and air together. This is a hint of the spa-emphasis that complements the offerings inside. The hotel is an Aveda Destination Spa, which means that the full array of Aveda spa treatments is available. But the hotel adds another twist, "vinotherapy," a locally influenced series of treatments involving grape and wine products.

Guestrooms follow the cork theme with cork-shaped lamps, and a map of the underground cellars is the basis of a motif that appears throughout the hotel, including on textiles – an innovative way of running the same design through several levels of décor and furnishings. Rooms are airy, with large windows directly overlooking the vineyards; furniture is largely by Steven Holl and done exclusively for the hotel. Dark wood abounds to set off the open feeling, and the bathrooms are a series of light, mirrored spaces crisscrossed by latticework, all laid out in a functional, modern style.

The great effort that the Nidetzky family poured into the Loisium has already paid off: the resort won the Austrian National Prize for Culture and Tourism in 2006 in recognition both of the innovation displayed and the respect for existing structures. The vaults themselves date back 900 years; after all, the Loisium is but the tip of the iceberg. *In vino veritas,* indeed.

DAS TRIEST → **Austria**
Vienna

→ **Open**
01/1996

→ **Rates**
EUR 212 –
EUR 525

→ **Rooms**
72

DAS TRIEST

Architecture / Interior Design
Peter Lorenz / Sir Terence Conran

→ **Address**
Wiedner Hauptstrasse 12
1040 Vienna
Austria

DAS TRIEST   → **Austria**
                    Vienna

One of Vienna's first design hotels was born in 1996 in an old coach station used by travellers en route to the recuperative spas in the Italian city Trieste, once part of the Austro-Hungarian Empire. Austrian architect Peter Lorenz and British interior designer Sir Terence Conran preserved parts of the original structure, combining elements of imperial elegance with sober lines. The modern architecture stands out amongst the city's mix of monumental façades and late 19th-century Art Nouveau buildings.

Cross-vaulted rooms give the building a distinctive flair, but rooms are casually broken up by Conran's solid colour blocks of reds, yellows and royal blues, be it for the carpeting or the upholstered armchairs. Great care was taken also in selecting and pairing designer pieces by a host of renowned manufacturers and designers including Conran himself, B&B Italia and Casa Milano. The interiors strike a distinctly contemporary note: every upholstered piece by the Austrian firm Wittmann is handcrafted. Conran's choice of instantly recognisable near modern classics includes Artemide light fixtures and table lamps by Philippe Starck for Flos. The clean-cut bathrooms feature stainless-steel fittings by CP Hart and charming porthole windows, which, along with railings and flag motifs in the rest of the hotel, create an emotional link to the port of Trieste.

Another highlight is one of the suites: a dining table and side chair set made of vertical steel wire rods by Warren Platner for Knoll adorns the space and is perfectly matched by the celebrated standing lamp Arco by Achille Casteglioni. Specially commissioned black-and-white photographs of Trieste and Vienna underline the nostalgic link to the hotel's former role in international travel.

DO & CO HOTEL   → **Austria**
Vienna

→ **Open**
04/2006

→ **Rates**
EUR 310 –
EUR 350

→ **Rooms**
43

DO & CO HOTEL

Architecture / Interior Design
Hans Hollein / FG Stijl

DO & CO may already be known around the globe as gastronomic genius Attila Dogudan's exclusive catering company, but, with a brilliant renovation of its stunning flagship property in the Haas Haus adjacent to Vienna's St. Stephen's Cathedral, the Viennese firm has jumped into the hotel arena with an ultrastylish splash.

Seminal Austrian architect Hans Hollein – a Pritzker prize winner and one of the true pioneers of postmodernism – has created the ultimate upgrade to a building he originally designed and has never ceased to be identified with. An architectural landmark, it has stood the test of time, but FJ Stijl has now successfully taken the interior design into the future with a sophisticated blend of high- and low-tech. Four floors of the sparkling glass and metal structure have been transformed into 44 unique cone-shaped guestrooms that offer visitors to the Austrian capital unparalleled views of the city's best-known and arguably most majestic square as well as luxurious comfort. Each is a truly extravagant living environment on two levels: rooms are based on solid,

high-quality natural materials such as teak and stone, yet offer the kind of extreme modernism one has come to expect from the likes of James Bond. Generous two-square-metre showers, private fitness equipment equal to that of the most luxurious gym and even state-of-the-art flat-screen televisions – and that's just in the bathrooms.

Sophistication is also reflected in the culinary offerings, which are given an equally sparkling setting: DO & CO Hotel's exclusive restaurants on the building's upper floors offer an opportunity to taste the secret of the caterer's success; a lounge to elegantly slouch about in while deciding on whether to go up to the roof garden and sip on something delicious while marvelling at the sights; and the aptly named "temple" – a private dining pavilion with only 12 seats. Whether dining or living in the highly prized cantilevered structure, you may feel as if you are in an elegantly revamped futuristic spaceship – both reassuringly anchored in and happily mirroring Viennese tradition.

→ **Address**
Stephansplatz 12
1010 Vienna
Austria

DO & CO HOTEL → **Austria**
Vienna

THE LEVANTE
PARLIAMENT

→ **Austria**
Vienna

→ **Open**
05/2006

→ **Rates**
EUR 200 –
EUR 550

→ **Rooms**
70

THE LEVANTE PARLIAMENT

Architecture / Interior Design

Atelier DI Michael Stepanek / August Hufnagl

THE LEVANTE
PARLIAMENT

→ Austria
Vienna

The Levante Parliament's overall design concept is based on a visual and spatial interpretation of the four natural elements: transparency and light represent fire, the natural building materials symbolise earth, the generously sized rooms with 3.3-metre ceilings stand for air, and the linear forms and flexibility represent water. A wide range of core materials, including light natural stone, glass, chrome and dark mahogany wood, were selected to communicate the relationship to nature and harmonise with the classic modern design of the building, from the clean public spaces to the sleek, comfortable guestrooms.

The original building dates back to 1911, and is a perfect example of the Modernist architecture that was initiated by the Vienna School and Bauhaus. Its main characteristics, still evident today, are an emphasis on rationalism, the elimination of ornament and the use of technological advances in materials that allow for flexibility in design.

These are also the guiding principles by which the multidisciplinary team of architects, designers and artists transformed the building into an innovative space that integrates a gallery and the hotel. Noted Viennese photographer Carl Themessl's black-and-white images of dancers from the Viennese State Opera grace the hotel's public spaces, and glass design objects by artist Ioan Nemtoi have been given 4,600 square metres of prominent exhibition space. Nemtoi was also instrumental in the hotel's design – and a restaurant-bar bearing his name pays homage to his vision with both eye-catching works of glass art and seasonally rotating multi-cultural fusion cuisine. The undefined borders between gallery and conventional hotel space have resulted in a challenging synthesis of art and contemporary design.

MAVIDA
BALANCE
HOTEL & SPA

→ Austria
Zell am See

→ Open
12/2005

→ Rates
EUR 105 –
EUR 290

→ Rooms
47

MAVIDA BALANCE
HOTEL & SPA

Architecture / Interior Design
Niki Szilagyi / Interior Architecture, Munich

Architect Niki Szilagyi designed the Mavida for a sense of flowing privacy, blending holistic architecture with largely natural materials. The hotel is conceived as a homogenous space, a balance that places the individual at the centre. Wrapped in sensual textures, this is a serious comfort zone.

The lobby, which is painted in the hotel's signature shade of orange, features sleek modern lines rather than old-fashioned grandeur. Set in the warm cosy light that the elegant Italian Flos standing lamps provide, the understated armchairs rest comfortably on the polished beige natural stone floor. An overall light look extends to the inviting brown leather seating islands that flow along one side of the lobby floor – areas that allow for discreet gatherings within the public space. Framed by structural pillars, the reception desk is situated to one side to underline the intimate, personal approach.

The 47 guestrooms are unusually large and feature an equally unusual arrangement – the Casami-lano bed is placed right in the middle of each room. Midnight-blue and burgundy textiles have been carefully chosen to complement the abstract floral pattern of scattered cushions by British textile designer Tricia Guild. Balconies extend seamlessly from floor-length windows and doors so that guests may feel centred both in the hotel and in the spectacular mountains just outside. Lusciously thick natural-fibre rugs soothe the senses even more. The interior design scheme of wood and stone has been chosen for the bathrooms as well – but real bathing pleasure is found in the state-of-the-art spa. Massive blocks of slate create a dramatic backdrop for utter relaxation. Handcrafted elm furniture set in a smooth palette of earthy tones completes the deluxe feel-good look. If you are feeling particularly invigorated and energised, then Lake Zell and the surrounding alpine region, peaking up to 9,000 feet high, both eagerly await you.

→ **Address**
Kirchenweg 11
5700 Zell am See
Austria

/ 135

MAVIDA
BALANCE
HOTEL & SPA

→ Austria
Zell am See

THE DOMINICAN → Belgium
Brussels

→ Open
11/2007

→ Rates
EUR 200 –
EUR 1250

→ Rooms
150

THE DOMINICAN
Architecture / Interior Design
Lens Ass Architects / FG stijl

Tucked behind Brussels's famous theatre and opera house Le Monnaie is a new hotel that offers a strong sense of history mixed with forward-thinking, eclectic design in the European Union's capital city.

Public spaces and rooms were carefully curated and designed by the renowned Dutch design duo FG stijl, whose members, Colin Finnegan and Gerard Glintmeijer, won the prestigious Prix-Villegiature Paris for Best Interior Design in 2005. The hotel's sweeping archways are a clear reference to a Dominican abbey that stood on this site in the 15th century; acclaimed French painter Jacques-Louis David later lived – and painted – here. The original façade has been integrated into the new construction. Guests enter the lofty, high-ceiling public spaces and their breath is taken away by the attention to detail and what the hotel has dubbed "dramatic intimacy." A stroll through the Monastery Corridor evokes an almost medieval feeling of elegance with original Belgian stone flooring, and the Grand Lounge, considered the heart of the hotel, calls to mind the spirit of old European decadence with its soaring windows and metalwork, and at the same time attracts a definitively style-conscious modern clientele with its cutting-edge design.

The 150 guestrooms and suites – each with an individual look – are situated around a quiet inner courtyard and feature a rich combination of contemporary design and luxurious textiles, offering tranquil comfort in a cloister-like setting. It's a wonderful respite from the Continent's governmental hub, and a space in which old and new Europe effortlessly meld.

→ **Address**
Rue Léopold / Leopoldstraat 9
1000 Brussels
Belgium

CARBON HOTEL → Belgium
Genk

→ Open
04/2008

→ Rates
EUR 105 –
EUR 300

→ Rooms
60

CARBON HOTEL

Architecture / Interior Design
Peter Cornoedus

The newly built Carbon Hotel and Wellness Experience is part of the vibrant rejuvenation of the commercial centre of Genk, the heart of the 19th-century Limburg coal-mining industry. The Carbon dedicates itself to life's vital element in both name and design.

The architecture office PCP developed both the building and the interiors, choosing materials based on carbon and the five basic elements – wood, fire, earth, metal and water. The façade is a succinct reference to the mining fields: jutting beyond the ground floor's wall of glass is a solid front of dark brown bricks that glisten in the sunlight. Creating another striking effect is the windows' asymmetric pattern: small square panes are recessed, while thin rectangular sections protrude as if clinging by magnetic force to the brick face. Interior walls have high-quality paints and wallpaper by Arte, which alternate matt and gloss finishes for a subtle contrast of texture and light. Attention to texture is also evident in the restaurant's black floor tiles and in the woven, black vinyl Bolon flooring in the corridors and rooms. These Swedish-designed floors allow light to play off surfaces as they both radiate warmth and absorb sound.

Whether in the lobby lounge or in each of the 60 rooms, furnishings were selected for their honest use of materials: metal tables, wooden chairs, solid trunks as occasional tables, and fragments of stone. Black-glazed, free-standing bathtubs and ceramic tiles are by Porcelanosa, and showers include rain showerheads and coloured LED lighting by Kreon. The use of indirect, coloured light in the rooms allows for easy adjustments to suit one's mood. And for the ultimate in positive mood enhancement, head to the vast (608-square-metre) spa on the top floor. Here, a spacious hammam, sauna cabins, chromotherapy and even a 204-square-metre terrace with southern exposure keep all the elements in balance.

→ **Address**
Europalaan
3600 Genk
Belgium

ALMYRA

→ **Cyprus**
Pafos

→ **Open**
06/2003

→ **Rates**
EUR 90 –
EUR 845

→ **Rooms**
158

ALMYRA

Architecture / Interior Design
Joelle Pleot

→ **Address**
Poseidonos Avenue
8042 Pafos
Cyprus

ALMYRA

→ **Cyprus**
Pafos

Impeccable craftsmanship and an aversion to trends guide the clean, terraced architecture of Cyprus's Almyra. Following a major renovation by Thanos Michaelides, the hotel has undergone an ultra-chic metamorphosis and now features a subtle kind of interior elegance inspired by the island's patron goddess of love and beauty, Aphrodite.

Banquettes and low iroko and oak wood tables face windows that afford the first glimpse of the breathtaking ocean views available throughout the hotel. Sleek modern furniture and black and white interiors have been selected by Tristan Auer and Joelle Pleot, who designed one of Karl Lagerfeld's houses, an have been vamped up by hand-assembled Byzantine chandeliers that hang in both the lobby and Mosaics restaurant. Splashes of 1970s boldness – such as white leather sofas and ottomans – are enhanced by a combination of natural and artificial lighting. Because the hotel places as much emphasis on an outstanding family experience as on good design, the concept also focuses on the practical.

All of the hotel's guestrooms and suites are generous in size, to provide ample space for families – who will most certainly also appreciate the Almyra's two freshwater pools, both built in Spanish slate. Auer and Pleot have gone for lots of natural materials as well as glass and Carrera marble to create a calming effect in the rooms. Charming details, such as room numbers engraved on the floors, are further enhanced by displayed artworks. Wide terraces covered by glowing white trellises surround the pool area and afford sweeping views of the harbour; landscaped gardens with lavender walkways surrounding the hotel complete the picture-perfect setting. Given the stunning results of the makeover, it is indeed surprising that this is Pleot's first-ever hotel project – but it has earned her and Auer oodles of industry.

HOTEL JOSEF → Czech Republic
Prague

→ Open
06/2002

→ Rates
EUR 149 –
EUR 398

→ Rooms
109

HOTEL JOSEF

Architecture / Interior Design
Eva Jiricna

In the very heart of one of Europe's most beautiful medieval cities, designer Eva Jiricna has managed to create a modern masterpiece unique to its surroundings, yet which fits into them beautifully at the same time.

The 109-room Hotel Josef in Prague's old town is a study in understatement and offers an unusually smooth transition between itself and its majestic environment – this is not merely a slick interior renovation of a centuries-old building. Jiricna, who has raised eyebrows with her innovative interior designs in London, Paris and New York, created two buildings around a peaceful landscaped courtyard that gives the hotel a clear focus and point of orientation. Invigorating contrasts abound in the hotel's public spaces: a steel and glass staircase, the reception area and bar are given a calming foundation by the limestone in the lobby.

Guestrooms are designed with the efficiency that pervades the rest of the hotel. Classy, functional elements such as the rooms' lacquered finishes are offset by warmer design influences, including relaxed limestone floors. Baleri armchairs and Philippe Starck fittings in the bathrooms are a testament to the Josef's attention to detail. All are created with the limited amount of space in mind, making the hotel a well-proportioned mix of design efficiency and luxury without forfeiting any of the creature comforts one expects.

→ **Address**
Rybná 20
110 00 Prague 1
Czech Republic

| HOTEL
SKT. PETRI | → Denmark
Copenhagen | → Open
07/2003 | → Rates
EUR 240 –
EUR 2800 | → Rooms
268 |

HOTEL SKT. PETRI

Architecture / Interior Design
Erik Møllers Tegnestue, Millimeter Arkitekter / Per Arnoldi

Given its location in the heart of Copenhagen, the Hotel Skt. Petri stands as a fine example of the very best in minimalist Scandinavian design – with a warm welcoming glow and a refreshing humorous edge.

Casually gliding up to the light-filled lobby on the escalator is the first of many quirky experiences created by local architect Erik Møllers Tegnestue at the Skt. Petri – a renovated 1930s department store designed by Wilhelm Lauritzen and named after the famous church nearby. The mezzanine reception area is filled with the clean lines and characteristic curves of functionalism, and the glamorous large rings of light hanging above seem to crown the space. Rotating art and design exhibitions add to the lobby's cosmopolitan flair. Adjoining the Bar Rouge, the Brasserie Bleue is another social hub, which features mirrors carefully placed to encourage stealing glances of unsuspecting guests sitting at other tables. Møllers Tegnestue collaborated with one of Denmark's leading visual artists, Per Arnoldi, on the colour concept. The artist selected a tricolour scheme for the public spaces: bright whites contrasting with his signature cool blues and vivid reds adorn the hotel's interiors down to the smallest accessory.

In fact, the 268-room hotel has everything that modern Scandinavian design has to offer: modern urban living comfort in a pared-down style and to-the-point functionality. Custom-made dark wood furnishings and grey and brown textiles are set against the white-washed walls hung with a selection of artworks by Arnoldi, who also designed the headboards. Cosy armchairs, standing lamps with light-coloured shades by Moooi and snug wool throws all go towards creating real comfort zones.

→ **Address**
Krystalgade 22
1172 Copenhagen
Denmark

HOTEL
SKT. PETRI

→ **Denmark**
Copenhagen

THE THREE
SISTERS HOTEL

→ Estonia
Tallinn

→ Open
10/2003

→ Rates
EUR 195 –
EUR 443

→ Rooms
23

THE THREE SISTERS HOTEL

Architecture / Interior Design
Martinus Schuurman, Külli Salum

The opportunity presented to architect Martinus Schuurman and designer Külli Salum was both thrilling and perplexing: how to turn three 14th-century buildings, each a maze of different levels and staircases, into a fluid design concept and hotel.

The answer the pair came up with has become one of the Three Sisters' greatest charms. The 23-room hotel in downtown Tallinn is an interconnecting flow of galleries, walkways and staircases. The organic nature of its design is mirrored in the materials, such as the oak and limestone floorboards, used in the buildings' refurbishment. The owners drew on traditional Estonian designs, and – in order to keep within regulations that limited the amount of chrome, glass and plastic that could be used – carpenters were commissioned to construct entire wooden staircases, window shutters and doors by hand.

In tackling the interiors, Salum, who was guided by the theory that no three sisters are truly alike, created rooms that reflect three different tastes. The bohemian whims of the youngest sister, evident in the mix of old and new and a love of photography, is offset by the classic chic of the middle sister, reflected in the antique furnishings in her seven large rooms. The eldest, and by far most contemporary of the three, is ready to entertain with livelier designs and furnishings from Casamilano and Le Corbusier. Try out one of them – or all three. If there is anything the Three Sisters guarantee, it's a new perspective gained with every single visit.

→ Address
Pikk 71/Tolli 2
10133 Tallinn
Estonia

KLAUS K → **Finland**
Helsinki

→ **Open**
11/2005

→ **Rates**
EUR 180 –
EUR 550

→ **Rooms**
137

KLAUS K

Architecture / Interior Design
SARC Architects Ltd / Stylt Trampoli

Inspired by the emotional contrasts of Finland's national epic, its nature and drama, Helsinki's Klaus K hotel arrives bearing the stamp of Finland's finest architectural and literary traditions.

The Klaus Kurki hotel, a landmark for many years, has been transformed into the Klaus K with the help of major Finnish firm SARC Architects Ltd and interior design by Stylt Trampoli. Located in the late 19th-century Rake building, the hotel brings Finland's national epic, the *Kalevala*, down to an intimate scale. The lead architects of the Klaus K, Antti-Matti Siikala and Sarlotta Narjos, have created some of Finland's foremost modern architectural projects including the Sanoma Talo and Helsinki's groundbreaking Kone Building. Their unusual concept for the three strikingly original restaurants includes one called Filmitahti, which takes Finnish movies dating back to the 1940s as its theme. Considering the unconventional works of Finnish filmmaker Aki Kaurismäki, this is as far from a nostalgic Hollywood theme with the likes of Marilyn Monroe or James Dean as you could imagine.

Each of the 137 guestrooms is given a theme illustrating the *Kalevala's* primary emotional elements of desire, passion, mysticism and envy. The Klaus K aspires to go further and "take the hotel out of the hotel". Creating an ultra-designed lifestyle experience where contrasts abound, such as the Renaissance-inspired space of the Sali ballroom and the playfully designed theme rooms and suites – the hotel delivers a luxurious experience of tradition and edgy Nordic modernity.

→ **Address**
Bulevardi 2–4
00120 Helsinki
Finland

ARTUS HOTEL → France
Paris

→ Open
03/1992

→ Rates
EUR 235 –
EUR 410

→ Rooms
27

ARTUS HOTEL

Architecture / Interior Design
Pierre Seignol

Now entirely renovated, the Artus Hotel, situated in the heart of the Saint Germain des Près neighbourhood, blends everything that lovers of Paris, art and innovation could hope to find. Here, modernity and tradition are wonderfully united in the décor's simplicity, fluidity and transparency.

The entry hall's airy, open space allows guests to catch their first glimpse of a universe that is luxurious, yet never ostentatious. Here, traditional decorative objects are preferred over faddish décor. On the wall of the grand staircase that leads to the hotel's breakfast room is a stunning enlargement of a detail of a Delacroix painting – a classic look that offers a glimpse of the painter who once lived mere steps from the hotel's location. The guestrooms – each of them unique – were conceptualised with the intention of creating a larger version of a traditional loft. Upon entering, guests unexpectedly discover lighting that unveils an authentic, unique artwork that both represents the combination of modernity and sophistication and reflects the neighbourhood's aesthetic and cultural atmosphere. The light, minimalist design is warmed by the mix of exquisite natural materials that enhance every element of the hotel: fired clay for the walls of the lower level, carved wood for the reception desk, and Murano glass, stucco or even Arabescato marble for the bright, open bathrooms.

Whether fine-art lovers or style mavens, those who choose the Artus will be warmly welcomed into a haven of ease and calm. The Artus is not just a place to sleep, but rather somewhere to truly live in the heart and soul of *la rive gauche.*

→ Address
34 Rue de Buci
75006 Paris
France

BEL AMI

→ France
Paris

→ Open
01/2000

→ Rates
EUR 270 –
EUR 750

→ Rooms
115

BEL AMI
Architecture / Interior Design
Pascal Allaman, Christian Lalande, Nathalie Battesti,
Veronique Terreaux, Michel Jouannet

A new generation of French designers has transformed an 18th-century abbey into a modern masterpiece of subtle colours and clean corners on the left bank in Paris. The Bel Ami on Rue Saint-Benoît dares to be fun and exerts an unpretentious appeal to the fashionista, while managing to create an atmosphere of pared-down luxury through its strong modern design. The hotel's colour palette aims to please without being distracting, from the inviting rich chocolate sofas in the pistachio reception area to the coffee-coloured throws in the guestrooms and suites – not to mention caramel-hued stools in the self-service espresso bar.

The fresh French interior designers Nathalie Battesti and Veronique Terreaux are known for giving boutiques, houses and apartment buildings in Paris and Tokyo their invigorating twist, but in this Parisian house of fun, the pair – supervised by architect Christian Lalande – gave equal consideration to style and comfort,

→ Address
7–11, rue Saint-Benoît
75006 Paris
France

BEL AMI

→ **France**
Paris

BEL AMI

→ **France**
Paris

hinging their design approach on a simplicity that lacks neither warmth no character. It culminates in understated elegance and artistic refinement that gently intertwines analogous themes of nature and urbanism.

In 2003, Parisian interior designer Michel Jouannet, inspired in part by Stanley Kubrick's *A Clockwork Orange*, created 23 new rooms with selected colour schemes of orange, olive green and azure blue, giving each room an air of calm and informal elegance, accompanied by simple white marble bathrooms. Making extensive use of natural materials, including black lacquered bedside tables and Wenge wood for the rooms' cupboards, the Bel Ami is a soothing backdrop to the invigorating bustle of the left bank outside.

HOTEL SEZZ → France
Paris

→ Open
05/2005

→ Rates
EUR 270 –
EUR 700

→ Rooms
27

HOTEL SEZZ

Architecture / Interior Design
Christophe Pillet

Located on a romantic 16th-arrondissement thoroughfare away from Paris's hustle, bustle and opulence is the charmingly avant-garde 27-room Hotel Sezz. Visually striking and unconventional, the hotel features a casually meticulous personal butler on hand day and night, and a breakfast room situated under a glorious glass dome.

The defining element in this haute design Mecca is space – the smallest room is 19 square metres, the largest 37 – a rare luxury in a city in which it is difficult to secure breathing room or even a parking space. Designer Christophe Pillet, a protégé of celebrated stone and chrome devotee Philippe Starck, centred the hotel's minimal aesthetic on the austere khaki-grey stones found in the Portuguese town Cascais. And as in the dazzling coastal town, relaxation is paramount here.

→ **Address**
6 Avenue Fremiet
75016 Paris
France

No intimidating concierge desk looms in the hotel's entrance – instead, two salons in muted colours wait in the lobby. The effect is elegant, low-key and more south of France than urban, although the palette of slate, blue-grey and red is strictly Parisian. Beds stand squarely in the centre of the suites, which are done in chrome and red leather – the interior-design equivalent of a Ferrari, and a two-person stone jacuzzi dominates the sleek bathroom. Furnishings are based on simple lines and exquisite accents; here, functionality is compatible with a highly evolved modern aesthetic, and reflection can be seen everywhere from the artisan-crafted faucets to the rose-petal seating nooks in the downstairs Veuve Clicquot champagne bar.

HOTEL SEZZ   → France
                 Paris

KUBE ROOMS
AND BARS

→ France
Paris

→ Open
11/2005

→ Rates
EUR 250 –
EUR 750

→ Rooms
41

KUBE ROOMS AND BARS

Architecture / Interior Design
Raymond Morel / Christiane Derory

As its name suggests, the Kube is dominated by one particular geometric form – "the most modern of shapes," according to the owners – in its interior design. The architecture and design duo Raymond Morel and Christiane Derory have given the U-shaped former townhouse, located in a quiet cul-de-sac in Paris's bubbling, traditionally working-class 18th arrondissement, a truly mind-bending revamp. In addition to, obviously, lots of cubes, the themes of coolness and transparency – which are emphasised throughout the public spaces – are offset by the warming sense of privacy and comfort that pervades the guestrooms.

The courtyard of the renovated 19th-century building features a glowing Plexiglas cube containing the necessary reception facilities in a structure reminiscent of I.M. Pei's pyramidal entrance to the Louvre. And this is just the beginning of the fun. A sashay past the almost Haussmannian façade takes guests into the cavernous lobby-restaurant-bar, which serves as the heart of the hotel. Here they will find themselves transported to a futuristic, low-lit universe of a space, complete with generously high ceilings, lots of stainless-steel gratings, floor-to-ceiling curtains and a long counter in tarnished silver to lean against as they get their wits back about them. The fantastically state-of-the-art sound system is camouflaged as red ceiling lanterns.

Cubic seats and lounge chairs accented in fur offset the black glass of the walls, which are in turn animated by a whole row of plasma-screen televisions and sprinkled with strands of red lights. Bars play a pivotal role in the hotel's concept, so you'll find designers Laurent Saksik and Jerome Foucaud's ultratrendy Ice Kube bar on the mezzanine, which sits directly above the central bar and invites you to get into the swing of things with Paris's jet set in Eero Aarnio's 1968 "Bubble Chairs" suspended in mid-air in front of the entrance. All of this despite, or perhaps because of, the bar's 22 tons of ice, subzero temperatures and vodka-only drinks menu.

Oozing a sleek iciness in its public spaces, the hotel's 31 guestrooms and 10 suites – spread around an open-air courtyard and accessible via lifts lined in florescent ponyskin – turn the heat back up with warm touches added to the arctic-geometric theme.

→ **Address**
1–5, Passage Ruelle
75018 Paris
France

Black and white faux-fur curtains give the predominantly white decor a cuddly feel whilst readily living up to the chic provided by hot-pink bean-bag chairs or the pastel-coloured furniture designed by Morel in tarnished glass. Beds are lit from beneath, creating the illusion of levitation that imparts a sense of spaciousness, clarity and calm. Spinning the crystalline look further in the bathrooms, star designer Philippe Starck's aptly named "Jelly Cubes" collection of rectangular elements sits squarely with specially made glass cube showers constructed from the high-tech material Corian. And high-tech can and does go even higher: Guestroom doors open with biometric fingerprint technology, and each room is equipped with integrated computer equipment that serves as a DVD and CD player as well as a television screen.

Despite the feeling of having walked onto the set of an achingly smart 1960s sci-fi classic film, the hotel's materials are distinctly modern, the service is surprisingly friendly and the design succeeds in breaking from any sense of conformity. Kube Rooms and Bars, an ode to the box but definitely an example of thinking far, far beyond it, is future-retro made real.

KUBE ROOMS
AND BARS

→ France
Paris

LA RÉSERVE
PARIS

→ France
Paris

→ Open
06/2007

→ Rates
EUR 1857 –
EUR 4333

→ Rooms
25

→ **Address**
10 Place du Trocadéro
75116 Paris
France

LA RÉSERVE PARIS

Architecture / Interior Design
Rémi Tessier

LA RÉSERVE
PARIS

→ France
Paris

Nestled within the Place du Trocadéro, directly across from the Eiffel Tower, La Réserve Paris is a place where comfort meets elegance, with high design results and an array of five-star services. True to its name, the hotel's 25 short- and long-term apartments shy away from outright opulence, preferring refined affluence to the cutting edge. La Réserve prides itself on soft lighting and a subdued monochromatic aesthetic – the hotel's most striking elements are smart lines and feng shui.

Interior architect Rémi Tessier is partial to noble materials such as rosewood, ebony, sycamore, stone and slate, and much of La Réserve's sleek furniture utilises natural colour palettes with contrasting shades of black and ecru. Tessier, who has collected accolades for his work designing luxury yachts, seems to have an iron grip on functional design, using space elegantly and efficiently in suites that could, because of their exceptional equilibrium, be compared to the extravagant watercrafts sailing the Mediterranean. Furnishings are sublimely modernist and feature designs by Andrée Putman, Flos and Vitra.

With the exception of the sumptuous four-poster beds and the high double windows, everything is symmetrically aligned, from the plush Flexform chairs to the twin marble sinks in the bathrooms. Nowhere will one come across a sofa or a nightstand without a mate, or a decorative accessory that is in the least bit jarring. Here, the emphasis is on privacy, and many of the 25 multilevel apartments boast private office, dining and landscaped garden areas. La Réserve offers guests the opportunity to contentedly explore classical beauty as interpreted by modern designers in the City of Lights.

LA RÉSERVE   → France
PARIS   Paris

CASADELMAR → **France**
South Corsica

→ **Open**
05/2004

→ **Rates**
EUR 350 –
EUR 3000

→ **Rooms**
34

CASADELMAR
Architecture / Interior Design
Bodin & Associés / Carole Marcellesi

Known for his large-scale museum commissions, French architect Jean François Bodin's aim in designing Casadelmar was to harmonise the property with nature. As a result, the low-lying hotel – situated on two hectares of private land on Corsica's south-eastern coast – is made entirely of red cedar wood, grey local stone and enormous windows that allow unobstructed views of the sea. Its brilliant blues, soothing sounds and salty aroma pleasantly pervade the senses and lend the hotel its name.

In the lobby, vintage glamour is suggested by the choice of old-fashioned standing metal spotlights and Frigerio chairs that are sumptuously upholstered in lipstick-red fabric. The boxed-in reception area and the canopy of cedar planks that cover Bodin's king-size beds display an unusual interpretation of the "shelter" theme, and

→ **Address**
Route de Palombaggia BP 93
20538 Porto-Vecchio Cedex
South Corsica
France

CASADELMAR   → **France**
South Corsica

classic design pieces are smattered throughout the spaces, including Le Corbusier's 1930s chaise longue in some of the suites. The 20 guestrooms have stone floors and are washed in shades of honey, straw, caramel and ivory splashed with bright red, deep blue, or rich violet textiles and furnishings.

Each also has a private cedar-wood terrace providing generous views of the bay and surroundings. Here, renowned landscape designer Jean Mus reshaped the hills and scenery, artfully placing Tuscan cypresses, Japanese pines, olive and orange trees and other typically Mediterranean plants around the hotel. Lighting by I Guzzini illuminates relaxed evening strolls across the grounds to wind down for the night in style. The overall effect is sleek, simple and a luxurious reflection of Corsica's pure beauty.

BLEIBTREU

→ Germany
Berlin

→ Open
11/2003

→ Rates
EUR 119 –
EUR 227

→ Rooms
60

BLEIBTREU

Architecture / Interior Design

Herbert J. Weinand

Named after the boutique-lined street it is on, the Bleibtreu is a place to truly feel at home in Berlin. You won't find a formal lobby when you arrive at this intimate hotel, but rather a kind of microcosm of Charlottenburg, the fashionable, well-heeled district it finds itself in.

The unassuming pavement tables of its deli and bar, a florist specialising in roses, and a mortadella terrazzo walkway all lead to an open courtyard with a soaring chestnut tree. An inconspicuous front desk at the back of the building finally confirms that this is indeed a hotel and not a residential townhouse – which in fact it once was. Literally trendsetting, the Bleibtreu opened in 1995 with the interior designed by Herbert Jacob Weinand and ecologically sound items that were exclusively handcrafted in Germany and Italy, making it quite ahead of its time. Both the Blue Bar's hand-knotted carpet and Berlin-based artist Elvira Bach's wall tapestry were manufactured in Ghent and form part of the hotel's art collection. In line with the overall concept of fitting into the surrounding environment, the serene spaces are decorated with untreated oak furnishings, virgin wool carpets, handles made from natural, semiprecious stones and environmentally friendly paints. Specially selected scents give each floor an individual aromatic note.

While muted colours provide a soothing tone in the guestrooms, the courtyard is vibrant with a 23-foot-long table glistening with deep-blue glazed ceramic mosaics. The entire staging of table and chairs on a bed of blue-glass pebbles was developed by a group of five artists including Wein and and a landscape architect. Taking the hotel's glass elevator affords great views of the courtyard scenery.

→ **Address**
Bleibtreustrasse 31
10707 Berlin
Germany

LUX 11

→ **Germany**
Berlin

→ **Open**
07/2005

→ **Rates**
EUR 120 –
EUR 185

→ **Rooms**
72

LUX 11

Architecture / Interior Design
Giuliana Salmaso / Goetz Maximilian Keller

Just steps away from the television tower that has come to symbolise eastern Berlin, a sparkling white façade adorns a sprawling building. This jewel is Lux 11, a place aimed at global individualists. Set in what was originally a late 19th-century residential building, the landmark structure has been refurbished to reflect Berlin's new dynamism. The entrance reflects the vibrance of the trendy streets nearby: a storefront spa and Italian-Asian fusion restaurant are situated on the ground floor, where a café lounge invites guests and locals into the German capital's coffee culture. Lux 11's unique flavour also emerges in its unusual materials and aesthetic contrasts.

 "The interiors of Lux 11 play with opposites: warm and cold, smooth and rough," says London-based architect Giuliana Salmaso, who, with Claudio Silvestrin, conceived the hotel's structure and feel. "Interiors in Berlin are mainly in concrete and wood, so we chose concrete in China green and warm wood." The cool colour scheme lends a modern ambience, yet tactile abundance permeates the hotel's 72 rooms, such as the curtains in brown leather or canvas upholstery.

Open floor plans allow flow but also create intimacy. Accessible via smooth concrete steps, a raised bath sits almost altar-like in the middle of the room. The elegant washroom area integrates a rain shower, a porcelain sink atop a concrete block, and other facilities separated from the main space with opaque glass. Lux 11 is also a place where guests can live in self-sufficient comfort for extended stays thanks to fully equipped white kitchen units. Contrasts are always evident, even in the name. While "Lux" may evoke luxury, the moniker also refers to the hotel's location on Rosa-Luxemburg-Strasse, named after a historic German champion of socialist causes. Like Berlin's ever-changing landscape, Lux 11 mixes history with modernity and blends energetic chic with sublime relaxation.

→ **Address**
Rosa-Luxemburg-Strasse 9–13
10178 Berlin
Germany

LUX 11

→ **Germany**
Berlin

THE MANDALA
HOTEL

→ Germany
Berlin

→ Open
05/1999

→ Rates
EUR 130 –
EUR 410

→ Rooms
166

THE MANDALA HOTEL

Architecture / Interior Design
Lauber & Wöhr / Lutz Hesse

In an urban centre built anew by international star architects, The Mandala is one of three projects on Berlin's sparkling Potsdamer Platz by Ulrike Lauber and Wolfram Wöhr.

With an unassuming entrance and small lobby, the residence is meant to provide long-term guests discreet relief from the area's hustle and bustle: most of the studios and suites face the inner courtyard. Interiors pare luxury down to its modern essence of serenity and subtle harmonies, but spare no expense with furnishings by Donghia and Chinese antiques handpicked by Lutz Hesse, who runs the hotel. Windows of the second floor QIU lounge hideaway offer glimpses of the rush outside, but the Donghia mohair sofas and water cascading down a Bisazza glass mosaic wall are welcome distractions. The restaurant FACIL is hidden away on the fifth-floor courtyard, which is nearly entirely open to the elements during summer months. Its glass ceiling retracts

→ Address
Potsdamer Strasse 3
10785 Berlin
Germany

THE MANDALA
HOTEL

→ **Germany**
Berlin

over tables that extend into a garden surrounded by bamboo. And crowning it all is the hotel's 11th-floor fitness lounge and wellness spa, offering views of the new Berlin's rooftops.

Guestrooms are spacious, modern and smartly devoid of trend. Handcrafted tables and ornamental items such as Chinese stacking drums provide solid, dark accents amongst the soft colour-palette of raw silk curtains, cherry wood floors and pear tree wood furnishings commissioned exclusively for the hotel. The design theme continues in the bathrooms, where segmented light boxes echo the visual effect of the doors' frosted panes. Even the windows work toward creating your inner balance. Invisible crystals inside neutralise electronic smog. Signed black-and-white photographs by Ellen Auerbach complete the serenely style-savvy picture.

CERÊS AM MEER   → Germany
Binz

→ Open
07/2007

→ Rates
EUR 190 –
EUR 700

→ Rooms
50

CERÊS AM MEER
Architecture / Interior Design
Moritz Lau-Engehausen

Located directly on the seaside in Binz, quite probably Rügen's most famous resort town, CERÊS am Meer is a fine example of a contemporary climate-centric building perched on the liveliest spot of Binz's beach promenade. Arguably the most varied and beautiful of the Baltic islands, Rügen is also Germany's most popular island destination – and CERÊS infuses it with a cosmopolitan flair down to its smallest, handcrafted detail.

Architect and interior designer Moritz Lau-Engehausen made his unique vision a reality in an idyllic haven that is reduced, clear and modern, yet always captures the spirit of the sea as well as a certain sensuality. Utilising natural elements like striking smoked-oak wood parquet flooring and natural black stone from China in a soft neutral palette of anthracite, black, white and platinum, the resort's 50 elegant, airy rooms and suites are governed by a generous use of space. Here, French windows are a sweeping four metres high and expansive king-size beds are dressed in luxurious white linens. Each room also has a balcony or terrace that showcases a panoramic view of the island's velvety white sand beaches long "sea bridge" pedestrian dock that juts into the glistening blue water. It's as if the Caribbean has been transplanted to northeastern Germany.

Water is also the central theme in the SENSO SPA, whose luxurious treatments focus on the element in all its forms and temperatures. The restaurant, NEGRO, also picks up on the aquatic theme. It, along with the roof terrace, offers spectacular seaside views, and the lounge makes for a lovely respite, but perhaps the most unusual vantage point lies at the hotel's apex, in a spectacular glass cupola perfect for night time stargazing from the tower suite it tops. After all, CERÊS is named after a small black star discovered 205 years ago. With its immaculate charm and classical lines, the Baltic's new star is a veritable love letter to purity, as well as Germany's ultimate seaside experience.

→ Address
Strandpromenade 24
18609 Ostseebad Binz
Germany

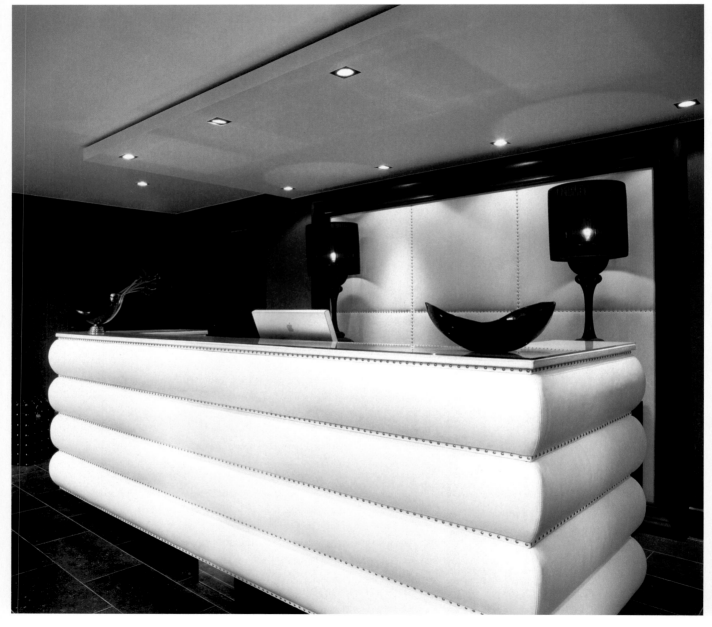

GERBERMÜHLE → **Germany**
Frankfurt
am Main

→ **Open**
08/2007

→ **Rates**
EUR 180 –
EUR 1000

→ **Rooms**
23

→ **Address**
Gerbermühlstraße 105
60594 Frankfurt am Main
Germany

GERBERMÜHLE
Architecture / Interior Design
Jochem Jourdan / Oana Rosen

GERBERMÜHLE → **Germany**
Frankfurt
am Main

Truly an exemplary marriage between medieval and contemporary Frankfurt, the Gerbermühle, which was a flourmill in the 1500s, intersperses cosy architecture such as a warmly lit stone bar, with sleek modern accoutrements, like a futuristic glass-walled dining area.

Positioned on the banks of the placidly breathtaking River Main, the newly built property also contrasts masculine elements like exposed beams and mezzanines with ultramodern feminine magenta lighting in the charmingly rustic stairwells and spacious supper space. A distinctively decorated café exudes a minimalist lodge vibe – complete with antlers on the wall and old-world light fixtures, while the modern yet lushly comfortable guest rooms and bedroom suites evoke the best of European hospitality with handsome leather furniture and glossy parquet floors. A smart king-size bed is placed squarely in the centre of each room, framed by the subdued décor's autumnal hues.

The old-world-meets-new atmosphere continues outdoors: channelling the idyllic river is a lovely 500-seat summer garden covered by ornate white umbrellas. An intense and well-documented romance began on the Gerbermühle – it was near this embankment that seminal German author Johann Wolfgang von Goethe met Marianne Willemer in 1814. This stunning new hotel carries on the lovely literary legacy on the outskirts of what is now Germany's financial capital.

GOLDMAN
25HOURS HOTEL

→ Germany
Frankfurt
am Main

→ Open
12/2006

→ Rates
EUR 90 –
EUR 250

→ Rooms
49

GOLDMAN 25HOURS HOTEL

Architecture / Interior Design
bernjus.gisbertz / Delphine Buhro, Michael Dreher

A repurposed hotel in Frankfurt's bustling Ostend district, the Goldman 25hours applies the spatial principles of the best nightclubs to a hotel space. The public rooms' layout prioritises flow in a multilevelled, multifunctional context, while the 49 guestrooms epitomise a funky international chic in concept and furnishings masterminded by designers Delphine Buhro and Michael Dreher.

The architectural firm bernjus.gisbertz put a stunning new façade on an existing building, the old Henninger Hof. Behind the street entrance, guests enter a mix of hideaway and hotspot. An interconnected lobby, lounge, restaurant and bar give a feeling of transparency to the entire ground floor. A living room with its own door to the street emphasises the sense of free-flowing space; atop it is a newly created outdoor cocktail bar that offers a South Seas feel on balmy summer nights.

The guestrooms themselves are stacked on seven floors, each with its own colour scheme that dictates, among other things, carpet and wall coverings. Each has a "godfather," a local notable whose story is expressed by the room, giving a sense of Frankfurt's cosmopolitan feel, and plays off a basic plan: high-quality basic materials and rectilinear design, with floors by Object Carpet and a mix of vintage tapestry and modern wall treatments. Lamps from Flos, furnishings by Swedish design firm Snowcrash and fabrics by mfta and Romo provide a balance of timelessness and hipness – style with staying power. Themed rooms – like the Princess, Paris and Casino rooms – add to the sense of fun. Individuality asserts itself at every level, from the public to the private, in this new-wave take on increasingly buzz-worthy Frankfurt hospitality – something set to expand even further in an innovative sister property, opening soon.

→ Address
Hanauer Landstraße 127
60314 Frankfurt am Main
Germany

GOLDMAN
25HOURS HOTEL

→ **Germany**
Frankfurt
am Main

ROOMERS → **Germany**
Frankurt
am Main

→ **Open**
09/2008

→ **Rates**
EUR 200 –
EUR 800

→ **Rooms**
112

ROOMERS

Architecture / Interior Design
Oana Rosen / Biorhythm

Classic curves meet progressive design at Roomers, an ambitious new venture in Germany's business capital. With its gleaming glass façade set in specially glazed white concrete, Roomers is a glossy snapshot into the city it inhabits: all timeless charm, clean lines and modern architecture.

Conceptualised by Grübel, an architectural firm best known for its sleek work with BMW, and Romanian designer Oana Rosen, Roomers is an elegantly futuristic five-storey hotel full of electrifying design flourishes, such as an illuminated bubble-domed wellness centre emblazoned with ivy etchings. Formerly a quaint office building, Roomers has now morphed into the exact opposite: a fresh, cosy space full of swirling dark colours interpreted in new ways. Through its strategic use of bright colours and leather upholstery, the lobby now looks more like a posh Japanese club than what was once the entrance to a workplace.

The 112 guestrooms are decorated in the seemingly contradictory style of indulgent minimalism, but when these two concepts meet, the effect is superb. Continuing the modern theme are the four conference areas in Roomers' illuminated top level. Kitted out with the chicest accoutrements, these luxurious business rooms can accommodate up to 80 people. Rosen, who previously took Frankfurt by storm when she lent her creative hand to the ultra-modern Hotel The Pure, has created another conceptual yet wholly enjoyable hotel. Located just minutes away from the river Main, visitors would be hard pressed to find a better backdrop to relax and indulge in the city of Frankfurt.

→ **Address**
Gutleutstrasse 85
60329 Frankfurt am Main
Germany

THE PURE

→ Germany
Frankfurt
am Main

→ Open
09/2005

→ Rates
EUR 100 –
EUR 400

→ Rooms
50

THE PURE
Architecture / Interior Design
Oana Rosen

A 19th-century loft in the heart of Frankfurt was completely renovated to create The Pure – a hotel that both captures and expresses the German financial capital's open-minded, cosmopolitan spirit and bustling atmosphere.

The lobby, the breakfast room, the bar and the lounge form a harmonic open space known as the "Living Room." The choice of exclusively light-coloured materials such as white leather, Thassos marble, white lacquer and light grey floors allows the building and its structures to recede into the background and directs the focus to the energy and activity within the space. Lighting and music are skilfully implemented to enhance the experience. Mornings are filled with soft illumination and tunes to create an ambience of calm vitality. At night The Pure transforms into an oasis full of energy, underscored by vibrant orange-coloured visual effects. The Pure's patio is an extension of this communicative space. Its Timbertech decking is outfitted with oversized Fatboy beanbags, fountains, bamboo, mirrors, and stairs designed for comfortable sitting rather than climbing. And the new Pure Basement is a gargantuan loft-like event space featuring adjustable colour schemes, a long sleek bar and seating areas and a decidedly chic atmosphere for any occasion.

The idea of borderless space is continued in the guestrooms. Here, the sense of openness is emphasised by clean-lined furnishings and light fabrics, high ceilings from which custom-made plissé lampshades are suspended, and bathtubs partially enclosed by glass. High-gloss African zebrawood and oak parquet offset the pure, white elements and lend balance and warmth. Preferring reduced clarity to unnecessary additives, the design and overall concept remain true to the hotel's name.

→ **Address**
Niddastrasse 86
60329 Frankfurt am Main
Germany

THE PURE

→ **Germany**
Frankfurt
am Main

| 25HOURS HOTEL | → Germany Hamburg | → Open 11/2003 | → Rates EUR 105 – EUR 155 | → Rooms 104 |

25HOURS HOTEL

Architecture / Interior Design
3meta / Freiraum and Sibylle von Heyden

Surprise, seduction and vigour are the basis of the 25hours Hotel's concept. Even your arrival catches you pleasantly off-guard: 420 convex chrome mirrors stud the black, curved reception desk, reflecting your entrance manifold.

This is just one of the many playful elements on a designer set that pays homage to the 1960s and 1970s with flowing surface shapes, hand-tufted pile rugs from Kasthall, mod Brionvega television sets and spun-metal table lamps from Flos, who produced the prototype and first batch for the hotel. 25hours literally spreads design as far as furnishings and home accessories that can be ordered directly through the hotel itself. Interior-design firm 3meta's core concept was to create convertible spaces for public or private functions. Informal communal rooms have been designed to encourage the hotel's young clientele to communicate with one another. Circular

→ **Address**
Paul-Dessau-Strasse 2
22761 Hamburg
Germany

insets in the ceiling alter the moods, using bright, clear light by day, but as soon as the sushi master, DJ and bartenders move in behind the U-shaped breakfast bar, the lighting unfolds in hues of pinks and reds, creating a club-like feel by night. The third-floor "Living Room" is reserved for guests only and invites you to stretch out on low lounge seats by Alfa in front of a giant flat screen.

Public areas are dipped in warm pinks, reds and oranges, whereas guestrooms are cool retreats resplendent in pale blues or watery greens. Equally groovy, these are fitted out with a white fringe curtain, a retro chair and a desk that can be be turned into either a seat or a suitcase rack. Unsparingly stylish, 25hours Hotel is affordable fun where guests can make themselves at home.

25HOURS
HOTEL

→ Germany
Hamburg

EAST

→ Germany
Hamburg

→ Open
10/2004

→ Rates
EUR 155 –
EUR 850

→ Rooms
125

EAST

Architecture / Interior Design
Jordan Mozer and Associates

Bringing to life what he calls "a surreal mixture of East and West, old and new," Chicago-based star architect Jordan Mozer presents his signature narrative architecture and organic design to Hamburg's swankiest address. East features 125 rooms, lofts and suites in one of the booming northern German city's most daring structures. In a former iron foundry near Hamburg's notorious red-light district, the hotel blends gastronomy, hospitality and nightlife around a three-storey-high restaurant and courtyard. According to the architect, its design was inspired by the foundry, memories of surreal first trips to Asia and an appreciation of the Eastern recognition of a spiritual essence in nature.

Four pillars tower within the former factory hall, while dramatically lit parts of the original foundation divide the restaurant area. Spaces draped in resplendent floor-to-ceiling velvet curtains are decorated with handmade furnishings and wrought-iron fixtures and illuminated by candlelight. Alongside Asian accents that complement natural fabrics and pebble-grain leather, different floors are scented in ginger, lotus, jasmine, cinnamon, water or sun, making guests sensually aware of the spaces they move in. The restaurant area doubles as a party zone, and in warmer months the terrace serves as a pleasant extension to the restaurant.

Rooms display futuristic, curving forms and bright tones in a cosmopolitan, transcontinental design language. Extravagant details such as curvy headboards and original artwork add to the spaces' character, and free-standing tubs challenge the concept of separate wash and sleeping areas. The top floor has been developed as an arena for pleasure and rejuvenation; its with a low-key spa and roof terrace both follow Mozer's ultramodern lines. Throughout East, his amorphous accents generate a sense of movement and flow, resulting in an inevitably winning combination for any style-savvy urbanite.

→ **Address**
Simon-von-Utrecht Strasse 31
20359 Hamburg
Germany

EAST

→ **Germany**
Hamburg

GASTWERK
HOTEL

→ Germany
Hamburg

→ Open
01/2000

→ Rates
EUR 141 –
EUR 373

→ Rooms
141

GASTWERK HOTEL
Architecture / Interior Design
Klaus Peter Lange / Regine Schwethelm, Sybille von Heyden

Seasoned hotelier Kai Hollmann makes turning Hamburg's 19th-century municipal gasworks (or *Gaswerk*) into Europe's first loft-style hotel look as easy as dropping a "t" into its name, instantly transforming the complex into a "guest works."

Because the red-brick shell and even an enormous green industrial machine from the building's bygone days as a power station are both under a strict preservation order, a sensitive conversion was required of Hamburg architect Klaus Peter Lange. Rising to the occasion, he simply integrated the green monstrosity into the design of the 600-square-metre atrium lobby, in which a bridge leading to the guestrooms is suspended overhead. Natural light floods the atrium and gold leaf adorns the front desk, above which an old tower clock has stopped telling time. Sheer curtains on either side point the way to the bar and restaurant or to the twenty conference rooms, which also cater to grateful local professionals.

Pure functionality is still expressed by exposed pipes and naked brick walls, but interior designers Regine Schwethelm and Sybille von Heyden found that the brick actually provided a warm

→ Address
Beim Alten Gaswerk 3
22761 Hamburg
Germany

backdrop. They set about contrasting the building's rough edges with soothing textures, slick and simple MDF furniture, oversized armchairs and touches of Asia – an imported style prevalent in this seafaring city. The "old" rooms feature original brick walls and arched multipane windows that can be darkened with sliding panels of felt. Finest walnut wood trimmings, tall casement windows and unmasked concrete walls garnish "new" conference rooms and penthouse suites. Rotating propeller-headed ceiling fans pay homage to the many mechanical devices that once whirred away in the power station.

GASTWERK
HOTEL

→ Germany
Hamburg

SIDE

→ Germany
Hamburg

→ Open
04/2001

→ Rates
EUR 190 –
EUR 710

→ Rooms
178

→ Address
Drehbahn 49
20354 Hamburg
Germany

SIDE
Architecture / Interior Design
Jan Störmer / Matteo Thun

SIDE

→ **Germany**
Hamburg

Architect Jan Störmer's glass and steel façade towers 12 storeys above Hamburg – nestled in an area of the city where classy urban chic meets established normality.

The atrium lobby is encased in frosted glass, stretching storeys high like a luminescent sliver between skyscrapers. A computer system that controls the lighting of the hotel orchestrates a spectacular light show in the atrium, which was exclusively developed by visionary theatre director Robert Wilson. A focal point for arriving guests and to "dress up" an otherwise spartan space, the installation extends across multiple levels to the ceiling, pulsating in an ever-changing play of intensity that follows the natural course of daylight. Hovering above the futuristic atrium is the eighth-floor sky lounge where Milan-based designer Matteo Thun suggests weightlessness with improbably curved furniture and floating disk lighting. Stretching even further beyond, the lounge terrace presents a panoramic view across both Hamburg's gritty port and its genteel city centre. Test-sitting on Thun's orange and blue seating for Rossi di Albizzate is welcome anytime – whether to admire the contemporary light show or simply to take a breather. The interior is softened by voluptuously round furnishings and natural touches against the backdrop of Thun's masterpieces. Every decorative element has been painstakingly selected or specially developed as part of the overall design concept, which is actually a "superconcept" of sorts.

Buttery creams and sumptuous browns are the soothing canvas in guestrooms, against which the Italian designer cleverly decorates public areas using strategic splashes of garish colour: on ground level, bright red leather seating and lush velvets are set against natural stone flooring in the "fusion" bar. Going deeper underground, the energetic orange of the gym infuses it with warmth, and the mellow yellow in the restorative spa treatment rooms paints a perfect picture, contrasting with the fresh blue colour scheme of the swimming pool area.

THE GEORGE → Germany
Hamburg

→ Open
2008

→ Rates
EUR 157 –
EUR 357

→ Rooms
125

THE GEORGE

Architecture / Interior Design

GRS Architekturbüro Reimer + Partner / SynergyHamburg, Sibylle von Heyden

Hamburg's The George is a smart interpretation of an English-style social club, but here membership is not required. Injecting the classic sensibilities of English club-rooms with cutting-edge design motifs and stylish architecture, The George light-heartedly evokes the old, while lending a touch of timeless glamour to the new.

Offering 118 impeccably dressed guestrooms, five suites and two penthouses, The George is an ideal space for those seeking the utmost in privacy. Conversely, the hotel also offers regally designed common spaces – standouts include the austere smoker's lounge with striking leather furniture, handsome meeting rooms with dark timber flooring, a light-flooded rooftop spa, a restaurant-bar and a cosy, beautifully wallpapered library. All of the above offer visually varied takes on the hotel's exclusive club-like atmosphere, and can even be hired for private events. Here, sleeping, meeting and dining are made to measure.

The George is also a pioneer in the up-and-coming neighbourhood on whose border it is situated: buoyant and bustling, St. Georg is one of Hamburg's most multifaceted, multicultural districts, where trendy boutiques and street cafés mix with remnants of the area's slightly seedy past. The George is a shining example of elegant chic melding with the fashionable and funky; a brilliant symbiosis of liveliness and relaxation.

→ **Address**
Barcastrasse 3
22087 Hamburg
Germany

| HOTEL MAURITZHOF MÜNSTER | → Germany
Munster | → Open
10/2003 | → Rates
EUR 110 –
EUR 240 | → Rooms
39 |

HOTEL MAURITZHOF MÜNSTER

Architecture / Interior Design
Rainer Maria Kresing

A complete makeover by interior architect and designer Rainer Maria Kresing has given this red-brick hotel in northwestern Germany an ultramodern, four-metre glass-and-steel drawer structure at its base.

This central structure, which serves as a channel to the lobby and bar, also bathes these public spaces in natural light. When night falls, attractive standing lamps by Foscarini provide the necessary illumination. On arrival, chairs by De Sede and specially commissioned tables by Kusch+Co set the interior scene.

Individually designed, spacious rooms and suites are covered in warm beechwood parquet flooring, and a palette of natural colours has been chosen to calm and soothe. Exclusive built-in furnishings in glass, steel and cherrywood were especially developed for the hotel by Kresing himself. These framing elements are suitably complemented by hand-picked sofas and chairs by the likes of Le Corbusier, Montis, Cappellini and Philippe Starck. The latter also created the look of the distinctive fittings in the adjoining bathrooms. Kresing chose to pay homage to the American modern classics of Eileen Gray in the interior design concept of the junior suites.

→ Address
Eisenbahnstrasse 17
48143 Münster
Germany

BECKER'S HOTEL &
RESTAURANT

→ Germany
Trier

→ Open
2007

→ Rates
EUR 70 –
EUR 120

→ Rooms
30

BECKER'S HOTEL & RESTAURANT
Architecture / Interior Design
Dipl. Des. Ingbert and Jutta Schilz

→ **Address**
Olewiger Strasse 206
54295 Trier
Germany

BECKER'S HOTEL & → Germany
RESTAURANT   Trier

Amidst the vineyards and rolling hills of Trier, one of the oldest cities in Europe, dating back to Roman times, Becker's Hotel & Restaurant grounds itself both in nature and in a family tradition that goes back five generations.

Through the use of natural materials such as stone and wood, the property appears as if it is almost nestled within its surroundings. Seen from the outside, the lobby glows through large-paned windows, while the building's volcanic rock façade gives the impression of a warm hearth. Blocks of charcoal grey basalt form a recurring motif inside the hotel as well, their subtly varying patterns lending the design a dynamic yet truly classic timelessness.

Yet Becker's self-professed heart is its kitchen. Done in black and white, the restaurant it serves suggests a sophistication befitting a black-tie event or a white wedding, while the wine bar's deeper, darker tones evoke a cosmopolitan night out. Here, too, are the ubiquitous basalt stones, but the simple rectangular shelving for the wine glasses adds a repetitive, almost artistic visual element to the room, perhaps citing the reserved dignity of a Donald Judd sculpture. In the guestrooms, the stones give way to finely patterned dark wood floors combined with the glow of low spot lighting. A simple pane of glass separates the dark tiled shower from the sleeping area, adding a hint of airiness to the otherwise earthy elements embodied in the hotel's design. At Becker's, German wine-country hospitality is writ large, but is certainly footnoted with a sophisticated, modern touch.

FRESH HOTEL → Greece
Athens

→ Open
04/2004

→ Rates
EUR 140 –
EUR 450

→ Rooms
133

FRESH HOTEL

Architecture / Interior Design
Zeppos – Georgiadi & Associates

The aptly named Fresh Hotel, which opened in Athens in the spring of 2004, adds a candy-box kaleidoscope of splashy colour to an emerging industrial quarter.

Deliciously designed by Tassos Zeppos, Eleni Georgiadi and their associates, the Fresh boldly mixes rich natural materials such as oak and walnut wood with bright pinks and oranges, making it a sanctuary from the flurry of downtown Athens just outside its doors. The nine-storey building, with a pool and bar sporting a view of the Acropolis from the top floor, welcomes its guests into a lobby extending over two levels. Here, a generous fireplace surrounded by an imposing black wall stands opposite the reception, which is created by an attractive pink glass box and gives visitors a taste of the funky feel to come upstairs. A walnut floor extends from the lobby and, improbably, climbs up the wall as guests make their way up to their rooms.

The 133 guestrooms, six of them with private gardens, are temples to purity of form with sleek, modernist spaces broken up by bright slashes of orange, pink and green against mauve and beige. Furniture and fittings, including Tolomeo lamps by Artemide, Starck's transparent polycarbonate Eros chairs by Kartell and Lens tables by B&B Italia, are offset against other light oak pieces. The distinct look of the bathrooms, with brightly coloured light boxes behind the shower and translucent screens for the shower itself, is completed by mosaic flooring. The hotel was created in less than a year by ripping an old hotel down to its foundations and infusing Zeppos and Georgiadi's eye-catching design, which is indeed, well, fresh.

→ **Address**
26 Sofokleous & Klisthenous Street
105 52 Athens
Greece

LIFE GALLERY
ATHENS

→ Greece
Athens

→ Open
04/2004

→ Rates
EUR 260 –
EUR 900

→ Rooms
30

→ Address
103 Thisseos Avenue
14578 Ekali, Athens
Greece

LIFE GALLERY ATHENS
Architecture / Interior Design
Klein/Haller / Vassilios Rodatos

LIFE GALLERY
ATHENS

→ **Greece**
Athens

Gently nestled in lush grounds on the northern outskirts of Athens, the Life Gallery's elegant sea-green glass façade hints at an interior infused with Eastern influences and suburban Zen.

Spread across 3,200 square metres in Ekali, one of Athens's most sophisticated suburbs, the hotel has a contemporary style touched by Asian elements: bamboo wall coverings, traditional Indonesian furniture and typically Asian agave plants greet visitors in the lobby. The interiors, which are co-designed by owner Gina Mamidakis, create a metaphor for life's richer experiences, and double as a refined gallery setting for local artists. Encircling the building, the expansive landscaped gardens are dotted with mature pines and cedar trees and blend in harmoniously with their suburban surroundings. Two sundecks and swimming pools set in the greenery of the grounds offer guests a continuation of the tranquillity that characterises their rooms.

Following a spatial revitalisation of the 1970s five-storey block by German architects Klein and Haller, the hotel's 30 airy rooms feature stone floors and a muted colour scheme of grey, taupe and beige. Orange light recessed into panels on the threshold to the modern bathrooms sets a warm tone for the simple and functional Gervasoni bed with a black-stained bamboo surround, which Italian designer Paola Navone designed for every room. Balconies stretching out from 24 of the rooms are enclosed within a frame of clever multifunctional, high-tech glass panels that can be rotated to create an atrium, and the impressive views of Mount Parnes and Mount Penteli offer a finishing touch of natural grandeur to complete the picture.

SEMIRAMIS → **Greece**
Athens

→ **Open**
08/2004

→ **Rates**
EUR 165 –
EUR 750

→ **Rooms**
51

SEMIRAMIS

Architecture / Interior Design
Karim Rashid

Athens's Semiramis Hotel is a prime example of what happens when you give a hot designer like Karim Rashid carte blanche and control over every aspect of a building and its interior.

Commissioned by art patron Dakis Ioannou, the hotel in the leafy Athens suburb of Kiffisia is entirely the creation of Rashid. The Egyptian-British industrial designer's mark is on everything from the slippers under the bed to the placemats on his organically curved tables. Guests entering through the glowing pink glass cube into a lobby – which features a rotating collection of fine art including works by Tim Noble and Sue Webster or Jeff Koons on loan from international art galleries – know they are in store for something radically different than the city's classic architecture. Rashid's signature furniture, including his Wavelength Sofa, Swing Chair and even his bank of black sofas shaped like pouting lips in the lobby, gives this hotel its distinct look. Juicy pinks, oranges, greens and yellows make up the hotel's energising colour scheme, tinting everything from lobby couches to transparent glass partitions in the rooms. A lively lighting concept has been especially commissioned from Focus Lighting in New York under the direction of principal designer Paul Gregory.

Semiramis's guestrooms, suites and poolside bungalows offer both the use of creative materials (like the opaque glass bathroom wall) and playful design, such as the light-box art installations behind each bed. The designer takes an innovative approach in mixing textures and materials: coloured concrete with rubber floors, for example, or ceramic tiles with metal or epoxy with dark wood. Innovative technology is also a given in Rashid's 21st-century concept. For example, traditional "Do Not Disturb" or "Make Up This Room" signs have been replaced with electronic message boards. Guests can type in personalised messages from the in-room keyboard – Rashid suggests, "Hello, I'm single. Please come in."

→ **Address**
48 Charilaou Trikoupi
Kifissia, Athens
Greece

SEMIRAMIS → **Greece**
Athens

SEMIRAMIS → **Greece**
Athens

MYKONOS	→ Greece	→ Open	→ Rates	→ Rooms
THEOXENIA	Mykonos	04/2005	EUR 145 –	52
			EUR 830	

MYKONOS THEOXENIA

Architecture / Interior Design
Aris Konstantinidis, Angelos Angelopoulos

A legendary classic of 1960s hotel architecture has made a glamorous comeback on the Greek island of Mykonos, where cutting-edge chic meets breezy *joie de vivre*.

The low-rise building of the Mykonos Theoxenia stands on a prime location, right next to the white windmills that are the island's trademark, and offers stunning views of the Aegean Sea below. The hotel's original design by one of Greece's most revered architects of the 1960s, Aris Konstantinidis, which incorporates local stone and traditional Cycladic architecture, stood the test of time well enough to be considered for national preservation by the Greek Ministry of Civilisation. But its interiors desperately needed a makeover, something Yiannis Tsimas and Angelos Angelopoulos pulled off successfully in 2004. The designers didn't stray far from the late Konstantinidis's master plan, revamping the glam interiors while bringing the hotel up to the most modern design standards. Stone-clad walls, orange and turquoise hessian fabrics and sweeping minimal surfaces all create a backdrop for Patricia Urquiola's fjord deep-blue bar stools and sofas, designed for Moroso. The Italian designer also developed the white Moroso beach chairs in the pool area, which is surrounded by curtained four-poster beds and offers a tempting alternative to the beach.

In the hotel's 52 rooms, Angelopoulos has added accents in bright lime, orange and red to the Greek standards of white and blue. Period furniture made of light beech wood pays tribute to the design era in which Theoxenia exploded onto the Greek hotel scene. As guests marvel at the picture-perfect sea views while leaning back on retro period furniture on simple white balconies, Konstantinidis's vision has been turned into a timeless design statement.

→ **Address**
84600 Kato Mili
Mykonos
Greece

MYKONOS
THEOXENIA

→ **Greece**
Mykonos

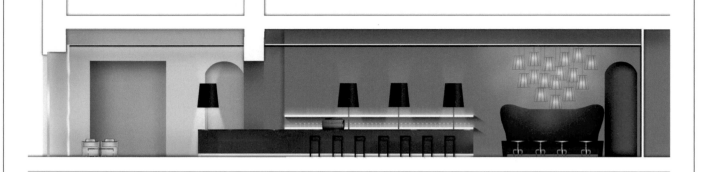

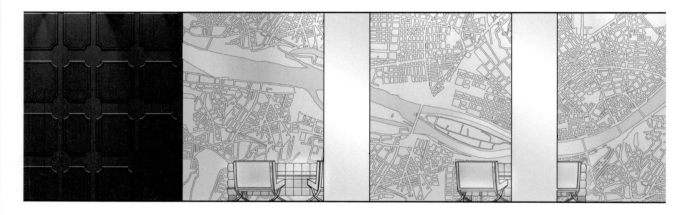

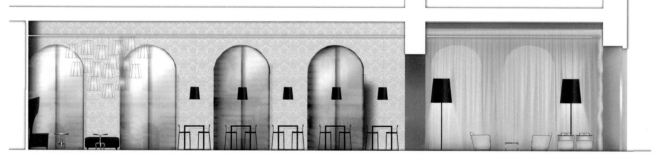

HOTEL ROSSLYN → **Hungary**
Budapest

→ **Open**
11/2008

→ **Rates**
TBA

→ **Rooms**
70

HOTEL ROSSLYN

Architecture / Interior Design

Konstruma Épitesz Iroda Kft. / Studio 63 Architecture & Design

On the border between Budapest's historic centre and its up-and-coming government quarter stands an old stone building with an elaborately decorated façade. Formerly a Freemasons Grand Lodge, this turn-of-the-century edifice is now home to the Rosslyn.

The historic building was completely refurbished, though many of its original features were retained – from abundant decorations, sculptures and paintings on the structure's exterior, to parts of the lobby's original *seminato veneziano* flooring in the interior. The frescoes, arches and main staircase were also kept intact, so that the interior continues to exude an antique look and feel despite the revamp. The Rosslyn's design references not only the building's historical aesthetic but also its specific functional history as a gathering place for Hungarian Freemasons. In a nod to the

fraternal organisation's minimal, almost rigid aesthetic, only clean lines and natural materials like stone, wood and leather are used in the hotel's communal spaces.

The property's 70 guestrooms and suites feature a similarly linear, pared-down design expressed in an elegant monochromatic colour scheme. Floors are dark wood, carpets are cream, walls are white, furniture is black and finishings are in various shades of grey. A line of writing in simple, black typeface wraps around each room, spelling out phrases of poetry in both English and Freemason symbols. This detail serves to enhance the hotel's intriguing yet exceedingly elegant historical atmosphere, which co-exists in balanced tension with the air of contemporary sophistication generated by modern spaces and minimalist fixtures.

→ **Address**
Podmaniczky u 45
1060 Budapest
Hungary

LÁNCHÍD 19 → **Hungary** → **Open** → **Rates** → **Rooms**
Budapest 08/2007 EUR 120 – 48
EUR 400

LÁNCHÍD 19

Architecture / Interior Design
Radius B+S Ltd. / KB-Design Ltd.

Named after Budapest's famed "Chain Bridge," which spans the Danube, Lánchíd 19 is a contemporary highlight in a neighbourhood of predominantly 19th-century architecture. This contrast is indicative of Budapest's evolving character, which celebrates both past and present. The architect and design team of Péter Sugár, Lászlo Benczur and Lászlo Kara created a movable accordion-like glass façade, further animated by the changing colours of an innovative lighting design concept.

Glass is one of the dominant materials in the interiors as well, creating a sense of openness and allowing movement and connectedness to become an integral part of the structure's character. A building-high glass atrium towers above the foyer, enabling natural light to flood the communal spaces and glass bridges that lead to the guestrooms. A glass and steel staircase connects the foyer with the lobby bar, which is located on a gallery above. Looking over the openwork glass and wood space separators, one has views of the restaurant and the intimate garden beyond.

The lobby itself is equally dramatic with its transparent floor revealing Roman ruins a level below. Here again history is well integrated into the interior design, where examples of classical modern design, such as chairs by Alvar Aalto, are mixed with custom-designed furnishings. In the guestrooms, the spatial connection of the living space and bathrooms picks up the concept of "flowing space" with their sliding glass doors.

→ Address
Lánchíd utca 19
1013 Budapest
Hungary

101 HOTEL

→ Iceland
Reykjavik

→ Open
03/2003

→ Rates
EUR 350 –
EUR 940

→ Rooms
38

→ **Address**
Hverfisgata 10
101 Reykjavik
Iceland

101 HOTEL

Architecture / Interior Design
Ingibjörg S.Pálmadóttir

101 HOTEL

→ Iceland
Reykjavik

An unapologetic Nordic coolness pervades the atmosphere of the 101 Hotel, Iceland's first entry into the league of boutique hotels. Owner and designer Ingibjörg S. Pálmadóttir has created a hot spot out of the 1930s office building that was once home to the Icelandic Social Democratic Party.

Modern dress-down egalitarianism can be lived out around the communal lounge fireplace, whose warm light illuminates an already spotlighted tree-trunk table and reflects off the metal frames of black leather seats. Pálmadóttir commissioned exclusive sofas and seating, and also went for modern classics by Eero Saarinen and the inevitable Philippe Starck. The cocktail bar is the central gathering point for guests and locals. The unadorned, masculine space in polished black – despite an eclectic mix of Chinese lacquered tables, wooden blocks and Edwardian chairs – finds its feminine counterpart in the stark white dimpled mural that runs alongside the glass roof of the restaurant, in which everyone sits pretty on Philippe Starck and Piero Lissoni's Eros chairs for Kartell. Monochromatic design and clear lines determine the architectural look and feel of the public areas, where changing exhibitions of the hotel's collection of works by Icelandic artists are showcased – including Pálmadóttir's sister, Lilja.

Stepping into the guestrooms, your feet are gently warmed by heated oak floors. Refreshing white Italian bed linen by Quagliotti contrasts with both matt and glossy black furnishings accentuated by Artemide lamps. Opting for the slightly rustic touch, the open-plan design leads straight into the bathroom, where a free-standing bathtub is firmly grounded by metal claw feet and can be filled to the brim with geothermal water.

In the heart of Reykjavik's city centre, this gem strengthens its connection to the art scene by being just next door to the Icelandic Opera House and close to Pálmadóttir's 101 Gallery.

THE MORGAN   → Ireland
              Dublin

→ Open   → Rates   → Rooms
11/1997   EUR 140 –   121
              EUR 2500

THE MORGAN

Architecture / Interior Design
Niall D Brennan / Helen Kilmartin / Minima Co.

Architect Niall D Brennan and designer Helen Kilmartin have created a haven of understated elegance with The Morgan in Dublin's vibrant Temple Bar district.

The slender check-in desk jutting from a support column hangs like an afterthought in this chic hotel. Brennan and Kilmartin's spatial concept relies on a modern structure that stresses function, though the white stone slabs, inviting white furniture and open fireplace in the foyer are befitting of a showroom for modern design. Mid-century furniture by Le Corbusier, Eileen Gray and Verner Panton elegantly complement the use of North European beech, aluminium and glass throughout.

In the guestrooms, a light and cosy atmosphere is brought out by hues of beige, cream and coffee. The beds of reddish pear wood are a spacious 1.82 metres wide and covered in crisp white Egyptian cotton bed linens supplied by Mitre Furnishing – beautifully framed by light fixtures by French designer Pascal Morgue. The bathrooms feature vanity tops and natural beech bath panels that contrast with white tiles. A feeling of timeless elegance sets the tone of the minimalist design.

→ **Address**
10 Fleet Street
Temple Bar
Dublin 2
Ireland

HOTEL GREIF   → Italy
Bolzano

→ Open
01/2000

→ Rates
EUR 175 –
EUR 350

→ Rooms
33

HOTEL GREIF

Architecture / Interior Design
Boris Podrecca and 33 contemporary artists

Greif is the German word for "griffin" – the mythical creature with a lion's body and the wings, beak and talons of an eagle. Just as the griffin combines diverse strengths, so does this centuries-old hotel with a view of the Dolomites of northern Italy. However, there is nothing antiquated about this modern space infused with traditional architectural details.

Viennese architect Boris Podrecca has used a steel and glass entrance to mirror the modernity found within, but because elements such as the façade are under a preservation order, Podrecca has incorporated the wood of the original portal in the final design. Creative tension is generally encouraged by this juxtaposition of historic and modern elements, which follows principles of *chiaroscuro* – light versus dark – and pairs contemporary artworks with ones from the 17th, 18th or 19th centuries.

The hotel has been in the hands of the Staffler family since 1816, and the current owner, Franz Staffler, collaborated with Podrecca on composing 33 individual guestrooms from scratch: Some are split-level loft spaces, some have terraces and bay windows, others have steam saunas or whirlpool baths. Natural, untreated materials are used throughout – from non-lacquered parquet floors and raw silk curtains to hand-woven gaberdine carpets and bathrooms lined with exclusive marble and even featuring silver-leaf-covered walls. If the chair in your room is not one of the fine antique examples of Biedermeier craftsmanship on display at the hotel, then it will definitely be one that has been especially handcrafted in maple or walnut in the local carpentry workshop. Each room features a specially commissioned work by a different artist – hand-picked by Staffler, who was assisted by art historian Carl Kraus from Innsbruck and Andreas Hapkemeyer of the Bolzano Modern Art Museum.

→ Address
Piazza Walther
39100 Bolzano
Italy

FALCONARA
CHARMING HOUSE
& RESORT

→ Italy
Butera

→ Open
07/2007

→ Rates
EUR 200 –
EUR 640

→ Rooms
65

FALCONARA
CHARMING HOUSE & RESORT

Architecture / Interior Design
Antonio Vitale, B. Castrense / Roberto and Antonella Chiaramonte Bordonaro

Overlooking the clear blues of the Mediterranean Sea and Africa beyond, the new Falconara Charming House & Resort is neighbour to a Norman castle, setting an unusual atmosphere in which traditions, history and even a touch of decadence meld with utter beauty. Yet this is a place where one also can find pure lines and contemporary ambience … all in all, perhaps an embodiment of the contrasts inherent in this southern Sicilian property.

The resort dedicates its updated design and impeccable amenities to its guests in two remarkable buildings: La Fattoria is an update of what was once an annex to the nearby medieval Castle of Falconara; meanwhile, the sleek, newly built

→ **Address**
Località Falconara
93011 Butera (CL)
Sicily
Italy

Club House boasts a restaurant, bar and 39 rooms and junior suites, in addition to modern spa facilities and a nearby swimming pool. La Fattoria's 26 guestrooms include 12 junior suites and prestigious suites, some of which are identified by the names of the castle's former owners. Barons Roberto and Antonella Chiaramonte Bordonaro, the owners of both the adjacent castle and the resort, personally managed the latter's interior design, outfitting rooms that reflect two aesthetics. The Club House's contemporary aesthetic is up-to-the-minute, whereas La Fattoria's rooms are embellished with traditional elements. Here, unique pieces draw their

FALCONARA
CHARMING HOUSE
& RESORT

→ Italy
Butera

FALCONARA
CHARMING HOUSE
& RESORT

→ Italy
Butera

inspiration from Sicilian or Moorish influences – as does the eclectic collection of art objects and curiosities on view in the resort's breathtakingly airy public spaces.

It is a perfect synthesis of apparent contradictions: the overall effect is airy, yet aristocratic. Medieval, yet modern. Original elements – such as wood-beam ceilings, sweeping archways, rugged floors made of local stone and even Caltagirone ceramics decorating the stairs and windows – are expertly combined with contemporary conveniences and visual clarity. Outdoors, the sweeping views of blue and the dangerous drop are grounded by the Falconara gardens' Mediterranean beauty.

CONTINENTALE   → Italy
                        Florence

→ Open
01/2003

→ Rates
EUR 300 –
EUR 1110

→ Rooms
43

CONTINENTALE

Architecture / Interior Design
Michele Bönan

Considered by many to be the crown jewel of designer Salvatore Ferragamo's small chain of hotels, the Continentale in Florence pays homage to the happy-go-lucky feel of the 1950s and 1960s with bubble-gum pink accents for a totally zeitgeist experience in the middle of the romantic Italian city.

Designer Michele Bönan was "looking for ways to tap into the senses through music, light and aroma" and approached the property with a mix of harmony and irony. Mission definitely accomplished and softened by billowy drapes of light pink, lemon and pistachio tones in the reception: upon entering the hotel, guests find themselves in a quiet envelope of white walls and floors in light-grey *pietra serena,* a stone native to Florence that even incorporates serenity into its name. A blend of zebrano wood and steel, cerused oak, floor lamps by Haans Group and vintage pieces complemented by Bönan's custom-designed creations give you a first impression of the careful mix throughout. The second floor has more public areas, including Ferragamo's favourite "relaxation room" complete with five Bönan-designed chaises longues, the lounge with an acrylic bar that glows in, yes, pink, but also orange or simply white, and the breakfast room highlighted by a pink wool-covered banquette sitting pretty next to Arne Jacobsen tables.

In the private domain from the third floor upwards, 43 guestrooms are appointed with sheer-draped beds, light wood furniture on oak floors and flowing curtains that catch the Tuscan light. The designer created oak desks and chairs trimmed with leather and steel to evoke the feeling of a 19th-century steamer trunk. Simple bathrooms gleam in white with Corian sinks elegantly perched on oak bases crafted by Ginetti Co., who also worked their Italian magic on all the wood in the hotel. Reassuringly retro black-and-white photomontages from the studio of Faye Heller complete the modern look that goes hand in hand with a positive mid-century feel.

→ Address
Vicolo dell'Oro 6r
50123 Florence
Italy

GALLERY
HOTEL ART

→ Italy
Florence

→ Open
05/1999

→ Rates
EUR 270 –
EUR 1110

→ Rooms
74

GALLERY HOTEL ART
Architecture / Interior Design
Michele Bönan

The Ferragamo family has bestowed a chic, contemplative and cosmopolitan hotel on the beautiful city of Florence – sitting pretty on a tiny square just steps from the Ponte Vecchio. The property is a constantly evolving project created by interior designer Michele Bönan for lovers of art and good living.

True to its name, the Gallery Hotel Art is a temple to contemporary art and culture. The concept team of Lungarno Hotels has transformed public areas into truly multifunctional spaces without succumbing to the coolness of pure functionality – earthy ceramics and sensuous floral arrangements are just two examples of this warmth. *Objets d'art* ranging from paintings and photography to sculptures accent the walls of the lobby, where exhibitions regularly take place. The hotel sees itself as a project as well as a dynamic engine of cultural exchange, a concept exemplified by the Fusion Bar/Shozan Gallery, where Mediterranean and Japanese cultures meet in an expression of culinary panache. Taken as a whole, the hotel's modernity, lighting, careful selection of furnishings and unique peculiarities are all vital elements of its successful balance between aesthetic beauty and physical well-being.

The architect has created richly elegant spaces for the hotel's guestrooms – as well as the seventh-floor penthouse suites, which offer unrivalled views over Florence's rooftops. The bedrooms' linen sheets, cashmere blankets and linear pigskin headboards all add a truly unique touch. All decorative details stress a sense of craftsmanship, such as the elements in dark Wenge wood that ground the rooms' brightness. Delicately pinstriped walls are adorned by black-and-white studies of Florentine monuments. A savvy Mecca for aficionados of good taste.

→ **Address**
Vicolo dell´Oro 5
50123 Florence
Italy

STRAF

→ Italy
Milan

→ Open
01/2004

→ Rates
EUR 264 –
EUR 605

→ Rooms
64

STRAF
Architecture / Interior Design
Vincenzo de Cotiis

→ **Address**
Via San Raffaele 3
20121 Milan
Italy

Blending recycled materials into new surroundings in a concept that shakes up the interior of a 19th-century Milan palazzo, architect, artist and fashion designer Vincenzo de Cotiis has achieved his goal of creating a visually striking alternative to standard hotel design in his very first project in the field. "The hotel is almost like an installation, where the concept lies in the choice of materials and in their transformation as a result of reusing and repositioning them in new contexts of salvaged objects and components," says de Cotiis, describing the rough handmade and deliberately "aged" materials he assembled to create an atmosphere of luxury and opulence that permeates the property.

De Cotiis's eclectic, modernist (or even postmodernist) taste is reflected in the Straf, which, like his fashion collections, strives for individuality and a reconsideration of accepted philosophies and methods. In rethinking what began as a palazzo and then spent years as a "normal" hotel, the Milan architect takes more than a few risks: he uses bare cement for stairs and floors as well as oxidised copper and split slate in room interiors. He slips torn and aged gauze between sheets of glass. These are just examples of how the designer succeeds in creating an atmosphere of warmth, despite the hard aspects of the materials used.

Located on a quiet side street a few steps from Milan's Duomo Cathedral and La Scala opera house, the hotel's look and feel also reflects the city it is situated in from the minute one passes through its high glass portal doors – but in, of course, a highly unusual way that is meant to open the senses and minds of those visiting it. "My design concept could be described as provocative, because I translated the materials and colours usually seen on the outskirts of cities into the context of a luxury hotel. Basically, the colours

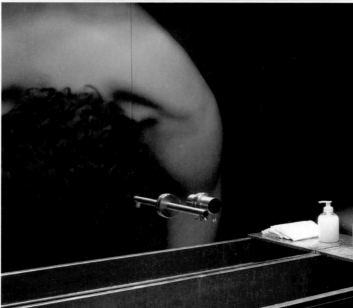

STRAF   → Italy
                                                        Milan

STRAF

→ **Italy**
Milan

I have chosen harmonise with the Milanese environment, which is predominantly grey," says De Cotiis. Indeed. But here, greys become polished dark concrete, and are mixed with browns, beiges and golds – even brick red and green – in a palette that reflects the full spectrum of the sophisticated stylin Italy's fashion capital.

Despite (or perhaps because of) the scratched mirrors, burnished brass, black slate and iron, however, there is a comfort and warmth that attracts the jet set and fashion fans from around the world, who come for major events like Fashion Week or simply a stylish weekend parading around the world's finest shopping outlets. The hotel's 64 guestrooms come in either a light or a dark colour palette and are oddly intimate, in spite of the hints of industrial design. Seven of them include a massaging armchair and five boast a so-called well-being corner that de Cotiis has designed. The corners pass on technological modern conveniences in favour of a simple separate area where guests can unwind in style. Some rooms even boast chromotherapy light panels on the ceilings for colour therapy, and all offer tactile pleasures in fine textiles, lusciously decadent bathrooms and interestingly mirrored surfaces throughout. Public areas, too, are slightly unfinished odes to fashion and relaxation: A reading area invites guests to a C-shaped couch formation under a glass courtyard, and the slick Straf Bar has become a magnet for sunglass-wearing mavens from around the world.

Given the singularity of his work, it is no surprise that de Cotiis thinks of the project as an artistic endeavour. And in doing so, he has managed to reach new levels of comfort and offer a truly unusual experience – as the Straf's guests can readily attest to.

THE CHEDI	→ Italy	→ Open	→ Rates	→ Rooms
MILAN	Milan	03/2007	EUR 128 –	250
			EUR 258	

→ **Address**
Via Villapizzone 24
20156 Milan
Italy

THE CHEDI MILAN

Architecture / Interior Design
Jaya Ibrahim – Jaya Associates

THE CHEDI
MILAN

→ Italy
Milan

In design circles, Indonesia is a country best known for sensual buildings and attention-grabbing textiles, whereas Italy is world-famous for revolutionary industrial design and transcendental sculptural forms. Naturally, an amalgamation of the two great countries and cultures would produce a veritable monument to highly individualistic architecture and design.

Luckily, renowned hotelier Adrian Zecha, who is already a trend-setter in Asia, decided to traverse the Indian Ocean and spice up Milan's stylish Bovisa district by combining the most innovative aspects of Indonesia with extraordinary Italian style and hospitality. The GHM group of hotels is known for redefining standards of luxury and elegance, and The Chedi Milan, GHM's inaugural European hotel, does just that in 250 tastefully chic rooms.

It is natural, then, that The Chedi, under the direction of Indonesian interior designer Jaya Ibrahim, combines alluring Eastern décor with touches of exquisite modernism, all supported by a gleaming Neoclassical pedigree. Here, Balinese art hangs on high white or beige walls under soft inset lighting, while fine materials such as bronze, stone, mosaic and ceramic elicit a refined Asian influence at each unique panorama.

Ibrahim, whose impressive oeuvre also includes the stunning Setai in Miami and the luminous Chedi Muscat in Oman, is partial to an autumnal palette of earth tones. Sand, brown, ochre and orange dominate the hotel's upholstery, and red accents along with dark woodwork provide a contrasting signature. Guestrooms

are minimally decorated – Ibrahim prefers to save his innovative textiles and flashy symmetrical touches for the world-class restaurant, the glass-walled bar and the spa and swimming pools.

This exemplary marriage of East and West is enhanced even more by Nathan Thompson's lighting design. Thompson, who has lent his expert hand to Chedi enterprises in Oman, Indonesia and Bali, has infused the hotel with a warm ambience, as well as an inviting lobby and double-sided sconces illuminating a dazzling marble staircase. Sensual touches even extend to the olfactory: the hotel's signature fragrance – a mix of mandarin and green tea – gently permeates each space.

Although not apparent at first glance, Milan is much more than the fashion capital of Europe – it is also a melting pot of brilliant design work, from Achille Castiglione's iconic Arco lamp to Mario Botta's virtuoso restoration of the Teatro alla Scala. The same goes for Jakarta, which, in addition to having fish that climb trees, is an ethnological and cultural goldmine. The Chedi, which means "spiritual monument" in Thai, is the synthesis of two thrilling and influential design Meccas.

THE CHEDI → Italy
MILAN Milan

THE GRAY

→ Italy
Milan

→ Open
06/2004

→ Rates
EUR 330 –
EUR 990

→ Rooms
21

THE GRAY
Architecture / Interior Design
Guido Ciompi

Designed with Milan's most exclusive fashionista set in mind, the simply named Gray treads a careful line between elegance and opulence. Unashamedly elitist and purely residential, only the most established names are granted access to The Gray's private club-like atmosphere.

The hotel is hidden away in two five-storey buildings that used to house residences and businesses. The Florentine architect Guido Ciompi, known for his work on Gucci and Armani stores around the world, has created a sumptuous lobby in which to welcome guests, with a red-velvet-covered divan swinging above the reception. Ciompi also has included a light installation that bathes the walls, top-to-toe drapes and the lobby's black flagstones in an ever-changing myriad of colours. A new open-air lounge, called Aria, offers guests exotic ambiance under the stars with soft-lined pouffe chairs and low tables.

Each of the 21 guestrooms in Milan's most closely guarded secret offers its guests completely unique interiors. One room features its own gym, for example, whereas another is spread out over two storeys connected by a filigree steel staircase. At the same time, all share high-quality craftsmanship, evident in the limed wood closets, the ebony tables and the headboards upholstered in white or ostrich leather. Ciompi pursues his stylistic hallmark, a formal expression of clean, geometric lines, through-out the hotel's interior. This alone is enough to make The Gray a modern classic.

→ Address
Via San Raffaele 6
20121 Milan
Italy

THE GRAY

→ **Italy**
Milan

SANTA TERESA
RESORT

→ Italy
Pantelleria

→ Open
04/2006

→ Rates
EUR 140 –
EUR 380

→ Houses
18

→ **Address**
Via Contrada Monastero Alto-Sibà
91010 Scauri Siculo (TP)
Pantelleria
Sicily, Italy

SANTA TERESA RESORT
Architecture / Interior Design
Gabriella Giuntoli

Set amidst breathtaking natural beauty on the volcanic island of Pantelleria – the largest of the Sicilian islands – Santa Teresa Resort embodies a rustic simplicity that is perfect for any traveller looking for the true and untouched.

Situated on a working farm that extends over 40 hectares of vineyards, olive trees and lush flora, the resort is a collection of intriguing structures dotting the rugged landscape in both the Sibà plain and the adjacent Monastero Valley. These four mini-villages consist of 18 beautifully restored *dammusi*, which are ancient buildings made of the same cut stone found in the low walls winding their way through the hills. Once lived in by Pantelleria's native inhabitants and infused with the area's Arabian past, the dammusi have been transformed into modern abodes by architect Gabriella Giuntoli, who has created interiors that are a study in purity, even a certain austerity. Whitewashed walls frame minimalist interiors in white and light grey, whose arched ceilings and narrow windows lend the serenity of a cool, calm sanctuary. A few more colourful touches – in soft blue, green and yellow – can be found in the kitchen, bathroom and niches of the dammusi in Monastero. While each building's façade and interior simplicity recall the past, Giuntoli's clean-lined furnishings and subtle use of both natural and artificial lighting evoke a sense of contemporary well-being to anyone staying here.

Some of the buildings have their own shaded outdoor sitting area surrounded by seasonal blooms, while others face a wide common terrace where one can sit and enjoy an enchanting view of the surrounding countryside. The dammusi allow sweet seclusion after a day of splashing in isolated coves, golfing or relaxing by one of the resort's clear blue pools. Santa Teresa is a perfect combination of privacy, age-old tradition and simple living in a natural setting.

SANTA TERESA
RESORT

→ Italy
Pantelleria

DUOMO HOTEL → Italy
Rimini

→ Open
05/2006

→ Rates
EUR 180 –
EUR 400

→ Rooms
43

→ **Address**
Via G. Bruno 28
47900 Rimini
Italy

DUOMO HOTEL

Architecture / Interior Design
Ron Arad Associates

DUOMO HOTEL   → Italy
                Rimini

Long a fixture in the historic heart of Rimini, one of Italy's long-standing and established seaside resorts, the duoMo hotel was untouched for many years until the owners decided to bring celebrated designer Ron Arad and his team into the picture in 2003, resulting in a unique and exciting transformation. The main concept revolved around the need to embrace the past while simultaneously creating space for a thorough look into the future. This need for dynamism has created a unique design identity, where subtle contrasts, light, shadow and transparent elements were infused into the existing building, emerging into a new hotel.

Situated on a narrow street, typical for the Emilia-Romagna region, the façade lies in proximity to the opposite façade, begging for the unique interpretation that has carved its new identity by connecting the street to the building. The existing structure has been wrapped in a skin of Corian, which

meanders its way inside the building, forming the back wall of the bar and ending in a bench seat. The shiny metallic coating articulates the design language used throughout the property immediately upon viewing its exterior.

Guests enter the hotel through giant pinball-flipper doors. These frame the view to the reception area, which inevitably becomes the hotel's focal point. The front desk is an oversized circular stainless steel structure, dramatically leaning at an angle, looking like a large inclined wedding ring dancing on a plate. Shelves are built into this ring, defining the horizontal topography of the desk. The wall behind the reception is formed by a series of aluminium fin-shapes that allow natural daylight to flood the space while affording an edited view of the offices located behind it. Although ultra-futuristic in its design, the entrance area exudes a bouncy lightness. The original features, daring colours and adventurous shapes inevitably make a major impact.

The much-hyped noMi club is a large island with fjord-like scoops spreading outwards from the main structure to provide guests with surfaces to sit at. The bar's surface is made of brushed steel and its sides finished in mirrored polished steel, creating distorted reflections of the people and the surrounding environment. On balmy summer nights, cleverly retractable glass walls allow for the activity in the bar to be taken outside onto the streets of Rimini's lively historic centre. World-renowned DJs regularly entertain guests and locals, and the Sunday beach parties promoted by the hotel already feature high on the in-crowd's agenda. Unconventional and exciting design is also present in the private champagne room. It has been set up in an exclusive atmosphere for guests to indulge in after a long day of work or leisure.

Arad's audacious design philosophy is reflected throughout the rooms as well. Individually formed bathroom pods create the backdrops to the sleeping areas. Each pod is a wet room with teak-slatted timber flooring and a large circular glazed window. The exterior of this uniquely designed structure forms the bed's headboard. Arad visually provokes and experiments with basic spatial perceptions while maintaining the highest level of comfort in the rooms. The careful management of the movement of light and shadow evokes the idea of infinite spaces.

This tour de force is meant to aid the planned transformation of Rimini from a somewhat forgotten beach resort into a trendy destination. If one judges by the response the hotel has had so far, Rimini is once again firmly plotted on the maps of fashionable summer city breakers and stylish beach aficionados.

　　　　　　　　DUOMO HOTEL　　→ Italy
　　　　　　　　　　　　　　　　　　　　　　　　Rimini

HOTEL
LA COLUCCIA

→ Italy
Sardinia

→ Open
06/2003

→ Rates
EUR 260 –
EUR 640

→ Rooms
45

→ **Address**
Località Conca Verde
07028 Santa Teresa Gallura (SS)
Sardinia
Italy

HOTEL LA COLUCCIA

Architecture / Interior Design

Julio César Ayllón / Alvin Grassi

HOTEL
LA COLUCCIA

→ Italy
Sardinia

The bold, wave-crested façade of La Coluccia both harmonises with its Sardinian surroundings and stands out as a distinctive presence. The design by architect Julio César Ayllón and designer Alvin Grassi features a welcoming minaret that stands guard over the isle of Spargi, just opposite.

A flowing, dynamic screening wall presents La Coluccia's face to the world, while traditional Mediterranean tile roofs and other local motifs anchor the hotel in its spectacular setting, which includes pines and cypresses, rock formations and the sea. Sails cover an open square in the hotel's centre, which is paved with locally sourced Orosei marble. Lattice-roofed walkways lead around the compound, melding with the pine and bougainvillea that provide shade and privacy for the sculpted swimming pool. The entire complex lies low and takes advantage of its sea-sloping location to maximise exposure to the Mediterranean – to be enjoyed even from the comfort of the pool.

The use of only light colours is another distinguishing feature: sheer white, dove and ivory stand out against the green sea, but are paired with inserts in earth and red clay tones. As directed by Grassi, a protégé of the Italian designer Alberta Ferretti, the interior integrates high-fashion accents, featuring sleek, flowing forms and a mix of modern and traditional materials ranging from polished cement and soft leather to rich dark woods. Deep-set windows, as well as a mix of hard and cushioned surfaces, simplicity and softness, provide visual and tactile relief throughout this elegantly discreet gem.

ONE HOTEL → Italy
Siracusa

→ Open
05/2007

→ Rates
EUR 119 –
EUR 229

→ Rooms
44

→ **Address**
Diodoro Siculo, 4
96100 Siracusa
Italy

ONE HOTEL
Architecture / Interior Design
Mario Rizza

ONE HOTEL

→ Italy
Siracusa

Dramatically situated on the side of a cliff in Sicily and not far from the archaeological site of Syracuse – where Archimedes once lived and worked – One Hotel combines its ancient surroundings with the urbane contemporary world. Local architect Mario Rizza designed the three-storey building with its cage-like façade made from a steel frame and microperforated plates, which gives an impression of simultaneous power and grace.

From the lobby featuring Jean Marie Massaud's Auckland chairs and wave-like Aspen sofa, guests can access the sushi bar and restaurant, where walls and benches are covered with jet-black crocodile leather. The equally sleek Fly Chairs by Marco Acerbis complete the set. Directly next to the restaurant is an immaculate fitness studio offering a wide range of sport activities for sculpting its guests' bodies. Carved directly into the natural rock beneath the hotel, an area for a hammam, sauna and hydrotherapy offers a quiet haven in which to retreat.

All four guestroom styles are rigorously composed in black, white and grey. The executive room includes a balcony complete with its own mini Kyoto garden; other guests can sunbathe on a large roof terrace. Central to each room is a washbasin, situated outside the dark-tiled bathroom, that utilises LED lighting. Black-on-black floral pattern wallpaper highlighted by soft, indirect tinted lighting also endows a Zen-like elegance. It is this exquisite combination of black, white and coloured lighting that gently helps guests navigate through – and make fitting use of – the hotel's heady contrasts of energising activity and peaceful reflection.

VIGILIUS
MOUNTAIN
RESORT

→ Italy
South Tyrol

→ Open
11/2003

→ Rates
EUR 235 –
EUR 605

→ Rooms
41

VIGILIUS MOUNTAIN RESORT

Architecture / Interior Design
Matteo Thun, Studio Thun

In the soaring mountains of the south Tyrolean region of northern Italy, Milan-based architect Matteo Thun – being a south Tyrolean by birth – has created an environmentally minded mountain hideaway that perfectly illustrates his idea of "getting away from it all."

"Everything here revolves around nature and everything is landscape. From the outside, you hardly notice the hotel, and when you're inside, you see so much you could be outside. Put in another way, it's not like looking at a postcard; it's as if you were in the postcard," says Thun. Indeed. The Vigilius Mountain Resort can be reached only by travelling up 1,500 metres by cable car, and affords panoramic views of vineyards and apple farms near the town Bolzano as well as utter tranquillity at altitude. In keeping with his philosophy of blending his architecture into the context of its surroundings, Thun has used wood and glass in a way that blends into the sweeping vistas surrounding the hotel.

Also true to Thun's ecologically friendly approach to design, the resort is built with energy and nature conservation firmly rooted in the founding ethos of "organic architecture." The roof is covered in grass, local wood is used for heating and internally heated stone partitions in the hotel's 41 rooms and suites warm the interiors in the most efficient and pleasant way possible. These features, along with biomass heating, are just some of the very practical yet equally aesthetically pleasing solutions to fulfilling these laudable aims, which have won the hotel several awards, including the Wallpaper Design Award for Best New Eco Retreat in 2004.

But all this awareness does not detract from aesthetics. An attractive stylistic mix of unpolished silver quartz floors offsets well-placed sofas covered in black-and-white spotted cow hides – after which the unmistakably modern orange hue of the reception area beckons, glowing beyond a translucent partition. Wholeheartedly embracing the new has not precluded, however, the inclusion of a cosy tile-covered oven from the original late 19th-century structure or the 300-year-old timbers in the restaurant, appropriately named 1500. A destination spa – highlights of which are a spring-water pool behind an enormous window overlooking the valley below and beautiful outdoor terraces – echoes the well-considered, clean-lined architectural aspects of the rest of the resort while offering a wide array of holistic spa services, such as yoga courses, watsu Alpine treatments and the "move & explore" sports programme.

A unique sensory experience is created through the use of the naturally scented larch wood throughout, which has been painstakingly crafted to achieve three different finishes: Floors are covered in roughly patterned larch, a fine grain has been used for all panelling and finishes, and a fluted look graces the doors. All guestrooms face either east or west, allowing, as Thun says, "the colours of either dawn or sunset to transform them into theatres of light." The outdoors is brought even closer by floor-to-ceiling windows leading to generous balconies overlooking the Dolomites. Fireplaces are found inside, and not even a single piece of art on the walls distracts from the personal dialogue with nature.

"If 'landscape' can be translated as 'endlessness,' then 'landscape' is an endless topic to be examined. If 'nature' can be equated with 'freedom,' then many explorations can be considered," says Thun. His ability to both combine these ideas and find the perfect transition from the traditional to the modern simply reinforces the feeling that the Vigilius Mountain Resort is a perfectly organic extension of the ancient mountain on which it is perched.

→ **Address**
Vigiljoch
39011 Lana
South Tyrol
Italy

VIGILIUS
MOUNTAIN
RESORT

→ Italy
South Tyrol

CA' PISANI   → Italy
Venice

→ Open
12/2000

→ Rates
EUR 218 –
EUR 550

→ Rooms
29

CA' PISANI

Architecture / Interior Design
Roberto Luigi Canovaro / Pierluigi Perscolderung

A revived merchant's townhouse, nearly 500 years old, provides the setting for Venice's noble Ca'Pisani hotel. The building's traditional elements are on full display – but look closer and you will discover a Futurist palace.

Designers Roberto Luigi Canovaro and Pierluigi Pescolderung's concept includes elements of the Futurist movement of the 1930s and 1940s, whose polished, geometric forms are amplified by works created by renowned Italian artist Fortunato Depero. Yet original architectural features of the former townhouse – such as exposed wooden beams over the main hallway – are consistently integrated. The design theme is continued in the hotel's restaurant, La Rivista, where sparkling blue tables underscore a dreamy atmosphere.

"Starlight" is the name of the special type of masonry work – a unique technique that creates the effect of small, shining stars – that was developed to embellish the bathrooms in the hotel's 29 guestrooms. Each of the beds is an original piece from the 1930s or 1940s collected from all over Italy by the Serandrei family, Ca'Pisani's owners. Finer details in silver and amaranth and unique wooden inlays on each guestroom door only add to the feeling that the hotel is designed to give guests a sense of individuality. The hotel's location in a quiet, picturesque part of the city contributes to the calming effect of the interior designer's clean sharp lines, making Ca'Pisani a very special destination in Venice in which to experience the successful melding of two sharply contrasting design eras in a supremely relaxed setting.

→ **Address**
Dorsoduro 979/A
30123 Venezia
Italy

PALAZZINA
GRASSI HOTEL &
RESIDENCE

→ Italy
Venice

→ Open
12/2007

→ Rates
EUR 190 –
EUR 950

→ Rooms
32

PALAZZINA GRASSI HOTEL & RESIDENCE

Architecture / Interior Design
Susann-Kathrin Scharfen-Quellmann

Taking its diminutive name from the neighbouring art museum Palazzo Grassi, the small residence hotel Palazzina Grassi Hotel & Residence embodies two eras of Venetian history, yet unites them in a distinctly modern way.

Nestled between two larger palaces and accented with petite balconies and short, twisted columns, the property puts its noble 15th-century face forward on the Grand Canal. In joining the building's two sections built four centuries apart, the studio Susann-Kathrin Scharfen-Quellmann respected much of the original structure and used Venetian lamps and red fabrics to embellish the subtle, predominately white colour scheme and dark-wood modern furnishings. Here is where antique boiserie provides a contrast to the clean-lined, geometric furnishings within the suites' living and kitchen areas and bedroom, whose centre is a taut white canopy bed. In the bar on the ground floor, red tapestries by the historic Venetian firm Fortuny have been reinterpreted by a local artist and lie behind a glass panel on two walls. It is a colour that acts as a leitmotif joining the 15th-century architecture to the hotel's main area in the back, which was built in 1850 as a bathhouse. Although the latter's original colonnaded hall – rising through two floors – is no longer open to the sky, it has been painstakingly preserved.

Each of the hotel's 28 rooms and four suites has a different layout, but they share a truly modern design aesthetic, and some suites have private terraces overlooking the romantic, age-old landscape of Venice's interior courtyards. The lamps and fabrics join other materials representing local craftsmanship, such as terrazzo and glass mosaics. The marmorino plaster technique used on the walls is yet another nod to the city's legacy; it follows methods developed in Venice in the 15th-century to avoid heavy materials yet still create walls that look like marble. This little palace is an unfussy ode to contemporary, understated luxury melding seamlessly with elements of true Venetian history.

→ **Address**
San Marco 3247
30124 Venice
Italy

PALAZZO
BARBARIGO SUL
CANAL GRANDE

→ Italy
Venice

→ Open
09/2007

→ Rates
EUR 180 –
EUR 520

→ Rooms
18

PALAZZO BARBARIGO SUL CANAL GRANDE

Architecture / Interior Design
Elisabetta Coletti / Alvin Grassi

Enjoy an authentic Venetian atmosphere in a refurbished 16th-century palazzo lying directly on the city's most famous waterway. Near Ponte Rialto and Piazzale Roma, the building's red-brick bilevel façade and private gondola landing exude an understated, exclusive experience.

The six deluxe junior suites face the Canal Grande, the other twelve guestrooms overlook the romantic Rio San Polo. In updating a historic building dating back to 1569 – it was once a nobleman's dwelling – Hotelphilosophy creative director Alvin Grassi decided to bring contemporary architectural concepts to the existing volume and space, wich in turn became integral to developing the subtle interior design. In both public spaces and guestrooms, all interiors contain a touch of Art Deco-inspired glamour brought up to the present minute. Grassi's fashion-industry background is evident in the elegant choice of fabrics and textures found throughout the property: living areas are completely lined with damask fabrics inspired by the famed Venetian artist Fortuny, and Grassi himself designed original lamps. Furnishings also hearken back to another bygone era, lending the property a sense of elegant intimacy with curved leg chairs by designer Jacques Garcia and furnishings designed by Hotelphilosophy's creative team. Colours from dove grey and understated browns move into black and charcoal in a continuous tone-on-tone symphony that quietly yet steadily crescendoes through the visual spaces.

The modernised Art Deco theme is beautifully continued in the hotel's bar – a cavernous black space that might best be described as awe-inspiring. The overall result is a blend of past, present and a suggestion of the future; an example of Belle Époque-inspired luxury and just an air of the mystery and romance that modern-day artistes are longing for.

→ **Address**
San Polo 2765
Venice
Italy

LUTE SUITES   → Netherlands   → Open   → Rates   → Rooms

Amsterdam   01/2005   EUR 285 –   7

EUR 395

LUTE SUITES

Architecture / Interior Design
Marcel Wanders

Facing the Amstel River in the village of Ouderkerk, seven freestanding structures embody the exclusivity of luxury accommodations: at Lute Suites, guests literally have it all in the form of petite, three-level gabled cottages, each with a kitchenette and living room. But what could simply be a bucolic getaway is also a design aficionado's dream. Staying here, on the reclaimed site of an 18th-century gunpowder factory, is the closest you can come to inhabiting the studio of one of Europe's most acclaimed young designers, Marcel Wanders, artistic director of the Netherlands-based design collective Moooi.

Renowned Dutch chef Peter Lute's eponymous restaurant – occupying a portion of the factory with a distinctive bell-shaped gable and arches passageway – began this location's renaissance in 2003. Rotterdam architect Eline Strijkers honoured the historic preservation orders for the designated national monument and created "satellite" spaces to accommodate a working restaurant. The result includes structures within structures, such as the glass and steel greenhouse dining area beneath a hayloft.

Wanders first came to Lute for a meal, but ultimately became the creator and co-owner of Lute Suites, infusing the seven adjacent structures with his playful imagination. The reconstructed wonderland is filled with creations by Wanders, Karin

→ **Address**
Amsteldijk Zuid 54 – 58
1184 VD Ouderkerk a/d Amstel
Netherlands

LUTE SUITES   → Netherlands
                 Amsterdam

Krautgardner and fellow Moooi designers. Wanders jumped at the opportunity to work with Lute. "Interiors offer me a chance to look at the products I've designed and test their usability," he says.

Like the river framed by the suites' ten-foot windows, water is an interior centrepiece, showcasing Wanders's work with Italian manufacturers Bisazza and Boffi. Wanders's white "soap bath" for Bisazza resembles a futuristic vehicle or prehistoric egg and even grants a river view. In other bathrooms, his Gobi line basins and fixtures for Boffi include a flower knob tap control, reminiscent of a garden hose attachment. All "wet rooms" have intricately patterned Bisazza mosaic-tile walls designed by Wanders. The suites' architectural framework is designed to offer views of the bathroom itself, whether through smoked glass, a metal or teak spiral staircase, or a flower-patterned metal screen. The steeply pitched roofs and heavy support beams are also highlighted. In two suites, the bedroom is a tent-like nest beneath the roof, connected to the mezzanine via a ladder.

Each suite is individually decorated, some with a signature Wanders "knotted chair," a hammock-like piece of carbon and epoxy-coated aramid fibres, a design held by the Museum of Modern Art in New York. Its macramé motif is picked up in a stairwell's suspension support. Wanders's plastic webbed Gwapa chairs, oversize

LUTE SUITES → Netherlands
Amsterdam

LUTE SUITES → **Netherlands**
Amsterdam

lamps, exuberantly colourful side table and prototypes created especially for Lute round out the fun, modish looks. Slim Bottoni sofas get custom-made fabric by Paul Smith, who also outfitted the restaurant's staff.

Other Moooi designer pieces include the black leather and "burnt" wood Smoke chair by Maarten Baas and Light Shade Shade lamps by Jurgen Bey. To "wrap" these collector furnishings, surfaces are composed like decoratively crafted gift boxes: wallpaper has a Baroque pattern, a ceiling is painted gold, floors are made with inlaid steel and, of course, there's Bisazza mosaic tiling.

In Wanders's opinion, "A hotel should offer experience, it should be exciting and surprising with a strong visual rationale that elicits a strong emotional response." In this case, he puts his figurative message literally on the walls and conveys a sense of optimism. In one living room, multiple shelves stretching the length of the wall hold his one-minute sculptures – coral-like clay forms painted gold. It is proof of what can be accomplished when seizing not only the day, but 60 seconds. In the "boardroom" conference cottage, newspaper headlines and articles bearing good news paper the wall. Lute Suites is true to the unapologetically earnest philosophy of Wanders's design studio: "Here to create an environment of love, live with passion, and make our most exciting dreams come true."

KRUISHERENHOTEL → Netherlands
MAASTRICHT   Maastricht

→ Open
04/2005

→ Rates
EUR 240 –
EUR 375

→ Rooms
60

KRUISHERENHOTEL MAASTRICHT

Architecture / Interior Design
Rob Brouwers at Satijn plus Architects, Wil Snelder at Kragten /
Henk Vos of Vos Interior Designs, Ingo Maurer

Fusing austere Gothicism with chic modern design, the Kruisherenhotel opens into the inner shell of a monastery dating from 1438. Situated on the picturesque *Kommelplein* square in central Maastricht, the complex once served as a monastery and church for the Order of Crutched Friars, but late in 2000, renowned developer Camille Oostwegel transformed the derelict buildings into a luxurious hotel while retaining respect for its celebrated legacy.

The contrast between past and present is highlighted through the visual language of Henk Vos with creations by Le Corbusier and Rietveld as well as contemporary designers like Marc Newson and Philippe Starck. Three interconnected locations house the hotel's 60 rooms and suites. The monastery hosts most guestrooms, while the Renaissance-style concierge building and a new annex accommodate the remaining spaces, including two carefully appointed gastronomic establishments that cater to a distinguished clientele with Michelin-starred cuisine and panoramic views. The church contains the integrated reception area, conference rooms, a library, boutique and coffee bar. Surrounded by cloister corridors, the gardens match the historic architectural lines and interiors, and an inner court sets the tone for a modern interpretation of the outside space. German artist Ingo Maurer's light installations add the finishing touches.

Vos composed various colour schemes, styles and furnishings to create an individual character for each of the rooms. Resting on the design principles of transparency, space and comfort, interiors are enhanced by the intriguing contrasts resulting from the stained glass windows, authentic original wall and ceiling paintings. Paying tribute to contemporary design while honouring age-old construction and detailing, the Kruisherenhotel is an architectural journey through the ages.

→ **Address**
Kruisherengang 19–23
6211 NW Maastricht
Netherlands

KRUISHERENHOTEL → Netherlands
MAASTRICHT   Maastricht

THE OTHER SIDE → **Norway**
Neiden

→ **Open**
03/2008

→ **Rates**
EUR 225 –
EUR 520

→ **Rooms**
24

THE OTHER SIDE

Architecture / Interior Design
Birgitta Ralston and Alexandre Bau

Atop a plateau in Norway's northern stretches, The Other Side strives to live up to its name with a view that seems to extend endlessly and a truly innovative concept. Swedish/French design duo Birgitta Ralston and Alexandre Bau based the resort's architecture and building layout on the traditions of the local Sámi people, complete with shamanism and a sense of otherworldly magic. This inspiration is accompanied by an ultramodern interpretation of luxury that takes in as much of the unusual natural ambience as possible.

A panoramic view of the Neiden Plateau, near Norway's borders with Russia and Finland, is bounded by the Barents Sea and the Neidenelven, a famous salmon river. The architecture is designed for maximum environment, from the northern lights in winter to the midnight sun in the summer, from viewing the surrounding tundra's elk and reindeer to gliding in a sleigh behind a team of sled dogs. Twelve houses are laid out in groups of three, following a pattern based on a Sámi shaman drum. Each structure takes its inspiration from elemental forces: the Wind House is perched in the air, the Water House over a pond and the Fire House in front of an enormous ritual fireplace.

Each cluster is accompanied by a multi-storey bathhouse, which provides a fireplace, library and panoramic view of the countryside in addition to the facilities promised by its name. Russian design elements, connoted by crackling fireplaces and decadent fur accents, adorn the Goddess Suites as well as the Other Side of the Moon, the hotel's innovative restaurant. The contrasts come alive most in the Goddess Suites, where a roaring fire plays off a sweeping vista of perfect Nordic placidity.

→ Address
9930 Neiden
Norway

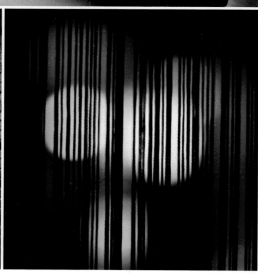

GRIMS GRENKA → Norway
Oslo

→ Open
01/2008

→ Rates
NOK 1495 –
NOK 20000

→ Rooms
66

GRIMS GRENKA

Architecture / Interior Design
Kristin Jarmund Architects

Situated in the heart of Oslo, Grims Grenka's focus on refined and modern design elements is combined with traditionally Norwegian features to create a luxurious and sensual atmosphere. Tactile natural materials such as stone, wood and leather are paired with glass and painted surfaces. Eye-catching flourishes include folk art, lamps made from reindeer antlers and a moss garden embedded in the reception desk.

That desk, its front backlit and made of satinated blue glass, stretches for eight metres within the vast lobby. Ancient Norwegian log-houses are the inspiration for the long, continuous walnut panelling throughout the space, but an ultramodern and three-dimensional twist is added with integrated lighting and niches for seating and bars.

Lighting is closely integrated with the interiors and furnishings, creating different atmospheres for different rooms and zones, and variation according to time of day and season. To draw out the pervasive horizontal lines and "floating" concept of the interiors, light sources often are cleverly hidden and placed at a low level – such as under beds, tables and shelves.

The furniture designs are both Nordic and European, with custom-made writing desks, benches and night shelves in the guestrooms. "Summer rooms" are done in black and green tones with natural oak, and "winter rooms" are predictably grey, white and blue in combination with a darker, warmer oak. The colour of the ceiling is always carried down one of the walls, and the colour of the floor is taken up on the opposite wall, resulting in a cosy "wrapping" effect. Exposure comes with the bathrooms, which either have semi-transparent glass walls or are totally opened up and integrated into the entire room. Entrances to guestrooms are made via individual "wooden bridges" sheltered by wood walls and a ceiling and accented with mirrors. Talk about dramatic entrances and exits – Grims Grenka keeps both natural and exciting.

→ **Address**
Kongens gate 5
0153 Oslo
Norway

FAROL DESIGN
HOTEL

→ Portugal
Cascais

→ Open
05/2002

→ Rates
EUR 110 –
EUR 370

→ Rooms
34

FAROL DESIGN HOTEL

Architecture / Interior Design
CM Dias Arquitectos

Mounted on the rocky shoreline of the Estoril Coast, this daring property, created by CM Dias Arquitectos, practically falls into the Atlantic Ocean – and right into the lap of the sophisticated fashionistas who frequent it.

To complete the modern transformation of the Count of Cabral's 19th-century mansion, selected players culled from Portugal's fashion-world elite were successfully courted to each "dress a room." Ana Salazar, Fátima Lopez, Miguel Vieira and Manuel Alves & José Manuel Gonçalves were among the designers who created individual looks to rival the latest catwalk impressions for every room. Public spaces offer splashes of red in both furnishings and on interior and exterior walls, adding to the building's almost regal splendour.

Beautiful aquatic retreats have been integrated throughout the property and include an outdoor saltwater pool and hydro-massage bathtubs in each of the guestrooms. The Rosa Maria restaurant serves delectable Mediterranean fusion cuisine by chef Bernhard Pfister in a subdued, chic atmosphere. Certainly a setting fit for a count, if not a fashionable king.

→ **Address**
Av. Rei Humberto II de Itália, No. 7
2750-461 Cascais
Portugal

FONTANA PARK
HOTEL

→ Portugal
Lisbon

→ Open
10/2007

→ Rates
EUR 170 –
EUR 565

→ Rooms
139

FONTANA PARK HOTEL

Architecture / Interior Design
Francisco Aires Mateus / Nini Andrade Silva

As part of a project focused on refashioning old buildings in Portugal's emerging metropolis, the Fontana Park Hotel has preserved the original theme of its structure, which was an iron factory in the early 1900s. The iron motif is visible from floor to ceiling in this 139-room hotel located on a hill above Lisbon's old city, most noticeably in the eye-catching reception area.

Prominent Portuguese architect Francisco Aires Mateus has lent a strong modern flourish to the project, and award-winning designer Nini Andrade Silva has injected her signature blend of minimalism ("ninimalist") and soulful personality into the space. Guestroom furnishings incorporate a palette of black and white with occasional flirtations with green, and all is simple and unfussy to emphasise the beauty and appeal of both the surrounding architecture and the cosmopolitan Portuguese capital.

/ 333

→ **Address**
Rua Engenheiro Vieira Da Silva, 2
1050-105, Lisbon
Portugal

Even the bathrooms are haute design – guests can relax in an illuminated bathtub after dining at the hotel's upscale seafood restaurant Saldanha Mar, which is all in white, or at the hotel's chic Asian fusion boîte spot Bonsai, which contains a 100-year-old namesake tree as well as imperial purple rugs and luminous inset lighting. The bar embraces an approach different from the restaurants and guestrooms, using bold colour blocking to elicit a visual intensity: black bar stools stand in front of a black lacquer counter and an interactive screen wall. Old has never felt so new.

FONTANA PARK
HOTEL

→ Portugal
Lisbon

JERÓNIMOS 8 → Portugal
Lisbon

→ Open
08/2007

→ Rates
EUR 220 –
EUR 325

→ Rooms
65

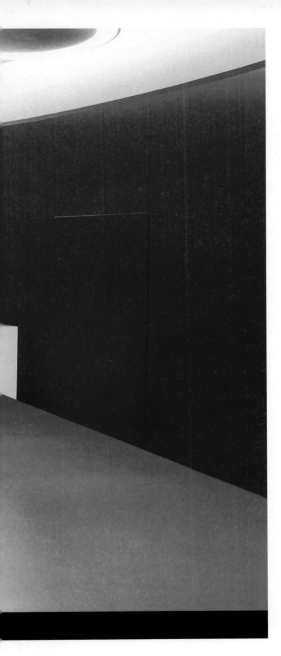

JERÓNIMOS 8

Architecture / Interior Design
Sofia Tavares / Capinha Lopes & Associates;
Project Director – Sofia Freire

Where the tidal waters of the Atlantic flow into the estuary of the Tagus River, old and new come together in the hotel Jerónimos 8. Located in Lisbon's historic district of Belém and surrounded by museums and monuments, the 1940s building has been given new life by the Lisbon-based architects Capinha Lopes & Associates, whose renovation of the hotel liaises with its surroundings.

The ornate gables, statues and reliefs of the nearby 16th-century Jerónimos Monastery accentuate the modern renovation. Windows afford a view of the monastery from the hotel's wine bar, where one can taste the rare and much sought-after Bussaco wine that has been produced for generations by the Alexandre de Almeida family, which also owns the hotel. As if to reflect the wines, the bar is designed in a rich savoury palette of red, white and brown, with a dark-wood floor and floating lamps. The welcoming reception desk – a lustrous, dark chocolate cube of Wenge wood

→ **Address**
Rua dos Jerónimos, 8
1400-211 Lisboa
Portugal

before a crimson wall – greets guests in the same colour scheme. The passage to their rooms follows a brightly lit corridor carpeted in alternating stripes of browns and reds, with the room numbers on the floor in front of each door.

Despite the proximity to the monastery, the rooms are anything but ascetic. Instead, they are snugly appointed in shades of chestnut, burnt sienna and cream. Each of the 65 rooms and suites has a pale marble bathroom generously bathed in natural light. Throughout the hotel, the abundance of natural lighting blends the interior with the Lisbon sky outside.

CHOUPANA HILLS
RESORT & SPA

→ Portugal
Madeira

→ Open
03/2002

→ Rates
EUR 275 –
EUR 788

→ Rooms
62

CHOUPANA HILLS RESORT & SPA
Architecture / Interior Design
Michael de Camaret / Didier Lefort

French architect Michel de Camaret and designer Didier Lefort have brought both Asian and African flair to this subtropical retreat, which they composed using local wood and volcanic stone.

On a south-facing slope high above the Madeiran capital of Funchal, individual bungalows stand on stilts, their verandas and wooden peaked ceilings providing an airy, safari tent-like haven 500 metres above the Atlantic. Decorating the rooms are coconut mats, fine linens and custom-made furniture such as a canopied four-poster bed inspired by the construction of the island's old-fashioned ox-drawn carts. Sliding doors are made of the willow trees from the neighbouring village. Local volcanic basalt is used around the pool area or to create walkways in various forms – ranging from raw, polished or whole to broken down into pebbles. In the larger communal building, a "post and beams" concept is attractively applied to marking wide-open spaces through the use of massive Tali wood pillars. The bar Basalt is suspended above the Asian-styled Xôpana Restaurant. In the lounge, the modern sofas are Lefort's version of the famous sleds that provide rides from Monte to Funchal.

Antiques have been brought in from other parts of the world: the oldest are 17th-century Italian and Spanish dressers adorned with ivory, gold leaf and tortoiseshell. Two 18th-century stone Buddhas are examples of newer rarities. Despite the exquisite attention to detail indoors, it is the spectacle of city rooftops and endless ocean that is truly breathtaking, especially when savoured from the comfort of a jacuzzi on the suite terraces or the tranquillity of the outdoor infinity-edge pool.

→ Address
Travessa do Largo da Choupana
9060-348 Funchal
Portugal

ESTALAGEM DA
PONTA DO SOL

→ Portugal
Madeira

→ Open
2001

→ Rates
EUR 90 –
EUR 130

→ Rooms
54

ESTALAGEM DA PONTA DO SOL

Architecture / Interior Design
Tiago Oliveira / Tiago Oliveira, Carvalho Araújo

Confident in its simplicity and conceding to what Mother Nature offers, this stark white getaway by architect Tiago Oliveira is all straight edges but still conforms to the slate outcroppings high above the village of Ponta do Sol.

The raw magnificence of the cliff setting demanded that the hotel layer itself in sections down a slope terraced by thick stone walls. Given the overwhelming view, the challenge was to establish a sequence of eye-catchers and wind barriers that create points of interest all over the grounds. In the end several circuits were created – some through a covered bridge, others on the ground – which intersect or even join at certain points. The hotel's flat surfaces and many angles create stark shadows that seem to carve the entire space as well.

Aiming to highlight the natural surrounding beauty, Portuguese interior designer Carvalho Araújo painted rooms' walls white and chose minimalist furnishings in light wood. Floors of black stone are strewn with grey rugs, and classic black-and-white photography on the walls underlines the monochrome look.

All rooms have balconies and the swimming pool has an infinity edge, which makes the Atlantic seem just a dive away. Sitting on its very own perch, the rectangular shape of the restaurant raises the level of originality even further. Other than the choice of sterling silver cutlery and table accessories placed on bare white linens, it is completely stripped of any superfluous décor, emphasising the stunning view across the coastline of Madeira, extensive banana plantations and the Ponta do Sol village through the floor-to-ceiling windows, which are merely framed by the sides of the box.

→ Address
Quinta da Rochinha
9360 Ponta do Sol, Madeira
Portugal

HOSPES
AMÉRIGO

→ **Spain**
Alicante

→ **Open**
06/2004

→ **Rates**
EUR 185 –
EUR 720

→ **Rooms**
81

→ **Address**
C/Rafael Altamira, 7
03002 Alicante
Spain

HOSPES AMÉRIGO
Architecture / Interior Design
Hospes Design Team

In the centre of Alicante, close to the popular La Esplanada avenue as well as El Postiguet beach, the grand façade of the hotel Hospes Amérigo draws your attention skywards to the arched neo-Gothic windows and Juliet balconies.

The exceptional property has experienced previous incarnations as a Dominican convent, then a complex of commercial offices and, lastly, an apartment block before being saved and wholly refurbished and updated by the Hospes Design Team. Parts of the historic façade have been preserved and some of the old stones salvaged from the original convent structure, which now form parts of the walls on each floor. The modern light-filled lobby gleams with polished white marble and glass surfaces, but the past is present again in the wrought iron work that surrounds the balcony above it.

Guestrooms have been decorated in a warm cosy palette of neutral colours and simple textures: Cream-coloured armchairs sit comfortably on pale hand-woven carpets, and a touch of unobtrusive, bourgeois decorative elements probably would also have pleased the mid-19th century residents of the Amérigo. If you're inspired by the romance of the Juliet balconies, then simply head to the roof terrace from which the fantastic views of Alicante's castle are best enjoyed while lying in the heated pool, enjoying a romantic dinner under the stars or having a natural treatment in the crystal Bodyna Spa. Or, back downstairs, allow yourself a taste of the region in the Senzone Restaurant and Tapas Bar. It all adds up to sensual aesthetics that promise utter enchantment.

HOSPES
AMÉRIGO

→ Spain
Alicante

CASA CAMPER   → Spain
               Barcelona

→ Open
01/2005

→ Rates
EUR 180 –
EUR 260

→ Rooms
25

→ **Address**
Carrer Elisabets nº11
08001 Barcelona
Spain

CASA CAMPER

Architecture / Interior Design
Jordi Tio / Fernando Amat

CASA CAMPER → **Spain**
Barcelona

Young, fresh and quirky, Casa Camper is as easy to slip into as a pair of your favourite shoes. "The name *camper* means 'peasant' in Catalan," says Miguel Fluxá, Camper heir, head of business development and one of the minds behind the Mallorca-based shoe company's first hotel diversification. "We still believe that everything we do should be connected to the land." In a renovated 19th-century building nestled in a lively side street of Barcelona's new trendy El Reval district, the 25-room hotel offers hip urban nomads a retreat from the city's and neighbourhood's bustle with a casually modernist and eco-friendly space that goes hand-in-hand with the firm's basic philosophies.

El Reval's mix of old corner shops and new restaurants, thousands of passers-by and Richard Meier's MACBA contemporary art museum may not exactly be rural, but Casa Camper exudes a homey yet hip, active atmosphere that begins with the bicycles hanging on pulleys from the front foyer's ceiling. These can be lowered and ridden freely around the city. Entering the hotel's island-style lobby, a luxurious marble and wood reception counter decorated with Pop Art contrasts with an antique window display cabinet. The rear of the lobby, done in Camper's signature blood-red and equipped with sleek silver tables and benches, looks like an upscale cafeteria and features a 24-hour buffet offering *tentenpié* ("snack" in Spanish). Here, guests can relax and

CASA CAMPER   → Spain
Barcelona

reload on soups, sandwiches and juices while they gaze at Hannah Collins's photographs of the rapidly changing neighbourhood's distinctive buildings.

In the uncarpeted corridors upstairs, guests may think they are seeing double: each standard room is actually two spaces across the hall from each other. The quiet rooms to the back are compact bedrooms (*dormitorio*) in the same red as the lobby, while the front sitting rooms (*salita de estar*) in white offer either a getaway space or one from which to watch the colourful parade on the busy street below from the balcony. Nothing is overdone; everything has a purpose or visual appeal. The overall stylistic effect is modern, sparsely comfortable and, well, cool.

And many of the rooms' most eye-catching details come from Vinçon, arguably Barcelona's finest design shop. Vinçon's owner, the renowned Spanish interior designer Fernando Amat, was responsible for the design of Camper's very first Barcelona shoe store and also created the hotel's look and feel. "We chose the name Casa Camper because the idea is that the guests use the hotel in the same way they would use their house," explains Amat, who made sure that each room is as functional as it is funky. Bedrooms have extra-wide beds, cubbyholes for storage and pegs for hanging that cover an entire wall; the adjacent bathrooms are dominated by walk-in showers featuring oversized showerheads. A window above the wide sink in each room offers a view of a lush "vertical garden" of potted plants that completely cover the opposite courtyard wall. Across the hall, the living room area is equipped with a flat-screen TV, a foldout couch bed and a Mexican hammock for lazing around. Travellers need only bring their laptops: wireless Internet access is available in every room and also on the hotel's roof terrace.

While T-shirted staff members are glad to bring you breakfast or a pillow from the pillow menu, service has an inspirational human touch that goes far beyond just being friendly personnel. Sprinkled throughout the hotel are splashy graphics by designers América Sánchez and Albert Planas and signs with the Camper motto "Walk, don't run" or the motivational maxims "Express yourself" and "You are what you eat" – an eye-chart-like poster that reiterates the aphorisms graces the bathrooms. And the company's ecological, healthful attitude is reflected not only in Casa Camper's non-smoking policy, but also in a comprehensive recycling programme, solar panels and a unique system that reuses hotel water (don't worry … the first use is shower water, the second for the toilets). Camper authenticity is also obvious next door at the FoodBall restaurant, where guests can lounge on a set of stairs while they enjoy an array of fresh organic juices and delicate organic balls of free-range chicken and other fillings covered in a layer of brown rice.

Casa Camper believes that "the secret to true luxury lies in simplicity." With its clean lines, laid-back ambience and little surprises like jelly flip-flops in each room, Camper has succeeded in capturing the functionality and fun of its groovy shoe line in a space that is welcoming, comforting and devoted to keeping things simple.

GRANADOS 83 → Spain
Barcelona

→ Open
03/2006

→ Rates
EUR 242 –
EUR 533

→ Rooms
77

GRANADOS 83

Architecture / Interior Design
Carles Basso and Joseph Mª Vidal / Jordi Clos, Kim Castells, Jordi Cuenca

Built on an architecturally notable Neoclassical site, Barcelona's venerable Pujol i Brull clinic, the Granados 83 brings high-end materials and design to its Old City location.

The hotel is constructed around a luminous central courtyard that itself spreads out from an elevator shaft in the middle, which leads to a glass ceiling. This extraordinarily vertical public space is the guiding organisational principle for the whole hotel. The original colonnades are enhanced by modern steel, red marble, glass and iron, but the lobby is dotted by strategically placed antiques and *objects d'art*. Images are constantly projected onto the walls, giving a sense of constant low-level movement. Flooring is black and white stone slabs that provide the visual texture of carpeting, and the motif of light and dark continues elsewhere: hallways are covered in pale marble and zebrawood.

Further use of marble, steel and glass continues in the guestrooms, enhanced by bare slabs of brick. Through the extensive use of white Thassos marble, bathrooms are an oasis of purity. All furnishings are covered in phosphorescent iron plating in order to create visual and tactile consistency – including the desks, above which pieces of Asian art are on show, helping to soften the ultramodern choice of materials. Further warmth is lent by raw leather inserts on chairs and the bed's headboard, creating a mix of materials that is both inspiring and soothing.

→ Address
Enric Granados, 83
08008 Barcelona
Spain

GRAND HOTEL
CENTRAL

→ Spain
Barcelona

→ Open
11/2005

→ Rates
EUR 245 –
EUR 765

→ Rooms
147

30
na

GRAND HOTEL CENTRAL

Architecture / Interior Design
Adolph Forensa and Oriol Tintoré / Sandra Tarruella and Isabel López

Barcelona's Grand Hotel Central carries the signature of two architects working 85 years apart: Adolph Forensa, who designed the original building in 1924, and Oriol Tintoré, who created its recent new look.

The hotel is built around an open central patio, a diaphanous space that allows a unique diffusion of light and sound. The lobby itself is laid out largely in its original format, a kind of blast from the past to remind guests of the hotel's former function and design as an office building. The building's original entrance, a carriage path with sidewalks, and a main path have all been maintained. A library at the entrance and living rooms at the end of corridors provide common space and break up the typical hegemony of rooms and corridors.

Interior design by Sandra Tarruella and Isabel López emphasises urban modernity, but with a transparency motif operating as well: much is made of glass and semi-opaque dividing surfaces. Bedroom and bath merge into each other without overemphasising compartmentalised space, and wardrobes are open to further enhance this open, flowing feeling. Softness and subtlety come from sconce lighting and dark wooden floors, contrasting with the simple lines and oversized rectilinear shapes. All rooms have street views, owing to the gallery construction. Superior rooms benefit from the larger scale of the building's original layout of space. Graphics, interior design and architecture combine to make the Grand Hotel Central one of Barcelona's new design treats.

GRAND HOTEL
CENTRAL

→ Spain
Barcelona

HOTEL CLARIS → Spain
Barcelona

→ Open
02/1992

→ Rates
EUR 125 –
EUR 1500

→ Rooms
124

HOTEL CLARIS

Architecture / Interior Design
MBM Architects

Part of Barcelona's renaissance as a bustling centre for commerce and the arts, the Claris has offered a high standard of design and luxury since 1992. The façade, built one hundred years earlier in 1892 as the exterior part of the former 19th-century Neoclassical Verduna Palace, was reworked by MBM Architects and incorporated into a new hotel space.

Alcove lighting highlights the lobby with its plate-glass fronting and copper, steel and concrete interior. The elegant lines of the stair rails, for instance, complement the overall dynamism of the substantial staircase; it all ultimately leads to a rooftop pool that combines traditional tiling with modern glass and neutral-hued wood structures. Throughout the hotel, a quiet sense of determined modernism, clean lines and contemporary materials go hand in hand with the classic façade.

The 124 guestrooms, including 38 suites, reflect modern values with elegant lines and detailing in steel and copper. No two rooms are alike: from the design and construction of the furniture to the choice of marble and exotic wood, everything has been made by great craftsmen using traditional methods. Within this grand structure combinations of old and new, whimsy and logic, come in to their own. Over 400 o*bjets d'art* are strategically scattered throughout the building and rooms, and include a group of Indian and Burmese sculptures dating from the 5th to the 13th centuries, more than 100 original engravings commissioned by Napoleon in 1812 during the Egyptian campaign, Turkish kilims, Roman and Carthaginian mosaics and engravings by Guinovart exclusively produced for the hotel.

→ **Address**
Pau Claris 150
08009 Barcelona
Spain

HOTEL CRAM → Spain
Barcelona

→ Open
02/2005

→ Rates
EUR 143 –
EUR 532

→ Rooms
67

HOTEL CRAM

Architecture / Interior Design

GCA Arquitectes Associates, Josep Riu, Paco de Paz, Beatriz Cosials

Striking curves coil around a central space. Sumptuous oranges and vivid vermilion contrast with surfaces in stark black and white where water and light move and meld to create an unforgettable atmosphere. Set in Barcelona's historic yet bustling Eixample district, the design concept of Hotel Cram could be seen as a quieter reflection of the dynamic city it lives in. Here is a place that, like Barcelona, wraps itself around you in a way that's oddly contradictory and almost indescribable, but is, more often than not, a vibrant, pleasant surprise.

Behind the historical façade of this completely reconstructed 1892 corner building, Spanish architect Josep Riu of GCA Arquitectes Associates has created a modernist 67-room hotel around a central, cylindrical courtyard that carries natural illumination from above down the structure's seven floors. While one is immediately struck by a muted ambience upon entering the lobby – with its anthracite-hued granite and dark-wood floors, black ceilings and "Tibetan" toned textiles and accents – the open column acts as a beacon of

soft light. "It's like a lamp," says GCA architect Roser Huguet. "It takes the light down to the lowest level of the hotel."

The Cram's elegant ground-floor public spaces greet guests with the dark modernist aesthetic of interior designer Beatriz Cosials. Here, ceiling-to-floor curtains offer a sensation similar to, perhaps, being backstage in an theatre, while low-lying, sleek black couches and modernist seating invite guests to settle in to a drink at the Majreva Lobby cocktail bar – while gazing at the wall of water separating it from the reception. The lighting concept is designed to create a subdued atmosphere in that it is always indirect, at times even subtly whimsical: small points of light that spell the word "light" in Japanese are set into the bar's black ceiling.

For all the soft darkness below, the hotel's upper spaces offer contrasts of dark and light and a cleaner, cooler feel. Leading upward like a series of white rings, broken by the vertical colour blocks created by the elevators, the courtyard column acts as a centrepiece

→ **Address**
Calle Aribau 54
08011 Barcelona
Spain

HOTEL CRAM → **Spain**
Barcelona

for the hotel's unusual structure and unique aesthetic. It is further embellished by a filigree hanging sculpture-like fixture sprinkled with delicate points of light. "The rooms lead off from the floors that branch off from the courtyard column, and each floor's décor is done in either a deep orange or red," states Huguet.

Because of the building's unusual shape – which is the result of the architects cleverly conforming to Spanish codes of construction – each room is different. Ranging in size from 16 to 22 square meters, rooms are sleekly efficient with wood floors and fully integrated storage and light units in pristine white. The guestrooms also play with the established colour scheme of oranges and reds by contrasting the basic white with coloured textile accents and furnishings by Edison Barone and Derin Sariyer, thus making the overall experience chromatically harmonious. Even the ceilings in the elegantly curved, white-tiled bathrooms echo the same tones. Here, too, light plays an important role: illumination is adjustable and allows guests to create a variety of individual atmospheres according to the comfortably cliché settings for "welcome," "fiesta," "romantic" and "night light."

After one has reached the apex of the "lamp" and therefore the top of the building, an outdoor rooftop pool and bar offer breathtaking views of the city in all its colours. Dwindling just a little bit down again, a relaxed side to this vibrant city is also palpable in the acclaimed restaurant Gaig one floor below, where chef Carles Gaig serves delectable Catalan cuisine in a restaurant dating back to 1869 – now both spatially and aesthetically integrated into the overall theme of the Cram in elegant red and black tones.

A truly enlightening roller-coaster ride with all the necessary aesthetic safety features awaits you at the Hotel Cram – an experience that mixes light and dark, history and modernity, water and light. A fitting embodiment of what Barcelona has to offer.

HOTEL OMM
→ Spain
Barcelona

→ Open
12/2003

→ Rates
EUR 246 –
EUR 910

→ Rooms
91

HOTEL OMM

Architecture / Interior Design

Juli Capella, Isabel López, Sandra Tarruella

Situated within Barcelona's fashionable Passeig de Gràcia district, Hotel Omm is the function-driven creation of architect Juli Capella and renowned Spanish interior designers Sandra Tarruella and Isabel López.

Sections of the unusual limestone façade teasingly peel back like pages of a book about to reveal the rooms inside. Yet what seems like decorative fantasy is actually functional: the façade design puts windows at angles to the outside, thereby shielding guests from unwanted views into their rooms and, at the same time, allowing direct sunlight to flood in while also softening any disturbing street noise. Giving a high priority to spaciousness and cosmopolitan style, the lobby – cleverly flowing into a sleek bar, then the restaurant – is devoid of boutiques and stairwells, and furnishings are kept at a low, uniform height. Individual artworks are found in public areas, such as the restaurant Moo. There, diners' attention is drawn to the individual under-plate designs by Spanish artists and designers such as Frederic Amat, Mario Eskenazi and Antonio Miró. A recently added full-service spa in an adjacent wing echoes the hotel's chic, jet-set elegance, which attracts both international and local guests.

The interior concept by Tarruella and López is based on simple lines, a fine balance of colours and volumes, and the use of natural materials without extravagant adornments. In this case, functionality doesn't necessarily preclude elements of surprise. Yes, the black rubber-lined corridors absorb sound, but, with two tubes of light spanning their length, they also create a very futuristic, spacey atmosphere. Passing through the hotel's dark hallways and then entering the light-filled rooms adds to the experience: doors open directly into the guestrooms' wide-open spaces unrestricted by an intermediary corridor. Furnishings are limited to modular pieces, and only a lightweight metal wardrobe and an entertainment unit separate the bedroom from the bathroom – which again avoids the superfluous without forfeiting comfort in any way.

HOTEL OMM   → Spain
              Barcelona

HOTEL OMM → **Spain**
Barcelona

HOTEL OMM   → **Spain**
Barcelona

NERI H & R   → Spain
Barcelona

→ Open
07/2003

→ Rates
EUR 285 –
EUR 485

→ Rooms
22

→ **Address**
Carrer Sant Sever, 5
08002 Barcelona
Spain

NERI H & R / 375
Architecture / Interior Design
Julio Pérez Catalá / Cristina Gabás

NERI H & R

→ **Spain**
Barcelona

Interior designer Cristina Gabás has taken the historical class of this 18th-century palace in the oldest part of Barcelona and enriched it with dazzling modern luxury befitting its location nestled between the cathedral and Sant Jaume Square.

Gabás masterfully combined antiques from the building's original epoch with lushly rough furnishings to create a wholly contemporary but extremely luxurious style. An exclusive location, Neri's elegant restaurant and bar lounge has a seductive ambience. Here, even the vases surprisingly match the sheer, crinkled silver metallic fabric that serves as a blind in front of arched floor-to-ceiling windows. The senses are roused by tactile surfaces and scents from essential oils and candles as well as jasmine and orange blossom trees on the roof terrace. The terrace follows the dictates of feng shui, combining the five elements to achieve a perfect equilibrium. Time stands still in the library, where the original wainscoting has been preserved and novels set in Barcelona take you deeper into the city.

The hotel's spaciousness is the first sign of luxury in the rather cramped Gothic Quarter, but some of the most dazzling elements of the Neri H & R speak of more refined opulence: gold and silver leaf artworks, rich velvets and iridescent fabrics, and the rough grain of quartzite bathrooms offset by the smooth minimalism of Arne Jacobsen fittings. The silvers, reds, blacks and blues of the Renaissance are emphasised on the first floor, a more neutral colour palette has been chosen for the second floor, and gold and green accents highlight the third. Incidentally, if you fall in love with a piece of furniture at the Neri, you can simply commission a bespoke piece especially made for your own home.

MIRÓHOTEL → Spain
Bilbao

→ Open
10/2002

→ Rates
EUR 112 –
EUR 267

→ Rooms
50

MIRÓHOTEL
Architecture / Interior Design
Carmen Abad / Antonio Miró and Pilar Líbano

Using Markina black marble, pale beige tones and the simple strategy of using curtains to open or enclose space, fashion designer Antonio Miró has translated his sober and elegant fashion style into interior design with this innovative hotel.

Ideally located between Bilbao's Museum of Fine Arts and the Guggenheim Museum, this eight-storey property was converted from a music school by the architect Carmen Abad. Having such prestigious neighbours, its new façade simply had to make an architecturally strong statement: atop six white columns, a thin grid of stone frames 25 large windows, creating a light-box effect at night. Influenced by its environment and community, the hotel showcases its own art and photography collection, providing a platform for young local and international talent. Many works date to the 1960s, including those by Concha Prada and Marc Viaplana. Furnishings include Wenge-finished tables by French designer Christophe Delcourt, tripod lamps with woven cotton ribbon-shades by Spain's Santa & Cole and leather and chrome metal chairs by Italy's Flexform in the bar.

With the vivid stimulation provided by the museum collections nearby and the central socialising spot at the hotel's Miró bar, guestrooms are a welcome place of retreat. Other than the dark wool carpeting and two dashes of colour in the shape of scatter cushions on the bed, the room's bedding, walls, furnishings and curtains are kept in the palest beige. Not only the wall-sized window but also the working and bathroom areas can disappear at the easy pull of a curtain as soon as your full day of exploration draws to a close.

→ **Address**
Alameda Mazarredo 77
48009 Bilbao
Spain

HOSPES PALACIO
DEL BAILÍO

→ **Spain**
Cordoba

→ **Open**
11/2006

→ **Rates**
EUR 180 –
EUR 600

→ **Rooms**
54

HOSPES PALACIO DEL BAILÍO

Architecture / Interior Design
Hospes Design Team

Originally built between the 16th and 18th centuries, this traditional Andalusian agrarian estate, now in the historical heart of Cordoba, has been meticulously restored and finely balanced with contemporary design.

Original detailing such as wrought-iron balcony railings, terracotta tiles, Moorish decorative elements and a lavishly painted ceiling have been artfully combined with understated modern touches. Rich fabrics and textures in champagne and copper tones are offset by dark walnut wood and light polished marble floors throughout the interiors – solid slabs of black stone from Cordoba lead to the gardens outside, thus creating a stylish bridge from the interior to the exterior.

The estate is composed of several buildings – the palace, of course, which was declared a "place of cultural interest" in the 1980s, along with its couch houses, stables and granaries – arranged around a total of five patios. The main patio is also the most spectacular, as the traditional paving has been replaced with a glass floor, revealing a dramatic perspective on the Roman ruins four and a half metres below. The restored paintings and frescoes from the 19th century are a further example of the care and attention given to the revitalisation of past beauty at the Hospes Palacio del Bailío. The clean pure lines, sense of history and quiet luxury all reflect the peace you will enjoy at this Andalusian getaway.

→ Address
Ramirez de las Casas Deza, 10–12
14001 Córdoba
Spain

HOSPES PALACIO   → **Spain**
DEL BAILÍO   Cordoba

HOSPES PALACIO
DEL BAILÍO

→ Spain
Cordoba

| HOSPES PALACIO
DE LOS PATOS | → Spain
Granada | → Open
06/2005 | → Rates
EUR 160 –
EUR 900 | → Rooms
42 |

HOSPES PALACIO DE LOS PATOS

Architecture / Interior Design
Hospes Design Team

Converted from a 19th-century town palace in Granada's historic centre at the foothills of the stunning Sierra Nevada, the Hospes Palacio de los Patos is an urban oasis that combines classical design with industrial architecture. Working with a property constructed between 1885 and 1890, the Hospes Design Team has retained the splendour of such original elements as the grand staircase, whilst introducing contemporary design features to break the construction's uniformity.

Thirty-two modernist double rooms and ten suites are designed to make visitors feel very much at home within an environment of visual contrasts fusing the area's Arabic influence with Spanish-Iberian flavour. The hotel is divided into two buildings: one classical part situated in the heart of the palace and a newly built construction housing 12 rooms, the Senzone restaurant and the Bodyna Spa. The Hos pes Design Team ingeniously covered the subterranean area that seamlessly connects the two structures with water tanks, allowing natural light to shine through.

Rooms integrate the building's original proportions with a distinctive identity of multicultural, progressive design. White or black coconut leather is used throughout the interiors, combined with silver and stainless steel details. Light materials and hues add to the weightless textures of wood and stone and accentuate the rooms' symmetry. In the suites, silver textiles and details contrast with purple chaises longues and enliven the almost monochrome surroundings. The Senzone Restaurant merges archetypal architecture with modern interior design as it serves traditional Andalusian cuisine, and the lush Arabic garden showcases the influence of the region's former rulers. Modernised to incorporate contemporary conveniences, guests can use the Hospes Palacio de los Patos – just steps from the Alhambra – as a springboard into a world of historic delights.

→ **Address**
Solarillo de Gracia, 1
18002 Granada
Spain

HOSPES PALACIO
DE LOS PATOS

→ **Spain**
Granada

HOSPES PALACIO
DE LOS PATOS

→ **Spain**
Granada

HOSPES PALACIO
DE LOS PATOS

→ **Spain**
Granada

SEASIDE HOTEL PALM BEACH	→ Spain Gran Canaria	→ Open 10/2002	→ Rates EUR 260 – EUR 660	→ Rooms 328

SEASIDE HOTEL PALM BEACH

Architecture / Interior Design
Alberto Pinto

Alberto Pinto's redesign of the classic 1970s Palm Beach carries the original's design focus into a new era. Rather than a typical update that simply superimposes a new identity onto an old structure, Pinto clarified original design elements to bring them to the fore, resulting in a strong late-modernist statement.

Located in an old palm grove, the Miami Beach-inspired façade curves to provide visual relief and a constantly flowing sense of interior and exterior space. Turquoise-mosaic pools and public spaces in a muted palette play up sun and shade. Oversize spotlit areas create dramatic, glamorously retro lighting effects. Bold Pucci-style patterns are re-interpreted in an array of different textures and materials, whether sandblasted onto mirrors around the bar or transformed into expressive light shades. Materials such as chrome, mirrored glass, travertine and marble add strong accents of luxury and old-school elegance.

The 328 rooms reflect the distinct stylistic era of the building, a particularly decadent take on seaside glamour. Pinto's redesign involved playing up colour contrast to celebrate sunset, sea and sand. Walls are thus bathed in warm tones and floors come alive in cool colours. Furniture is uncluttered and displays clean, rounded lines, accented by chrome, varnish and brass. Bathrooms are adorned by the extensive use of travertine and marble. The overall effect is less retro than contemporary, as Pinto's scrubbing of unnecessary elements and emphasis on modern materials show just how forward-looking the original design was in the first place. For this effort the hotel was awarded the prestigious red dot design award in 2004.

→ **Address**
Avenida del Oasis s./n.
35100 Maspalomas
Gran Canaria
Spain

BAUZÁ H & R → Spain
Madrid

→ Open
1999

→ Rates
EUR 185 –
EUR 375

→ Rooms
177

BAUZÁ H & R
Architecture / Interior Design
Virginia Figueras

At the Bauzá Hotel, the debut of the Spanish Habitat Hotels group, interior designer Virginia Figueras mixed new ideas in décor and functionality with designs inspired by classics to create a hot spot in Madrid's coolest quarter.

Sr. De la Joya created the architectural backdrop against which the welcoming interiors and creative character, expressed through a careful selection of art and photography works on display, make it one of Madrid's most fashionable hotels – which is apt given its location at the core of the Calle Goya fashion and design district. Richly saturated colours warm the chrome and glass elements chosen for the interior design. In this instance design means creating comfortable settings where guests can relax – a sentiment that is perfectly displayed in the library, a favourite hideaway replete with a blazing hearth and deep, berry-coloured armchairs. As popular with the local fashionistas as it is with guests, the restaurant literally gives diners the red-carpet treatment and offers updates on Mediterranean cuisine set against the backdrop of a sweeping window affording views across the city.

Guestrooms feature four-punch, perforated desk chairs that are spin-offs of the classic Swiss aluminium Landi chair from 1938. These are elegantly complemented with simple light-wood furnishings and traditionally embroidered soft furnishings to give the rooms a cosy feel. The property's gem is the bridal suite that spans 77 metres and includes a 25-square-metre private teak terrace. Nine other guestrooms also have spacious terraces with incredible views across the rooftops of Salamanca, arguably Madrid's coolest quarter.

→ **Address**
Calle Goya, 79
28001 Madrid
Spain

DE LAS
LETRAS H & R

→ Spain
Madrid

→ Open
07/2005

→ Rates
EUR 195 –
EUR 450

→ Rooms
103

DE LAS LETRAS H & R

Architecture / Interior Design
Virginia Figueras

When entering the completely refurbished historic building located at No. 11 on Madrid's legendary Gran Vía, guests are immediately immersed in a warm, welcoming and intimate environment. Dating to 1917, the Belle Époque structure now housing the ultramodern De Las Letras H & R reflects the memories of this mythical avenue, which has witnessed some of the most significant events Spain has experienced over the past century. This is a place in which tradition rests in harmony with avant-garde interior design.

Some of the structure's most valuable design elements have been preserved, including the fantastic vintage woodwork, original tile mosaics, an old elevator and the noble staircase. A top-floor terrace offers vertiginous views over the Spanish capital's rooftops. Throughout the 103 rooms spread over six floors, high ceilings and wide windows create the sensation of additional space. Walls in the ultrastylish interiors are painted in rich shades of ochre, burgundy or orange and, befitting the hotel's name, are embellished with quota-tions of writers including Dylan Thomas and Friedrich Nietzsche. With different shapes, colours and layouts, each room possesses a special individual presence. Handmade Nepalese rugs add to the interiors' personal atmosphere, providing guests with avant-garde decoration in a warm, cosy and intimate environment.

In the street-level restaurant, glass walls allow natural light to flood in and help bring the outside world indoors, creating an electrifying buzz during peak hours. Here is where revellers queue up for the chic ambience, discretion and service of DL's Lounge, where traditionally conservative Madrid collides with its new face of foreign influences and bohemian aesthetics. The hotel also features a spacious library and reading room as well as a state-of-the-art spa. Full of charm, tradition and vitality, De Las Letras H & R offers a platform for culture and is alive with poetry, from the sun-drenched rooms to the subdued bar and restaurant, right in the very heart of Madrid.

→ **Address**
Gran Via, 11
28013 Madrid
Spain

HOSPES MADRID → **Spain**
Madrid

→ **Open**
09/2007

→ **Rates**
EUR 350 –
EUR 1400

→ **Rooms**
41

HOSPES MADRID

Architecture / Interior Design
Hospes Design Team

Located in Madrid's central Plaza de la Independencia, the Hospes Madrid offers superb views of the Alcalá Gate and the inspiring Retiro Park. The handsome red-brick building with wrought-iron balconies was designed by architect José María de Aguilar in 1883. Originally an apartment house for wealthy families, this fine example of the Bourbon Restoration period has been transformed into 41 uniquely decorated guestrooms, among them a grand suite, four grand suite duplexes and four junior suites. Because of the building's landmark status as part of the Historic District, the Hospes Design Team carefully complied with structural requirements and ensured that the modernisation was in perfect harmony with the existing historic elements.

The entrance is through an imposing court once used by arriving carriages – and its high ceiling, mouldings and magnificently restored wooden door make for an elegant welcome. Beyond the lobby is the luminous interior patio that leads to the Bodyna Spa in the former stables. The three levels of the Senzone restaurant include a formal dining room with an oak-coffered ceiling and stucco work, and a back patio where comfortable sofas and murmuring water beckon guests to linger over a drink.

Throughout the hotel, the ambience of light and tranquillity is achieved through the use of white marble and hues of white, silver and gold offset by dark fine wood. Even the Baroque-style furniture has been leavened with white finishes. The six rooms on the fourth floor faithfully reflect the establishment's personality. They are arranged on two levels, with a salon below and a staircase leading up to bedroom and bathroom. These rooms pay tribute to the old with their sloped ceilings of exposed wooden beams, and embrace the new with skylights.

→ **Address**
  Plaza de la Independencia, 3
  Madrid
  Spain

HOTEL URBAN   → Spain
Madrid

→ Open
11/2004

→ Rates
EUR 284 –
EUR 1151

→ Rooms
98

HOTEL URBAN

Architecture / Interior Design
Carles Bassó & Mariano Martitegui / Jordi Clos,
Kim Castells and Jordi Cuenca

Set in the centre of Madrid on the Carrera de San Jerónimo, the Hotel Urban welcomes guests with a fusion of avant-garde design, art and technology behind a façade of steel and glass. On the site of the former Duque de Ribas palace, a modern building crowns entrepreneur Jordi Clos's collection of hotels.

Through the double-height portico is a space in which every design feature reflects luxury without pretence. A tubular atrium crafted in stainless steel and alabaster leads to the majestic reception area. Panelled in black Zimbabwe stone with metallic seam finishes, the hall's initial impression is an interplay of shapes, energies and lights lending both tension and beauty. An alternative entrance is through the groovy-chic Glass Bar, an oyster bar graced by crystal floors, silver-shaded sofas and transparent seats and tables. In the Europa Decó restaurant, walls covered in rusted stone from Brazil create a backdrop of contrasting textures that

→ Address
Carrera de San Jerónimo, 34
28014 Madrid
Spain

HOTEL URBAN → **Spain**
Madrid

harmonises with the glass mosaics highlighting the wall. Rendered in marble and black steel, the venue stretches along the hotel's entire ground floor.

The Urban's 98 rooms and suites are reached through two elevators with transparent walls. Each elegant, modern room features an original artwork – such as a 200-year-old Buddhist figure – as well as leather headboards, antique furniture and bathrooms separated by glass screens that can be moved by the touch of a button. The top floor's breathtaking views can be enjoyed in a split-level space boasting the swimming pool, gym, sunroom and a restaurant. The Urban is all about luxury, but is never ostentatious. This is where high design meets art, achieving an otherwise elusive balance.

HOSPES
MARICEL

→ Spain
Mallorca

→ Open
08/2002

→ Rates
EUR 250 –
EUR 800

→ Rooms
29

→ **Address**
Carretera d'Andratx, 11
Cas Català
07184 Calvià, Mallorca
Spain

HOSPES MARICEL
Architecture / Interior Design
Hospes Design Team

HOSPES
MARICEL

→ **Spain**
Mallorca

Nestled into an idyllic landscape, the arcades and terraces of this proud, palatial building descend straight down into the rocks lapped by the Mediterranean.

In the past one of Mallorca's most elegant, exclusive international hangouts, Hospes Maricel's atmosphere today is stylishly leisurely. But a air of decadence remains, as seen in the retained details – neo-Gothic pillars, a Neoclassical entrance – of a building dating from 1949. After a revamp by the Hospes Design Team, traditional Balearic design elements of the original structure have been brought back in the form of archways, arcades and columns in marble, stone and dense sandstone from nearby Santanyí, while modern furnishings and accents add an undeniably contemporary feel. Whereas the seafront arcade and extended terraces resembling steps are grand, the deep wicker armchairs and the potted herbs on tables tell a more down-to-earth story, as do the private, grotto-like alcoves below, where guests can take in an array of spa treatments in the open air.

The 24 rooms and five suites fulfil simple modern priorities with interior design that maximises comfort, space and light. Born of this philosophy, they have a functional, minimalist edge, using neutral colours and fine textures. Carefully chosen accents are reminiscent of the building's illustrious history, highlighting its noble charm. Relax by the stunning infinity pool, which seems to flow into the seemingly endless blue of the sea; enjoy an oriental massage in one of the Bodyna Spa caves above the sea; or try the "best hotel breakfast in the world" at the Senzone Restaurant.

HOSPES
MARICEL

→ Spain
Mallorca

PURO

→ **Spain**
Mallorca

→ **Open**
04/2004

→ **Rates**
EUR 235 –
EUR 440

→ **Rooms**
26

PURO

Architecture / Interior Design
Alvaro Planchuelo / Erik and Katarina van Brabant

PURO

→ **Spain**
Mallorca

Madrid-based architect Alvaro Planchuelo has extensive experience restoring historic buildings in Spain and West Africa, but this time a Swedish hotelier client wanted a transformation that would make way for the 21st century by fusing global elements from Asia, Africa and Arabia.

Within Palma de Mallorca's old Muslim neighbourhood, which once had a commercial port, this 18th-century town mansion retains its signature arches and inviting courtyard but rejects past notions of decorative prestige. Instead, woods, stone and exotic accents are used to create a simple but bohemian look. Yet the interior by designers Erik and Katarina van Brabant is far from cluttered, and space is emphasised through the prevailing colour of white and low-lying furnishings. Fine, unusual details inspire curiosity.

White guinea goose feathers layer lampshades, cushions are made from hand-selected Rajasthani saris and above the beds are pale sculptural spheres of feathers that are actually ceremonial hats worn by Bandjon tribes in Cameroon.

The emphasis on hand-worked natural materials infuses the space with personality and an appreciation of quality and travel. Even pushing aside a room's massive hand-carved doors from Burma evokes a feeling of other-worldliness. The temple that lies beyond is a spa-size bath set in a spacious bathroom. Here, soaking in a tub is transformed into a luxurious activity simply by lying in a huge, square, black bath – as is your stay transformed simply by embracing the commodity of time and enjoying the simple cultural wealth around you.

HOSPES
VILLA PAULITA

→ **Spain**
Puigcerdà

→ **Open**
07/2007

→ **Rates**
EUR 139 –
EUR 550

→ **Rooms**
38

HOSPES VILLA PAULITA

Architecture / Interior Design
Hospes Design Team

Once a private summer residence, now a three-building haven equidistant to Toulouse and Barcelona, this villa and spa in a Catalan resort town is an ideal retreat from the urban fray. Framed by the Catalan Pyrenees and set directly on Puigcerdà Lake, the three-storey red mansion has a near-dollhouse quality to it, and its turreted octagonal tower adds an almost fairytale touch. The historic Neoclassical home is in fact a protected landmark; two new modern buildings flank it to create a truly unique property.

The Hospes Design Team restored many of the 19th-century building's original, decidedly French features, including the forged iron balustrades, grilles and balconies. Antiques have been incorporated, such as the former proprietor's late 19th-century wooden chairs, now painted white and cushioned with shimmering grey velvet. The ten guestrooms in the manor house are individually designed, with sloped ceilings on the top floor exposing original wood beams, adding a homey, rustic touch. The rooms are done mostly in black and white, with greys and creams softening the overall palette.

→ Address
Av. Pons i Gash, 15
17520 Puigcerdà (Girona)
Spain

Floors are laid with warm wood, with the exception of the ochre marble in the bathroom. The 28 rooms in a two-storey addition include private porches and fenced patios on the ground floor, and sweeping lake and mountain views on the second floor.

A captivating feature in each room, above the bed, is a black-and-white artwork featuring a drawing and text. This small piece is a portion of the house's *auca*, a traditional Catalan art form in which a series of drawings and short texts tells a story (the entire work hangs in the bar). With this, the Hospes team has made an ingenious link between history and the guests' journey to the villa: the *auca* is a copy of one created for the grandmother who once lived here, and announces the arrival of the railway in Puigcerdà. Another taste of Catalan tradition can be had in the Senzone L'Estany restaurant, which has stunning lake views from the modern building it shares with the Bodyna Spa.

HOSPES
VILLA PAULITA

→ Spain
Puigcerdà

HOSPES
LAS CASAS DEL
REY DE BAEZA

→ **Spain**
Seville

→ **Open**
01/2000

→ **Rates**
EUR 140 –
EUR 500

→ **Rooms**
41

HOSPES LAS CASAS DEL REY DE BAEZA

Architecture / Interior Design
Hospes Design Team

An 18th-century multi-dwelling in the fiery city of Seville is the privileged retreat of the Hospes Las Casas del Rey de Baeza. Drawing on Arabian and European styles that have influenced the Andalusian capital for centuries, the hotel is a relaxed, sophisticated fusion of past and present.

Rustic natural touches are added through woven pull-string window shades and riverbed rocks paving an idyllic path across the central courtyard. This is flanked by a forest of wooden posts and both painted and untouched stone columns – which provide an aesthetic support for the climbing vines – as well as two tiers of delicate carved wooden balconies. The posts were salvaged from the 19th-century Tavera de Toledo Hospital, which might have provided an inspiration for putting them to such good use. To emphasise the traditional Spanish flair on the exterior, the whitewashed walls are accentuated with the albero ochre colour typical for southern Spain.

Inside, the time-honoured feel is rooted in the terracotta flooring and curved, wooden slat chairs, which elaborate on the country theme. Upon entering the rooms, however, guests find interiors surprisingly reminiscent of chic urban apartments. Global

→ **Address**
Carrer Santiago,
Plaza Jesús de la Redención 2
41003 Sevilla
Spain

HOSPES
LAS CASAS DEL
REY DE BAEZA

→ **Spain**
Seville

modernity is evident in dark chocolate-coloured furnishings, including wooden beds from Indonesia, sweeping beech panelling, esparto carpets and oversize floor cushions to sink into or drape yourself across when the sultry Andalusian feeling moves you. On a more formal note, the headboard design mimics that of the window grates, creating a harmonious connection between inside and outside. Natural light has not been left to chance: its illuminating and sometimes beautifying properties are given an ideal stage in each of the rooms simply by shining through slim passages created by columns, bouncing off freestanding bowl sinks, water jugs and other ornaments from eras past – to be enjoyed in all their glory today.

HOSPES
PALAU
DE LA MAR

→ Spain
Valencia

→ Open
06/2004

→ Rates
EUR 200 –
EUR 650

→ Rooms
66

HOSPES
PALAU DE LA MAR

Architecture / Interior Design
Hospes Design Team

Flying on the high honours bestowed upon them for some of the hottest restaurant and hotel interiors in Spain, the Hospes Design Team took on the task of remodelling two adjacent 19th-century palaces in the centre of Valencia.

Hospes is known for restoring historic buildings and successfully updating them into luxurious properties. Under natural light pouring through a stained glass skylight, the grand loggia stairway with an intricately carved wood banister has been made all the more striking by simply painting the surrounding areas a stark ivory white. Once a carriage passageway, the vaulted foyer's wood floor evokes the feeling of walking along the deck of a boat, a reference to Valencia's involvement in America's Cup. The casual and contemporary interior patio pairs well with the classical nobility of the façade and interior architecture. Covered by sails and a glass and steel balcony leading to the guestrooms, the patio's raised boxes are lushly filled

→ **Address**
Navarro Reverter 14
46004 Valencia
Spain

HOSPES
PALAU
DE LA MAR

→ Spain
Valencia

with fragrant Mediterranean plants and herbs. And recently built upon the balcony, the Bodyna Spa offers a serene atmosphere and natural treatments for pure indulgence.

Although the design concept remains consistent, the two mansions' original architecture has brought about innovative uses of space. As for interior design, principles of modernity, rather than historicism, reign. Carefully coordinated design elements, mainly using Wenge wood, have been chosen for the rooms: the joinery work on the wardrobes complements the floor pattern, which is again mirrored in the Wenge headboards, tables and stools placed throughout. Some guestrooms are filled with light frrom ceiling windows; some feature oversized bathrooms where large bathtubs are either sectioned off from or opened up to the main living and sleeping space by means of a folding wooden screen.

AVALON HOTEL   → **Sweden**   → **Open**   → **Rates**   → **Rooms**

Gothenburg   06/2007   SEK 1290 –   101

SEK 8000

AVALON HOTEL

Architecture / Interior Design
Semrén & Månsson / Krister Stam

Situated in the heart of Gothenburg, the newly built Avalon Hotel follows a holistic concept that devotes as much consideration to subtle accents as to physical design.

Lighting, colours, fragrances, sounds and furnishings are all carefully composed to harmonious effect, making Avalon the first hotel in Sweden to earn feng shui certification. Most corners have been rounded off, and the fourth floor even has meandering lines. The architecture is clean and functional, making a guest's stay as uncomplicated as being at home, but with a few extra amenities. Of the 101 rooms, 24 have their own mini-spa, 3 have mini-gyms, and the penthouse suite unfolds over 83 square metres. Suite bathtubs even have a commanding view of the city.

The Avalon's team of architects, designers and artists also envisioned the hotel as a gallery for art and furniture. Contemporary Nordic architecture is combined with timeless classics such as Arne Jacobsen chairs. Hand-tufted Kasthall rugs, travertine or whitewashed oak flooring, Egyptian cotton linens and tailor-made duvets, and Bang & Olufsen entertainment systems are all part of the commitment to quality. Room design allows for personal preferences, from the choice of four pillows to the foldaway workplaces that disappear into the wall, truly separating work and relaxation time. To fully unwind, take a dip in the rooftop pool, read before the large open fireplace in the lobby or socialise at the 11-metre-long bar.

→ **Address**
Kungstorget 9
411 17 Göteborg
Sweden

ELITE PLAZA
HOTEL

→ Sweden
Gothenburg

→ Open
01/2000

→ Rates
EUR 240 –
EUR 445

→ Rooms
130

ELITE PLAZA HOTEL

Architecture / Interior Design
Lars Helling at Aavik & Helling Arkitekter AS /
Christer Svensson at Gunnar Svennson AB

In lovingly restoring parts of a century-old building in downtown Gothenburg, designers Christer Svensson and Lars Helling have created a masterpiece of refined tradition with the Elite Plaza Hotel.

Formerly the home of the Svea Fire & Life Insurance Company in the 1880s, and later the University of Gothenburg, The Elite Plaza Hotel opened its doors in 2000 and has showcased the elegant renovations undertaken by the two Scandinavian designers ever since. An entrance composed of fine-cut and partially polished granite and the English mosaic floor have both been meticulously restored to their original splendour.

Neo classical highlights throughout the 130-room hotel find their expression in fine details, such as the arches of Italian marble stucco from which guests can look down on the open lobby to carefully crafted wrought-iron work that perfectly reflects the New Renaissance style. Surrounding the groups of deep, comfortable armchairs, dark wood panelling lines the cosy bar; a material that Helling and Svensson also chose to integrate into the design of the guestrooms, where it is used to great effect in singular columns and on doors and ceilings.

And in recent months, the hotel's fifth floor has been modernised – with 12 spacious suites and doubles in relaxing shades of beige and greens and a slightly updated atmosphere replacing 25 smaller rooms. The understatement and historical references make Elite Plaza Hotel a place where guests – whether they stay for business or pleasure – can enjoy a unique melding of past and present.

→ Address
Västra Hamngatan 3
40422 Göteborg
Sweden

ELITE PLAZA
HOTEL

→ Sweden
Gothenburg

HOTEL J

→ Sweden
Stockholm

→ Open
05/2000

→ Rates
EUR 200 –
EUR 400

→ Rooms
45

HOTEL J

Architecture / Interior Design
Millimeter / R.O.O.M.

→ **Address**
Ellensviksvägen 1
13128 Nacka Strand
Stockholm
Sweden

Given its setting, it is only logical that Hotel J draws on the nautical design of historic America's Cup J-Class boats and the distinct seaside feel of New England for its concept.

On the water's edge at Nacka Strand, the hotel offers sweeping views of the Royal Djurgården, the world's first national park, the island of Lidingöand and the boats on Saltsjön. The architects at Millimeter and designers at R.O.O.M. turned the brick building, first constructed in 1912, into a stylish shrine to seafaring – and an American one at that. The infamous colours of the American flag – red, white and blue – are an integral part of the hotel's design concept, which the owners chose to make visitors from across the Atlantic feel completely at home. White-painted wooden boards, durable cotton textiles and solid oak furniture built by R.O.O.M. create a feeling of nautical intimacy. The hotel's architectural centre is its lobby, where fireside seats afford the same wide-angle views of the islands just off the coast of Stockholm.

Casting an eye over the hotel's 45 rooms reveals the same clean lines and classic simplicity evident in the lobby. The hotel is, after all, not far from Stockholm, undoubtedly one of the Meccas of Scandinavian design. For the interiors, R.O.O.M. selected natural materials and fine linens to create the same authentic feeling of comfort and ease. Highest quality materials and good craftsmanship are the distinguishing mark of Hotel J – just as they are for any favourite boat.

NORDIC LIGHT
HOTEL

→ Sweden
Stockholm

→ Open
1998

→ Rates
EUR 204 –
EUR 458

→ Rooms
175

→ **Address**
Vasaplan 7, Box 884
10137 Stockholm
Sweden

NORDIC LIGHT HOTEL
Architecture / Interior Design
FNNS Architects / Rolf Löfvenberg, Lars Pihl and Jan Söder

NORDIC LIGHT
HOTEL

→ Sweden
Stockholm

By night, subtle glowing colours emanate from the windows of an understated façade hinting at what is to come inside. Passing through the doors, one is welcomed into a world created by hundreds of different sources of light, varying in colour and intensity.

The team surrounding the architect Rolf Löfvenberg and interior designers Lars Pihl and Jan Söder has transformed an existing 1970s building into a modern design statement. Black and white are the dominant themes here, but aside from the well-chosen but nonetheless sober cubist furniture, the Nordic Light offers something truly unique.

The lobby's walls, ceiling and floor serve as a constant tapestry for lighting architect Kai Piippo to work with Sweden's naturally radical, atmosphere-transforming seasonal sunlight. From the shape of the stalactite lights hanging from a recessed circle in the ceiling to the ever-changing patterns of blue, orange and pink splashed onto the wall – sometimes even projecting images subtly evoking flowers or snowflakes – Piippo's installations are the strongest design theme throughout the Nordic Light's 175 rooms.

In some rooms, guests can even play with the lighting to suit their own changing moods. The special effect adds a remarkably pure, simple and transparent colour theme to the solid elements of the interior design, which include light wood floors, furniture in basic whites, blacks and greys, and Swedish Hästens beds. Because Stockholm gets little more than five hours of light during the day in the winter months, Piippo's lighting aesthetically manages to lift the more subdued atmosphere of the long dark months and generally creates an aura of variable experience.

LA RÉSERVE
GENÈVE
HOTEL & SPA

→ Switzerland
Geneva

→ Open
01/2003

→ Rates
EUR 340 –
EUR 1950

→ Rooms
102

LA RÉSERVE GENÈVE HOTEL & SPA

→ **Address**
301, Route de Lausanne
1293 Genève Bellevue
Switzerland

Architecture / Interior Design
Patrice Reynaud / Jacques Garcia

LA RÉSERVE
GENÈVE
HOTEL & SPA

→ Switzerland
Geneva

In a park on the shores of Lake Geneva, La Réserve takes you on a fanciful global safari and invites you into the playful indulgence of Parisian hotel interior designer Jacques Garcia.

Together with architect Patrice Reynaud, Garcia transformed the 1970s hotel into an explosion of extravagant colour, secluding shrubbery and revealing glass galleries. A gold leaf trim courses the lobby's upper wall, below which a frieze quotes philosopher Jean-Jacques Rousseau, a native son of the city, with "Back to Nature." Perched on every standing or mounted lamp are single coloured plastic cutouts in the shapes of parrots and peacocks. A band of leopard-print fabric cuts a horizontal line across lipstick red chairs and creates a vertical border along the red curtains that elegantly partition the lobby. Heralding the entrance to the Loti restaurant is a lifelike elephant poured in plaster. And a copper elephant's head, originally commissioned for the Colonial Exhibition in Paris in 1931, is now mounted on a wall in the restaurant – where bamboo tied up with leather strips, a cast-iron fireplace and deep brown woodwork define the rest of the décor.

Guestrooms are less ostentatious, with oiled parquet floors creating a stage for dramatic drapery, soft velvet bedspreads and black granite and mahogany fittings. Abstractly patterned wall hangings and wallpaper are echoed in the choice of woven frames for upholstered seating. The colonial theme is charmingly picked up again by the vintage travel photographs on the walls. Limitless in this design concept of cultural borrowing, a two-storey high painting by the Russian artist George Pusenkoff – a collage of visual quotations of Roy Lichtenstein, Da Vinci, the Japanese craft of woodblock prints and Mies van der Rohe – encapsulates this ethos well.

THE HOTEL → Switzerland
Lucerne

→ Open
04/2000

→ Rates
CHF 350 –
CHF 570

→ Rooms
25

→ **Address**
Sempacherstrasse 14
6002 Luzern
Switzerland

THE HOTEL
Architecture / Interior Design
Jean Nouvel

THE HOTEL → Switzerland
Lucerne

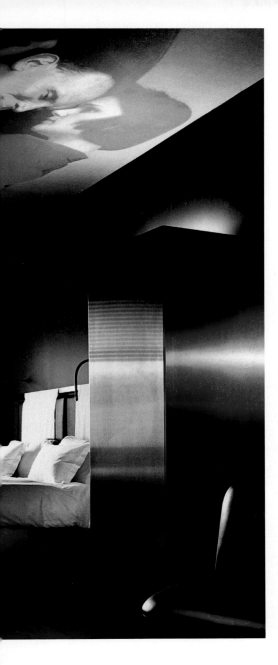

A small corner property built in 1907 has been transformed by none other than French star architect Jean Nouvel, whose celebrated Lucerne Culture and Convention Centre is just a few steps away.

Owner and hotelier Urs Karli wished not merely to meet his guests' expectations of creature comforts but rather to transcend any preconceived notions of how they should come alive in a hotel. The hotel's simple name is aptly chosen, seeing as it does not set out to be a "home away from home" but a place to be surprised and truly inspired. A tall order, to be sure, but one that Nouvel masterfully accomplishes by infusing his interior design with surprise, sensuality and elegance. People outside have the impression of being inside and those inside of being outside, artfully interpreting a familiar motif, displayed by Nouvel's restrained yet clever interplay of mirrors, which makes the tangible barrier between the pavement outside and the restaurant Bam Bou inside vanish in the eyes of the beholder.

Having designed every piece himself, the furnishing concept bears Nouvel's hallmark: vertical lines are drawn in wood, horizontal ones in stainless steel. Not one to rely on his skill alone, he chose his adviser and colour specialist, the Parisian Alain Bony, to create individual colour compositions for each of the 25 guestrooms. Perfecting the element of surprise, Nouvel selected film stills from his favourite directors, including Buñuel, Almodóvar and Greenaway, to project onto all the rooms' ceilings, making iconic scenes like one taken from Fellini's *Casanova* come alive when you lie in bed.

THE OMNIA → Switzerland → Open → Rates → Rooms
Zermatt 06/2006 CHF 280 – 30
CHF 3500

THE OMNIA

Architecture / Interior Design
Ali Tayar

For the Omnia, a Swiss mountain retreat in Zermatt with balcony views of the Matterhorn, architect and designer Ali Tayar has brought the American Modernist sensibility across the Atlantic and set it 1,649 metres above sea level with furnishings and spaces based on local materials, precision manufacturing and European craftsmanship. In a design philosophy and life combining Continental roots and a career in the United States, Tayar shares an aesthetic and history with forefathers Mies van der Rohe, Raymond Loewy, Jens Risom and Vladimir Kagan. Their work is incorporated with Tayar's in this small lodge with 30 rooms including 12 suites.

Timeless taste prevails over surprise or theatricality, but this doesn't preclude originality, especially in lighting design by Attila Uysal with fixtures by David Weeks and Tayar. Like the building's prominent interior support columns, Tayar's standing cylindrical lamps rise up through the lobby lounge floor more than they rest upon it, seemingly rooted somewhere metres beneath the bedrock. The lamp's solid oak post pierces a laser-cut anodised aluminium "shelf," positioned like an L-shaped bookend turned 90 degrees, its former vertical support now a horizontal one for an aperitif or coffee. A scallop edge, cut at the only edge touching the floor, allows the "table" to rotate on the lamp's axis. The simple design reflects Tayar's environmental philosophy: "If material is energy, then using less material saves energy." Consciousness of energy is also visible in the perforated white oak ceiling panels. The ceiling is treated as a system, with lighting, soundproofing, air-conditioning and heating elements glimpsed through circular and oval cut-outs.

Patterns are subtle at this property, which is full of solid neutral tones, leather, felt and smooth surfaces. There is the neatly layered but rough-edged granite slabs of the fireplaces, similar to the walls delineating vineyards outside. Alongside the hearths are the uniform triangular stumps of the chopped wood stacked along the walls. A rare textile pattern is that of the 1952 Heavenly area rug designed by Raymond Loewy for Edward Fields, meant to be a cost-effective option for a new era of families on the move. Loewy's concentric circles are reminiscent of a child's scribbling or perhaps a topographical map of elevations. The sedate lounge is more like a shared living room with dark maroon leather couches and seats by Mies van der Rohe marking subdivisions of space. The open dining area features Tayar's refectory-inspired tables, whose sturdy candle fixtures surrounded by a shade suggest a monastic reading room. The candle bases rise like a hardy mountain plant species from the tables' polished granite tops.

Guestrooms are streamlined and spacious, with entertainment packed away in USM Modular Furniture, a design classic in the collection of New York's Museum of Modern Art and a company committed to environmentally friendly production. Kagan's Erika chaise longue provides some soft curves, as does his semi-circular sofa, which follows the turret suite's contour. And Tayar's white-oak and aluminium coffee table has legs like sleigh runners – a reminder that transportation in Zermatt is only by horse-drawn sleigh or electric car. (Tayar also designed the Omnia's steel blue-lacquered electric car, which shuttles guests from the train station to the hotel.) Steel blue-lacquered doors separate the bedrooms from their wardrobes, where guests can unpack into various volumes.

The best place to relax after a hike or ski is the Japanese cedar bath, raised on a platform beneath a skylight. Each unique vertical slat was cut by a computer-run milling machine; the tension rods holding it all together are hidden, embedded within the wood. It is a piece of craftsmanship that hardly brings to mind industrial production, but is impossible without it. It's like the rest of this hotel – a study in local authenticity meeting international modernism, the Continent meeting America, and structure meeting style.

→ Address
Auf dem Fels
3920 Zermatt
Switzerland

THE OMNIA

→ **Switzerland**
Zermatt

THE OMNIA

→ Switzerland
Zermatt

| HOTEL GREULICH | → Switzerland Zurich | → Open 09/2003 | → Rates CHF 210 – CHF 360 | → Rooms 18 |

→ **Address**
Hermann Greulich-Strasse 56
8004 Zürich
Switzerland

HOTEL GREULICH

Architecture / Interior Design
Franz Romero, Markus Schaefle

In a residential area of Zurich, Hotel Greulich is a hotel of only 18 rooms, sparsely finished with simple furniture and a neutral colour scheme by Jean Pfaff, a Swiss painter known for his monochrome works in the late 1980s – all in all a fitting testament to his style.

The strongest colour statement in this otherwise neutral hotel was chosen for the new façade by architects Franz Romero and Markus Schaefle, who created the property by combining several buildings and a workshop area dating to the 1930s. In a comparatively bold move, they decided to give the façade a sensuous, slate blue curve that ends at an inconspicuous entrance. Another rather more unexpected element of warmth can be discovered in the cigar room, where a crackling fireplace glows invitingly. Yet the understated Swiss style is spun further: guests arrive in an intimate lobby before embarking on the journey to their rooms over dark grey terrazzo floors, past natural cedar wood walls and across the glass-covered courtyard. Here, landscape architect Günter Vogt added subtle, shimmering grey tones and intermittent textures by choosing a grove of silver birch trees to frame the space. A calming water trough and formal cedar-slatted wall, which separates the courtyard from a patio dining area, underlines the clarifying Zen feel.

Tasteful Japanese flavours don't stop there – the guestrooms feature specially defined sleeping areas with low beds, which are separated from the adjoining bathrooms by frosted glass panels. A simple yet effective decorative coup is achieved by placing a standout vase of fresh flowers amongst the understated furnishings and restrained colours. A shared terrace overlooking the landscaped courtyard is a welcome extension of the introspective mood for guests seeking the kind of rejuvenation to be had here.

WIDDER HOTEL   → Switzerland
Zurich

→ Open
03/1995

→ Rates
EUR 335 –
EUR 2060

→ Rooms
49

WIDDER HOTEL
Architecture / Interior Design
Tilla Theus

The Widder Hotel is a hamlet made of eight historical residences, many dating back to the Middle Ages. Swiss architect Tilla Theus preserved not only the individual façades, but also the internal floor plans and structures.

During the four-year construction phase, the ambitious project involved 20 architects working in shifts, 18 hours a day. The highly sensitive interior architecture links medieval wooden beams, Renaissance pillars and wall frescoes with present-day structures and construction methods. A glass ceiling tops the 12th-century stone house, and the polished curved wooden counter in the Widder Bar mimics the original ram head motifs from a guild's crest. Connecting the labyrinth of eight different buildings are seams that are smooth but refreshingly obvious, as well as nine elevator banks, including one of glass and chrome that rises alongside a wall of river stones. By subtly and cleverly intertwining the individual buildings via staircases and porticoes, a feeling of home-scale intimacy has been created in the hotel's public spaces.

Courtyards are utilised where the demands of a modern hotel's functions require more space. Each guestroom has its own layout and interior design. Some have classic designer furnishings such as a Le Corbusier's lounge chair and Eileen Gray's glass-top table. Others have partially restored *trompe l'œil* frames to recessed windows and real surprises such as leather bedspreads, and the latest Bang & Olufsen modern conveniences cons feature in all guestrooms. Even for those only interested in the study of architecture, the Widder is definitely worth a trip to Zurich.

→ Address
Rennweg 7
8001 Zürich
Switzerland

/ 461

HILLSIDE SU
HOTEL

→ Turkey
Antalya

→ Open
05/2003

→ Rates
USD 209 –
USD 378

→ Rooms
294

HILLSIDE SU HOTEL
Architecture / Interior Design
Eren Talu

On a green bank overlooking the Mediterranean, the Hillside Su Hotel offers itself as a clean white stage on which guests are invited to live out Turkish designer Eren Talu's dazzling disco dream.

The 1960s-inspired hotel in the popular tourist destination Antalya derives its name from the Turkish word for water and is a remarkable contemplation of clarity and transparency. White is the hotel's colour of choice, but Talu breaks up its monotony with a dazzling light display that begins the moment you enter the reception area. Six disco balls, each measuring six feet in diameter, hang in the six-floor atrium lobby. At dusk, they start to spin, launching a spectacular light show that is at once mesmerising and playful. Talu, one of Turkey's internationally known designers, has created a stage on which neither designer furniture nor fixed settings play the leading roles but rather funky details that never cease to surprise the guests. The lobby, as well as the Iroko-wood deck of the expansive pool area, which acts as a socialising magnet, serves his intentions very well indeed.

The Hillside Su's 294 rooms are sleek white cubes of calm. The low-level white plinths that serve as beds feature convenient pull-out tables. Lava lamps and the goldfish bowls each guest receives upon checking in provide the only quirky details to Talu's sparse interiors. If the breezy pace and soft beats of ambient music were a design concept, they would be embodied perfectly by the Su. Since opening in 2003, the hotel has become a destination in itself and a pretty hot one at that.

→ **Address**
Konyaalti
07050 Antalya
Turkey

/ 463

EV

→ Turkey
Bodrum

→ Open
05/2005

→ Rates
EUR 250 –
EUR 600

→ Rooms
48

EV

Architecture / Interior Design
Eren Talu

You might have to look twice at architect and designer Eren Talu's holiday resort overlooking Türkbükü Bay in order to shake the feeling that it's nothing more than a white shimmering mirage.

Eight buildings, in a shade of white that is quite blinding under the hot Turkish sun, cascade down a hillside overlooking the bay near the Turkish resort town of Bodrum. The buildings, which have been described as "eight giant steps towards heaven," are home to 48 separate residences. The starkly geometric lines and uniformity in the Turkish designer and architect's concept offer a sharp contrast to the natural elements of the rolling landscape on which it sits. His use of the colour white throughout, which represents purity, acts as a kind of backdrop against which guests can add their own tone or personality to the design. The layout, which includes a pool for each building, ensures the guest's privacy while creating a loose sense of community: everyone is given the freedom of choosing to share time with others or simply revel in the pleasure of having time to themselves.

Furthering this experience, some rooms feature their own kitchens, fitted with state-of-the-art equipment by the renowned manufacturers Euromobil and Smeg. Talu has taken the white motif through every room, aiming to provide a feeling of lush serenity as well as serve as a cool sanctuary from the hot sun outside. Terry-cloth linens and curtains provide a feeling of soft comfort, and well-positioned mirrors give the impression of endless space. Brightly coloured furnishings seemingly scattered at whim throughout each space and carefully chosen mood lighting are the only vivid accents – apart from those you provide yourself, of course.

→ **Address**
Türkbükü
Bodrum
Turkey

BENTLEY HOTEL → **Turkey**
Istanbul

→ **Open**
01/2003

→ **Rates**
EUR 180 –
EUR 800

→ **Rooms**
50

BENTLEY HOTEL

Architecture / Interior Design
Piero Lissoni / Nicoletta Canesi

The work of Milanese architect Piero Lissoni, the Bentley is a careful balance of Orient and Occident befitting its location in Istanbul – the bridge connecting Europe and Asia.

Under the guidance of Lissoni and Nicoletta Canesi, the Bentley opened in Istanbul in 2003 as a temple of radiance and light in the centre of the city's European section. Glass features heavily in Lissoni's design and is meant to invite visual stimulation from the streets outside into the interior of the hotel, which, in contrast, is full of the purity of form and subtle colours typical for Italian design. The first indications of Lissoni's blend of Eastern and Eestern influences are found in the hotel's lounge, where Ottoman-turquoise velvets covering chairs impart a voluptuous twist to the adjacent sleek table by Finnish architect Eero Saarinen.

The hotel's 40 guestrooms and 10 suites are a testament to minimalism and harmony: floor-to-ceiling windows continue the theme of glass and light. Pale hues of blue, beige, green and grey in the rooms' interiors set a transparent, light-flooded scene, where warm parquet flooring and lightbeige bouclé carpets lend something of the traditional to the overall cool atmosphere. Custom-made furniture and tables are all made of olive-stained oak. Penthouse guests step onto private terraces with panoramic views across the Bosphorus to the Golden Horn. Lissoni conceded to incorporating a single round element in the entire building: a brilliant white staircase wraps itself around an elliptical column that acts as the pure, understated backbone of the hotel's overwhelming elegance.

→ **Address**
Halaskargazi Cad. No. 75
Harbiye
34367 Istanbul
Turkey

SEAHAM HALL
HOTEL AND
SERENITY SPA

→ United Kingdom
Durham

→ Open
2001

→ Rates
GPB 225 –
GPB 575

→ Rooms
19

SEAHAM HALL HOTEL AND SERENITY SPA

Architecture / Interior Design

Jill Holst (Ward Robinson), Jocelyn Maxfield, Napper Architects

Just 20 minutes from the northern English city of Newcastle, Seaham Hall and Serenity Spa – the former a classic Georgian building dating from 1791, the latter a feng shui-inspired creation built in 2002 – are linked by an underground tunnel in which a teak and glass boardwalk is suspended over running water. Together they create a true destination getaway for discerning travellers looking for style alongside a subtle kind of indulgence.

Designed by Jill Holst of Ward Robinson, the hotel combines contemporary chic with the classic architecture of the period. References to the past are subtly integrated into the décor: a double-galleried landing and cantilevered staircase from 1850 showcase a modern stained-glass roof light by artist Bridget Jones depicting verses penned by Lord Byron at the time of his marriage to Annabella Milbanke at Seaham Hall in 1815. Byron's poetry also weaves itself into carpets designed by Hugh McKay, and the drawing room features furniture from Andrew Martin. The spacious, comfortable rooms – each of them unique – feature modern furnishings from Dialogica and B&B Italia and overlook the surrounding coasts or forests. Some even have original limestone fireplaces or exposed timbers that reveal the site's illustrious history.

Designed by Jocelyn Maxfield, the award-winning Serenity Spa uses its architecture and natural materials such as Portland stone, granite, limestone and teak to create a sense of space and tranquillity. Nestled into the natural hillside that gently conceals the interior's vast space, the spa is linked to the hotel by a curved underground tunnel so that guests need not go outside. The passage's underwater lighting spotlights a seated Buddha, and at the subterranean entrance a bronze elephant sculpture stands on a plinth surrounded by water. The spa's exterior is a series of seductive curves, while the main entrance soars to a glass-topped cone and leads to the water garden and the Zen garden designed by Japanese artist Hideo Furuta. Taken together, the property's two structures represent diverging architectural styles, yet complement each other in a bit of East meets West, old meets new and Lord Byron meets feng shui.

→ Address
Lord Byron's Walk
Seaham, County Durham, SR7 7AG
United Kingdom

SEAHAM HALL
HOTEL AND
SERENITY SPA

→ United Kingdom
Durham

42 THE CALLS → United Kingdom
Leeds

→ Open
1991

→ Rates
GBP 99 –
GBP 395

→ Rooms
41

42 THE CALLS

Architecture / Interior Design
David Clarke Associates / Juliet Jowett and Julia Laidlaw

Converted in 1991 from a vintage corn mill, 42 The Calls is an architecturally significant part of Leeds' urban renaissance. Along the way it has even helped to coin a new category in hospitality: the "mini grand" hotel, a hip, design-driven alternative to large-scale grand hotels.

Local designers Juliet Jowett and Julia Laidlaw retrofitted the mill with extensive modern conveniences, while placing emphasis on structural aspects of the original basis, including exposed beams and old machinery. The exterior's original brick and wood window sashes have been retained, while clean modern lines dominate public spaces – where they carefully complement the original structural details as well.

Each of the guestrooms has been uniquely designed, playing up charming factory elements such as grain chutes, massive wooden beams and girders. The interior design of the penthouse suite is defined by a high arched ceiling and a smorgasbord of original elements and modernist furniture, with views of the river Aire – a feature common to many other bedrooms as well. Each guestroom features handmade beds and a variety of comfort-enhancing touches – including the quirky idea of offering fishing rods in the rooms that face the river. Beds are covered in Egyptian cotton sheets and sumptuous velvet-backed mohair throws. In addition, a private hatch to the side of each guestroom door not only provides a nifty solution for room service to pass through requested delicacies, but also is evidence of the importance attached to real privacy, form and function in this urban retreat.

→ **Address**
42 The Calls
Leeds LS2 7EW
United Kingdom

HOPE STREET
HOTEL

→ United Kingdom
Liverpool

→ Open
02/2004

→ Rates
GBP 140 –
GBP 350

→ Rooms
48

HOPE STREET HOTEL

Architecture / Interior Design
Basia Chlebik / Maggie Pickles & Benjamin Favier of Archline Design

Hope Street Hotel brings a clean new style to Liverpool's historic Hope Street quarter. The landmark 1860 building, built in the style of a Venetian palazzo, was originally home to the London Carriage Works and now provides the perfect setting for this four-storey hotel.

Interior designer Basia Chlebik dramatically re-interpreted the space, using woods, stone and glass to complement original exposed brickwork, beams and cast iron columns. The sensational highlight is the central oak stairwell: two of the largest pieces of structural oak in Britain support the staircase that runs from the top to the bottom of the building. In place of a common balustrade, taut ropes of illuminated steel pierce the handrails, creating a spiralling pattern.

Guestrooms are individually decorated with bespoke furniture in maple, beech and American black walnut, wich is lit up by daylight pouring in through the picture windows. Creature comforts include king-size beds covered in Egyptian linens, under-floor heating and a wooden bath. Moving into the public spaces makes for a more dramatic communal experience: a sculptural installation of triangular glass slices creates a vertical cut through the restaurant area, which is offset by the charm of local community life figuratively "spilling into" the restaurant through expansive glazing.

→ **Address**
  40 Hope Street
  Liverpool L1 9DA
  United Kingdom

CHARLOTTE
STREET HOTEL

→ United Kingdom
London

→ Open
06/2000

→ Rates
GBP 210 –
GBP 950

→ Rooms
52

CHARLOTTE STREET HOTEL

Architecture / Interior Design
Kit Kemp

Individually decorated rooms and intimate drawing rooms make this London townhouse instantly feel like a home away from home. As with all hotels owned by interior designer Kit Kemp, the emphasis is on perfect detail and her collection of British art.

On entering, a squat Botero sculpture and two abstract landscapes by Welsh painter Roger Cecil create a welcoming atmosphere. Wood-panelled drawing rooms flanked by French stone fireplaces are filled with deliciously overstuffed furniture – and yet more hand-picked artworks such as those by Roger Fry and Vanessa Bell, who were both part of the famous early 20th-century British Bloomsbury group of intellectuals.

Another striking Bloomsbury period painting, a piece of hand made furniture or even a dressmaker's doll might be the eye-catching centrepiece of any given guestroom. Sumptuously patterned fabrics dominate the décor, such as those used to cover the tall, padded headboards. Kemp even came up with an exclusive wallpaper print using

→ **Address**
15 Charlotte Street
London W1T 1RJ
United Kingdom

details taken from an 18th-century Hogarth Press woodcut. Tall windows allow light to pour into the rooms and elegantly frame the views across the London rooftops outside. Catering to the needs of the many business travellers buzzing around the media-hub of North Soho, the architects have created a state-of-the-art private screening room equipped with the latest modern conveniences. A bustling mural taking Charlotte Street as its theme adorns the ground-floor bar and restaurant. Alexander Hollweg's tableau depicts scenes of 21st-century London and was commissioned by Kemp to revive the spirit of Roger Fry's 1916 frescoes *Scenes of Contemporary London Life* with a present-day vision.

CHARLOTTE
STREET HOTEL

→ United Kingdom
London

| COVENT GARDEN HOTEL | → United Kingdom London | → Open 05/1996 | → Rates GBP 225 – GBP 995 | → Rooms 58 |

COVENT GARDEN HOTEL

Architecture / Interior Design
Kit Kemp

Surrounded by 21 theatres, the Covent Garden Hotel has a choice location in the heart of London's entertainment district and is only a short walk to Soho and the Royal Opera House. In the midst of so much drama, the hotel certainly holds its own.

Guests are greeted by grand curtains adorned with English roses at the reception before entering the stage of aged woods, dignified architecture and head-turning interiors by Kit Kemp. Up stone stairs, the generously sized first-floor drawing room has maple-wood panelling, bright upholstery and a stunning writing desk of inlaid wood. For a more intimate retreat, withdraw to the adjoining Tiffany's Library with fireplace and honour bar. This charming hotel also meets modern travellers' needs, offering a gym and beauty spa, three private dining rooms and a private screening room. Brasserie Max, with its pewter bar framed by an arched and paned mirror and featuring cosy banquettes and tucked-away corners, is a favourite pre- or post-theatre haunt not only for Londoners.

The 58 individually designed rooms feature Kemp's trademark creative mixes of abstract and figurative upholstery patterns. Her "canvasses" are demi-canopies, decorative headboards, flowing drapes and even matching wallpaper and bedspreads. Bathrooms are kept elegantly simple in granite and mahogany.

→ **Address**
10 Monmouth Street
London WC2H 9HB
United Kingdom

COVENT
GARDEN HOTEL

→ United Kingdom
London

HAYMARKET
HOTEL

→ United Kingdom
London

→ Open
05/2007

→ Rates
GBP 245 –
GBP 2250

→ Rooms
50

→ Address
1 Suffolk Place
London SW1Y 4BP
United Kingdom

HAYMARKET HOTEL

Architecture / Interior Design
Kit Kemp

HAYMARKET
HOTEL

→ United Kingdom
London

HAYMARKET
HOTEL

→ United Kingdom
London

A bold step away from cookie-cutter minimalism, Haymarket Hotel fuses contemporary and classical references in an ultra-central London location. A landmark building designed by the legendary John Nash, the master architect who developed most of Regency London, including Buckingham Palace, Trafalgar Square and the adjoining Haymarket Theatre, the building comprises fifty bedrooms and two exclusive townhouse properties.

The façade features a dramatic row of columns that run the length of Suffolk Place. Interiors are a remarkable combination that honours the building's noble lineage while updating it with co-owner Kit Kemp's "modern English" interpretation of interior design. The lobby is a clean airy space featuring a large stainless steel sculpture by Tony Cragg and paintings by John Virtue, while the downstairs pool features a spectacular lighting scheme that uses strong contrasts of light and shadow. Sepia-grey oak dominates the lobby, library and conservatory, and hand-picked antiques help jumble past and present. Guestrooms are individually furnished and feature custom pieces, avoiding the "designer formula" look and emphasising rich texture and colour. From their shagreen coffee tables to ivory wood-toned pieces, they evoke contrast and comfort at every level. The two private townhouses have direct access to the hotel's services and facilities. Modern English indeed: Haymarket Hotel continues the contemporary rediscovery of specifically English traditions in their purest form, presented in a resolutely forward-looking context.

HAYMARKET
HOTEL

→ United Kingdom
London

KNIGHTSBRIDGE → United Kingdom   → Open   → Rates   → Rooms
HOTEL   London   05/2002   GBP 160 –   44
                                                          GBP 550

KNIGHTSBRIDGE HOTEL

Architecture / Interior Design
Kit Kemp

On a quiet leafy street not far from Harrods and Harvey Nichols, designer Kit Kemp has added a chic option to her collection of London luxury properties. Each of the Knightsbridge's 44 bedrooms and suites receive the same individual attention from Kemp, who has created a modern English style with both clean neutrals and bold colours.

The drawing room, library and lobby are full of original works by British artists, and the art is never an afterthought: in the centre of the lobby is a sculpture by Carol Sinclair that rises like stalagmites from the floor. Also on exhibit is Kemp's signature mixing of patterns, fabrics and furniture styles to harmonious effect. African sculpture and fabrics, tasselled curtains, unusual sofa legs and a ladder's blue neon rungs add touches of adventure to what could have been a staid library with a sandstone fireplace. Specially designed fabrics by Althea Wilson, fanciful book-lights by Dominic Berning and commissioned ceramics by Katherine Cuthbert are just some of the other elements that make the Knightsbridge unique.

On the first floor, suites have floor-to-ceiling windows, and equally grand oversize mirrors above the fireplace mantels. Rooms on the upper floors reveal a glimpse of Harrods over the rooftops. As quaint and cosy as the guestrooms are, enveloped with layers of eye-catching fabrics – stripes, florals and geometric shapes run riot – they are also fully up to date with high-speed wireless access and flat-screen LCD TVs.

→ **Address**
10 Beaufort Gardens
London SW3 1PT
United Kingdom

KNIGHTSBRIDGE
HOTEL

→ United Kingdom
London

| METROPOLITAN LONDON | → United Kingdom London | → Open 02/1997 | → Rates GBP 350 – GBP 3200 | → Rooms 150 |

METROPOLITAN LONDON

Architecture / Interior Design
United Designers, Linzi Coppick

e
1LB
om

Standing on elegant Park Lane and overlooking Hyde Park's urban oasis with floor-to-ceiling windows, the Metropolitan offers a cool haven for travellers to the British capital. Ten years ago, hotelier and perfectionist Christina Ong's charge to the Metropolitan's architects was strikingly straightforward: "Take a piece of paper and design me a hotel that precisely satisfies the desires and needs of the traveller." Back then, Keith Hobbs and Linzi Coppick of United Designers did away with all the non-essential elements of a "traditional" hotel to create something completely contemporary and yet utterly timeless, beginning with its unassuming and inviting glass-front entrance.

This timeless-simplicity aesthetic lives on in Coppick's solo renovation of the hotel, which was completed in stages ending in 2006. While the property's basic architectural elements and design concepts remain, her re-visitation – a "soft refurbishment," so to speak – was undertaken to provide a subtle update to both public spaces and guestrooms. Carpets, blinds and curtains, as well as some furnishings and the reception and concierge desks, were updated to reflect new trends and to keep pace with modern tastes. Yet the main focus of the new look is the lobby, which in its new incarnation allows for far more flexibility and invites guests to convene for informal, elegant business meetings or relax on voluptuously curved sofas by New York-based designer Vladimir Kagan. The lobby's screen was designed by Coppick herself and is completely movable, offering the choice of accessibility or privacy when open or closed, at the same time as allowing natural light to come through. Both reception and concierge desks appear in bespoke chocolate leather and have sleek surfaces in polished concrete, with the latter now in a new location to liberate space and optimise the already clean spatial feel of the hotel.

Still going strong are the hotel's internationally acclaimed Nobu restaurant and the absolutely happening, members-only Met Bar, an exclusive draw for London locals and guests alike. Also offering sublime respite is the COMO Shambhala spa, where visitors

METROPOLITAN
LONDON

→ United Kingdom
London

METROPOLITAN
LONDON

→ United Kingdom
London

METROPOLITAN
LONDON

→ United Kingdom
London

METROPOLITAN
LONDON

→ United Kingdom
London

can indulge in exquisite Eastern-inspired treatments, such as authentic Thai massage, in a sparely luxurious atmosphere. The hotel's otherwise modernist-cool lounge is decorated with curvy seating and unique wall displays, including a whimsical wall clock and a collection of *objets d'art* and vases set in a recessed, backlit grid that is reminiscent of an art installation.

Vases filled with elegantly simple fresh-flower arrangements echo this look in strategic, dramatic placements in the guestrooms. Here, coffee and cream colours prevail, but are accompanied by the occasional splash of peppermint or mauve. New carpets in the guestrooms are in a rich plum colour dyed especially for the Metropolitan, and bed coverings are in cream faux suede, all perfectly complementing the existing custom-made reddish, pear wood furnishings and carefully selected antique Asian pieces. Upholstery, curtains and carpets are all crafted from pure, natural materials – with the new Finnish-made blinds done in an intriguing paper yarn that elegantly diffuses natural light without distortion. Although all suites now feature Italian-made sofas and have been privy to the general update all around, possibly the most select room to enjoy is the penthouse – a light-flooded space featuring wrap-around windows and surrounded by a Japanese rock garden.

| NUMBER SIXTEEN | → United Kingdom London | → Open 06/2000 | → Rates GBP 110 – GBP 265 | → Rooms 42 |

NUMBER SIXTEEN

Architecture / Interior Design
Kit Kemp

With its wrought-iron balustrades and column-supported porticoes, Number Sixteen's crisp white-stucco Victorian townhouse presents a no-nonsense front in London's South Kensington neighbourhood. Situated just steps from the city's major museums and even Harrod's, only the corresponding house number suggests that this is a hotel and not a private residence.

Like the other Kit Kemp properties in town, Number Sixteen lavishes attention on the designer's penchant for custom fabrics. In each of the 42 individually outfitted guestrooms, textiles are a study in elegant detail: Fabric-covered headboards and armchairs are decorated with cross-stitch patterns or just a handful of stripes; the only accents on Kemp's centrepiece beds might be a bit of white-on-white hand embroidery on the throw. Kemp gets more playtime with window dressing – the two drawing rooms have floor-to-ceiling windows, and some guestrooms have private courtyards that overlook the hotel's stunning English garden. Bathrooms are in oak and granite, and furnishings are a mix of antique, modern and ethnic.

→ **Address**
16 Sumner Place
London SW7 3EG
United Kingdom

NUMBER
SIXTEEN

→ United Kingdom
London

One drawing room is fanciful with warm pinks and large rose prints on the draperies and cushions. A dove mobile hovers near the high ceiling, and on the walls are twin paintings of colourfully winged creatures from Australian artist Allyson Reynolds's *Moth* series. The lobby, however, turns more serious with an array of muted pastels. Number Sixteen's sense of subdued, relaxed modernity is brought to its apex in its conservatory and exquisite private garden, whose reflecting pool, fountain and lush foliage offer the kind of privacy that perfectly tops off a London afternoon.

SANCTUM
SOHO HOTEL

→ United Kingdom
London

→ Open
05/2008

→ Rates
GBP 145 –
GBP 945

→ Rooms
30

SANCTUM SOHO HOTEL

Architecture / Interior Design
Smith Caradoc-Hodgkins / Lesley Pierce

Paying homage to Soho's history as a centre of artistic activity and bohemia, London's Sanctum Soho Hotel is a celebration of edgy glamour that fluidly integrates art and individuality into its design. The spacious lobby is decorated with paintings and "living artworks" – trees whose branches grow through breaks in the metal sheaths encasing them – with scattered Gothic elements providing a touch of antique class. Light oaks, timbers and parquet flooring soften the ambience, as do two elegant fireplaces.

Striking furniture and handmade finishes by London design company Based Upon are interwoven throughout the hotel's lobby and the members bar, endowing both spaces with a discreet seduction perfect for those seeking both decadence and rejuvenation. Upstairs, a rooftop spa sports portholes and wavy railings that evoke a cruise-liner aesthetic, while an in-house cinema references classic odeons.

Lesley Purcell's 30 individually designed bedrooms range from crash pads to vast suites and are based on four different mood schemes. In the Silver Bullet rooms, clean-edged furniture is upholstered with sparkly, 1970s-inspired silver fabrics, whereas fired-earth browns and warm oranges colour the Espresso Deco rooms. Naked Baroque is all about soft beiges, pinks and creams decorated with understated swirl patterns, and plush furniture with touches of gilt. Purple Haze is glam rock, with shades of purple playing off sleek furnishings. No room feels formulaic or looks the same – and the personal touches are accentuated by the use of tasselled keys as opposed to the standard electronic variety.

→ **Address**
18–20 Warwick Street
London W1B 5NF
United Kingdom

| THE FRANKLIN
HOTEL | → United Kingdom
London | → Open
11/2007 | → Rates
GBP 195 –
GBP 1200 | → Rooms
40 |

THE FRANKLIN HOTEL

Architecture / Interior Design
Reardon Smith / J2 Design

Old and new come together in elegant synergy at the Franklin Hotel, which is situated in the heart of London's Knightsbridge. This intimate update of a cosy London inn spans four London townhouses adds and stands as a fine example of classicism brought into the 21st century.

Interiors reflect a truly holistic approach to design and bring a modern harmony to the building's new look: the open lobby overlooks a tree-lined garden and features a proper London aesthetic lightened by liberal use of glass and modish touches. Fired-oak floors, black onyx surfaces and engraved backlit screens complement the use of floral elements solidifying the classic English theme. Created exclusively for

→ **Address**
22–28 Egerton Gardens
London SW3 2DB
United Kingdom

the Franklin by Décor Arts, the wall finish is a mix of plaster and pigment with a pearlescent coating; a rare Chantilly pattern used in the wood floor surfaces is echoed in the stone floors. The reception desk is enhanced by a gold and brass surface with onyx atop the counter. Every surface has been thought out for maximum aesthetic and functional pleasure.

The 40 guestrooms feature the same meticulous attention to detail, unique handcraftsmanship and one-off productions. Walls are covered in a crushed-stone finish; backlit stencilled screens and hand-tufted rugs by Couristan provide a definitively luxurious experience.

THE FRANKLIN
HOTEL

→ United Kingdom
London

THE PELHAM
HOTEL

→ United Kingdom
London

→ Open
09/1989

→ Rates
GBP 155 –
GBP 750

→ Rooms
52

THE PELHAM HOTEL

Architecture / Interior Design
Kit Kemp

On Cromwell Place in London's posh South Kensington neighbourhood, a small white portico ushers you into this distinctive terrace house, where renowned interior designer Kit Kemp has translated the English country-house style into smart city living.

The hotel's interior is richly ornamented from top to bottom, making use of fine details such as tailored fabrics and original artworks. Large-scale oil paintings and carefully chosen antiques, including writing desks and upholstered chairs, further emphasise the property's well-heeled, luxurious atmosphere. Upon entering the drawing room, a mix of pinewood panelling, generous arrangements of fresh flowers and Victorian and Edwardian antiques creates a cosy, eclectic atmosphere. The library is magnificently done in mahogany and, like the drawing room, boasts an impressive period fireplace that invites guests to unwind before a fire that crackles well into the night.

The 52 guestrooms and suites vary according to their architecture – each is an individual creation of the designer, who draws upon her private art collection and enthusiasm for experimenting with colour in adding playful quirks to the traditional ambience. Kemp also juxtaposes bold patterns in her innovative use of fabrics on walls, headboards and soft furnishings. In one guestroom, a fabric-covered headboard with broad, vertical stripes of magenta, orange, brilliant red and chocolate brown provides a warm contrast to the Rococo-patterned red-and-white bedspread. Bathrooms in mahogany and granite feature cast-iron oversize bathtubs. Never settling for the tried and true, Kemp forges a surprising elegance.

→ **Address**
15 Cromwell Place
London SW7 2LA
United Kingdom

THE PELHAM
HOTEL

→ United Kingdom
London

THE ROCKWELL   → United Kingdom   → Open   → Rates   → Rooms
                      London   06/2006   GBP 120 –   40
                                                                    GBP 200

THE ROCKWELL

Architecture / Interior Design
Squire and Partners

Neatly situated in Earl's Court on South Kensington's Cromwell Road – just a hop from Harrod's – this intimate hotel is a new, understatedly luxurious restoration of a four-storey double-fronted Victorian terrace typical for this tony London neighbourhood.

London architects Squire and Partners have redesigned the public spaces to retain their original English charm, restoring the space's intricate wrought-iron banisters, two sweeping stone staircases and Victorian mosaic floor. These elements are, however, juxtaposed with splashes of contemporary design – something already obvious in the meticulously restored façade, where vivid green window reveals and glass balustrades along the hotel's ground level offset original mouldings and details. Once inside, guests can settle into cosy comfort in the lounge, an inviting haven with an open fireplace, walnut bookshelves and lush burgundy draperies, or in One-Eight-

One restaurant, which overlooks a landscaped garden whose lush foliage and teak garden benches offer a rare urban oasis. Within the interior, simple oak furnishings and wallpaper with a palm motif impart a calm modernity.

The floral-wallpaper theme is revisited in an array of variations in most of the 40 guestrooms, each of which also retains original architectural details for a twist on English tradition. Furnishings, however, are clean and pure, and bathrooms splendidly ultra modern, outfitted with glazed power showers and fittings by Philippe Starck and Hans Grohe. Garden rooms have private patios with southern exposure, and the two-level mezzanine suites give the feeling of living in a refined private apartment rather than a hotel. A fusion of contemporary luxury with past charm, the Rockwell's unpretentious design has already attracted clientele.

→ **Address**
181 Cromwell Road
London SW5 OSF
United Kingdom

THE ROCKWELL   → United Kingdom
London

THE SOHO HOTEL   → United Kingdom
London

→ Open
09/2004

→ Rates
GBP 255 –
GBP 2500

→ Rooms
91

→ **Address**
4 Richmond Mews
London W1D 3DH
United Kingdom

THE SOHO HOTEL
Architecture / Interior Design
Kit Kemp

A style feast awaits you: following in the footsteps of their previous London hotel successes, The Soho Hotel is celebrated hoteliers Tim and Kit Kemp's largest project.

The first deluxe hotel in the bubbling borough of Soho was created on the site of a former multi-storey car park. The hotel was built from scratch, yet still respects the original red-brick structure. This shrine to eclecticism boasts unusually large rooms, some of which feature floor-to-ceiling warehouse-style windows. All 91 guestrooms have been lovingly designed and furnished by Kit Kemp. She thrives on the exciting creative tension of not approaching a design with a fixed idea in her mind but rather creating her look in a very hands-on way by mixing, matching and experimenting.

Her contemporary British style is firmly founded on top-notch furnishings and materials in artful combination with a plethora of styles, colours and patterns. "'Eclecticism' means being interested in a lot of things: creating living interiors that aren't boring," says the designer, whose private art collection also enriches the distinguishing personal flavour of the guestrooms and public spaces. It's hard to miss the impressive ten-foot-tall Botero sculpture in the lobby or the mural adorning the hotel's Refuel Bar & Restaurant. She commissioned the latter to illustrate the humble automotive beginnings of the site, which represent a stark contrast to the far-from-humble beauty of the hotel.

THE SOHO HOTEL → **United Kingdom**
London

THE VINCENT

→ United Kingdom
Southport

→ Open
03/2008

→ Rates
GBP 140 –
GBP 695

→ Rooms
60

THE VINCENT

Architecture / Interior Design
Falconer Chester / designLSM

William Sutton, otherwise known as the Mad Duke, established the genteel resort of Southport in the late 18th century. So impressive was his creation that Napoleon returned to France after his exile here and instructed his architect to model the grand boulevards of Paris on the architecture of Lord Street. It is on this thoroughfare that The Vincent presents a series of contrasts – the new property is modern yet classical, functional yet luxurious, businesslike yet relaxing.

Behind the hotel's impressive glass and limestone façade are clean lines, bright walls punctuated with dark timber fixtures and muted, tonal furnishings. In public areas the décor revolves around earth tones, and in the spacious lobby the wood floor dramatically continues right up a white wall, creating a quirky effect. On the first floor, the Grand Galleria function room spans the width of the hotel and has a balcony terrace overlooking Lord Street.

The cool and contemporary theme is continued in the guestrooms, where visual clarity meets luxury finishes. Unlikely textures and dashes of colour break up soft shades of ecru and brown; Wenge wood panelling contrasts with bespoke art-print carpets. The hotel also vaunts a members' bar showcasing a stunning black granite bar, mirrored panels and gold accents. Situated in the heart of England's golf coast, The Vincent captivates golfers, design enthusiasts and business travellers alike. England's North West has landed.

→ **Address**
98 Lord Street
Southport PR8 1JR
United Kingdom

THE VINCENT
→ United Kingdom
Southport

Africa

→

SOUTH AFRICA
CAPE TOWN
JOHANNESBURG
KRUGER NATIONALPARK

METROPOLE HOTEL

Architecture / Interior Design
Kurt Buss / François du Plessis

→ South Africa
Cape Town

METROPOLE
HOTEL

→ South Africa
Cape Town

→ Open
01/2004

→ Rates
SAR 990 –
SAR 2400

→ Rooms
25

Past and present are superimposed at several levels at this newly restored Georgian townhouse on Cape Town's vibrant Long Street, redone to designer François du Plessis's specifications.

The house, constructed in 1870, acquired a Georgian façade in 1905. Over the years it has had terrorising rounds of renovations, excesses now worked into a funky concoction of modern, retro and classic elements. But "Afro glam" rules inside. Red is the dominant colour in public spaces, with all the passion and decadence it implies. Another eye-catcher in the lobby is South Africa's oldest working elevator, which is also a reminder of the building's long history. Despite the clean-lined restaurant Veranda with its un-interrupted view of Long Street, colour contrast is still the rule, and the M-Bar & Lounge goes all out with a poppy-hued lounge area and plush furnishings in a decadent space. On street level, the M-Café, with its chocolate and lime green interior, has a distinctly 1960s feel.

The 25 guestrooms provide a contrast of quiet, textured luxury brought up to modern speed by du Plessis's interior concept, which does away with heavy carpets and ageing wallpaper and instead implements a soothing minimalism. Nonetheless, the original gen-erous floor plan abides, with its large rooms and wide corridors providing an old-fashioned, spacious luxury – one that has been infused with contemporary elegance and an edgy choice of finishes and flavoured with a vibrant style that is indigenous to the land.

→ Address
38 Long Street, P.O. Box 173
Cape Town 8000
South Africa

TEN BOMPAS → South Africa
Johannesburg

→ Open
10/1996

→ Rates
USD 320 –
USD 400

→ Rooms
10

→ **Address**
10 Bompas Road, Dunkeld West
Sandton 2146
Gauteng, Johannesburg
South Africa

TEN BOMPAS
Architecture / Interior Design
Luc Zeghers & Associates

TEN BOMPAS → South Africa
Johannesburg

Johannesburg's Ten Bompas maximises design diversity in a small, modern suite-only hotel. Project architect Luc Zeghers & Associates created an overall atmosphere of warmth and tranquillity in public spaces – whereas the suites sparkle in a glorious marriage of ethnic and Edwardian.

The lobby and meeting rooms feature gracefully curved lines and neutral colours set off by deep-hued cotton prints covering custom furniture, as well as strategically placed African *objets d'art*. This peaceful yet lively space for business or pleasure leads onto outdoor patios, agarden and a pool, belying its location in the heart of Johannesburg's business district.

Each suite was assigned to a different designer following a brief by proprietor Christoff van Staden to provide natural light and outdoor access as well as a fireplace. Fulfilling van Staden's directive to create a "home away from home in Africa," the accomplished designer Gill Butler created an Edwardian suite with sand-hued walls and strongly coloured furnishings embossed with leather, combined with tile and steel for a full combination of comfort and modernity. Other suites blur cultures with military-style canvas and splashes of colour typical of the South African landscape. The ethno-African highlights in couturier Andre Croucamp's silk-enhanced suite provides a different slant than the "ethnic-turned-high-tech" approach taken in the suite designed by the project architects, Zeghers & Associates.

THE OUTPOST   → **South Africa**   → **Open**   → **Rates**   → **Rooms**

Kruger National   01/2003   SAR 2800   12
Park

THE OUTPOST

Architecture / Interior Design
Enrico Daffonchio

The philosophical underpinnings of modern architecture – that it should reflect and harmonise with its surroundings – find their fullest expression in the Outpost. Italy's Daffonchio & Associates designed the hotel for full integration into its environment.

And what an environment it is: Set in South Africa's Kruger National Park, the hotel only minimally encroaches upon the surrounding ecosystem and aims to expose guests to the world around them at every turn. The hotel was designed by Enrico Daffonchio, who has been building with an awareness of energy resources as well as placing a emphasis on integrating materials as graphic elements in their own right since 1966. As a result, visitors experience total immersion in the natural grandeur of Kruger National Park at the same time as taking a part in South Africa's ecotourism movement.

Unlike traditional bush lodges, the Outpost does not strive for a mix of colonial and local traditions but rather creates a totally new vocabulary using the elements of steel, canvas and aluminium in a very contemporary design concept. Foldaway sides allow maximum views. Indeed, the spectacle outside is turned into a real treat by being given a 180-degree panorama of the park from the bathroom, where organically shaped bathtubs sit on polished concrete floors. A more public refreshment is the starkly simple rectangular pool, alongside which the clean lines of the bespoke lounge furniture, covered in blue-and-white striped canvas, give an edge to the abundant natural shapes around it.

The hotel is part of a unique partnership with the local Makulele tribe, which will eventually take ownership and meanwhile benefits from part of the proceeds, as well as gaining quality training in the worldly ways of hotel management and also employment at the hotel. If you happen to need any further reason to go to the Outpost, then that is surely a good one.

/ 543

→ **Address**
Makuleke Region
Kruger National Park
Limpopo Provenience
South Africa

THE OUTPOST   → South Africa
                 Kruger National
                 Park

THE OUTPOST   → South Africa
               Kruger National
               Park

Asia/Pacific

UMA PARO
Architecture / Interior Design
Kathryn Kng

→ Bhutan
Paro

UMA PARO → Bhutan → Open → Rates → Rooms
Paro 2004 USD 250 – 29
USD 1200

UMA PARO

→ **Bhutan**
Paro

Perched on a tree-clad hill in one of the most untouched countries on earth is Uma Paro, a spectacularly unique resort enveloped by towering, snow-capped mountains, uninterrupted pine forests and an ancient mountain culture.

The inland resort stands on a 38-acre site near the town of Paro, one of Bhutan's main cultural centres, located amidst the Paro Valley's rice paddies, wheat fields, scattered villages and snaking rivers. The Bhutanese king's conscious policy of protecting the country from tourism has helped keep the landlocked Himalayan nation refreshingly pristine, and the designers of Uma Paro have embraced this unspoiled quality. The resort itself was designed by traditional Bhutanese artisans in collaboration with Singaporean architect Cheong Yew Kwan; the interiors by Kathryn Kng, also from Singapore, consistently pay homage to cultural context.

Exteriors and interiors are simple, clean-lined and clutter-free. Stone, wood and tiles constitute the primary building materials, which are all handcrafted using age-old techniques. Spacious guestrooms in clean whites, beiges and browns provide dazzling views of the surrounding valleys, forests and mountains. All of the interiors are adorned with indigenous detailing such as carved windows and intricate doors; the white villa walls and shesham-wood furniture are even hand-painted by local artists with brightly coloured flower motifs. Bedcovers made of natural Indian cottons are hand-stitched with designs that reference Bhutan's thriving Buddhist culture. And in further allusion to the geographic milieu, each villa comes equipped with a traditional bukhari wood-burning stove, whose smoke darkens the timber framing above, and around which friends, families and lovers can gather for cosy conversation or contemplation.

Trevor Hillier's understated landscaping gracefully blends with the dramatic surroundings, melting into the blue-pine forests. The design is reminiscent of local Bhutanese villages, with orchards, lawns and ramped pathways following the land's contours. Glades are planted with azaleas, rhododendrons, camellias and hydrangeas, and buildings are scattered on different levels, lending the resort a fluid feel. Below, plentiful fields provide red rice for Uma Paro's Bukhari restaurant, which is housed in a circular pavilion with floor-to-ceiling windows that offer unobstructed views.

There are twenty rooms and nine villas in all, six of which come with balconies and two of which include separate sitting, dining and study areas. The eight one-bedroom villas have luxurious private spa facilities, and the sole two-bedroom villa includes an outdoor stone tub and open-air courtyard with a fire pit. Once the home of a Bhutanese nobleman, the resort's main building serves as the property's visual focus, with peach-flowering roses climbing its walls and plentiful magnolias adorning it inside and out. A yoga room on the grounds overlooks the Paro Valley, its doors opening to mountain breezes. Further into the forest, a 90-square-metre hot stone bathhouse is available for guests, as are an indoor pool with outdoor sundeck, multiple steam rooms, four treatment rooms and a gym. In these buildings, as in all of Uma Paro, clean, locally influenced design incorporates as much sunlight and visible nature as possible, providing visitors with profound access to the magical mountain kingdom that surrounds them.

UMA PARO   → Bhutan
Paro

VATULELE
ISLAND RESORT

→ Fiji
Vatulele Resort

→ Open
05/1990

→ Rates
USD 810 –
USD 2940

→ Villas
19

VATULELE ISLAND RESORT

Architecture / Interior Design
Henry Crawford

→ Address
PO Box 9936
Nadi Airport
Fiji

VATULELE
ISLAND RESORT

→ **Fiji**
Vatulele Resort

Set along a stunning stretch of white sand beach on the western coast of Fiji's largest island, the Vatulele Island Resort is governed by a philosophy of unfussy relaxation and low-key luxury, in line with the resort's "redefining experiences" theme. Televisions, newspapers, phones and money transactions are nowhere to be seen at this South Pacific oasis, and the peaceful atmosphere created through their absence is enhanced by a rustic chic aesthetic and a commitment to personalised pampering.

The Vatulele's 19 spacious *bures* represent a blend of Sante Fe and Fiji design, featuring stucco walls in bright colours or whitewash, sunken living rooms, thatched roofs, native-wood furnishings and terra cotta floors. Each bure features an expansive terrace, private pool and easy access to the ocean. And 50 metres of dense jungle separate each structure from the next as well as provide cover and seclusion. At either end of the property are two additional over-sized villas, The Point and Vale Viqi (the "Grand Bure"), remote mini-palaces that serve as the resort's ultimate hideaways. True to the Vatulele's lavish yet laid-back ambience, their elegant façades boast impressive architectural detailing, while inside the simple, modern furniture stands in pleasant contrast to traditional African sculptures and austere clay vases. Generous windows let in cool ocean breezes and afford stunning lagoon views, and a permanent, full-time villa butler provides for all needs and desires.

For a break from the extreme privacy of these deluxe bures, Vatulele guests can take advantage of the on-site PADI dive facility or attend one of the communal meals hosted by the management in the style of a ship-captain's table. For the more romantically inclined, a private dinner for two can be set at water's edge, illuminated by candlelight and by the stars above, or guests can enjoy private dining in the beach wine cellar.

THE PARK
BANGALORE

→ India
Bangalore

→ Open
02/2001

→ Rates
USD 350 –
USD 600

→ Rooms
109

THE PARK BANGALORE

Architecture / Interior Design
Conran & Partners

Architects Conran & Partners of London took a four-storey former low-budget hotel in the heart of Bangalore's business district and turned it into one of India's foremost design hotels.

Despite looking pristine and basic in white on the outside, Park Bangalore's interiors reflect a transcontinental internationalism without forgetting their Indian roots. A spacious lobby with a glass façade welcomes guests into the hotel. There, as in the rest of the hotel, the design team of the British design icon Sir Terence Conran has balanced modern polished marble floors with local highlights such as an impressive black Indian column that immediately catches the eye. The elevators up to the hotel's 109 rooms are decked out in black leather and each floor has been given its own unique, strong colour scheme.

Aqua tones interspersed with splashes of orange dominate the first floor; lime is prevalent on the next two storeys, evoking an abstract, jungle-like feel highlighted by burnt amber and deep purple. The top floor of the hotel, known simply as The Residence, offers guestrooms resplendent in luxurious silks, leathers and woods, which add a pinch of Eastern opulence and are reserved for those seeking a sumptuous setting in which to relax. Conran & Partners have successfully fused modern European chic with toned-down Indian design characteristics, creating an abundance of style.

→ Address
14/7 Mahatma Gandhi Road
Bangalore 560 042
India

THE PARK
CHENNAI

→ India
Chennai

→ Open
05/2002

→ Rates
USD 290 –
USD 420

→ Rooms
214

THE PARK CHENNAI

Architecture / Interior Design
Hirsch Bedner & Associates, Los Angeles

The Park, Chennai stands on the historic premises of the erstwhile Gemini film studios. The Park Hotels took over this site and built an urban haven of 214 rooms in the heart of the business district of Tamil Nadu's vibrant capital in May 2002 and made sure to artfully weave the site's legacy into the hotel's concept.

Los Angeles architects Hirsch Bedner & Associates have pulled off a hotel that pays homage to its glittering cinematic past without dissolving into Bollywood kitsch. A traditional welcome with giant lotuses is interpreted in a modern way by artist Hemi Bawa. The multi-layered lobby has a screen that displays an ever-changing line-up of projected films. Guests are then beckoned across an atrium area, where the design team has selected pale cream limestone, aqua-coloured leather and cocoa velvets to create a soothing ambience. However, when night falls on the city of almost eight million, the lobby turns from an oasis of calm into one of Chennai's hottest spots, where locals mingle with the international clientele.

The design of the hotel's guestrooms is light and breezy, with modern furniture in muted colours set upon beech wood floors. The understated décor is subtly broken up by light ornamental extravagances, such as the coconut-shell inlaid tables or parchment lamps. Film posters from the 1960s scattered throughout the hotel hallways are among the few direct references to the Chennai's past, ensuring that Hirsch Bedner & Associates' cool, contemporary aesthetic remains the star of the show.

→ **Address**
601 Anna Salai
Chennai 600 006
India

THE PARK
CHENNAI

→ India
Chennai

THE PARK
KOLKATA

→ India
Kolkata

→ Open
11/1967

→ Rates
USD 300 –
USD 500

→ Rooms
149

THE PARK KOLKATA

Architecture / Interior Design
Prakash Mankar & Associates / Made Wijaya / Carl Ettensperger

The perfect example of an eclectic mix, the Park Kolkata has it all – quite naturally blending the stylistic footprints left throughout its history with an artistic contemporary heart.

Built 40 years ago, the Park Hotel group's flagship offers up a truly eclectic blend of styles and interiors, each part of a renovation done by a different team of architects over time. In 2000, architects Prakash Mankar & Associates, Made Wijaya and Carl Ettensperger gave the hotel its current contemporary spice. The concept weaves in past and present traditions of the Bengal region, where the hotel is situated. Elegant modern-colonial spaces blend seamlessly with polished, modern highlights of marble and light wood. Bengali features, such as the embroidery panels, called *Kantha,* are a distinctive feature throughout the hotel and its 149 guestrooms. The embroidery panels repeat their perpendicular pattern on bedspreads and bed frames, and even find expression in the polished marble floors.

Celebrating the region's rich artistic history and taking the hotel into its undoubtedly colourful future, the design team has managed to turn the public spaces into something of a fashionable downtown art gallery. Artworks by well-known Indian artists, including M.F. Husain, Yusuf Arakkal and Bikash Bhattacharya, adorn the walls of the Kolkata, happily sharing the space with bronze and brass sculptures, terracotta and murals created by local artists. Ensuring Bengali tradition and promoting a continuously evolving, up-to-date expression remain just two of the Park Kolkata's most endearing features.

→ **Address**
17 Park Street
Kolkata 700 016
India

THE PARK
NEW DELHI

→ India
New Delhi

→ Open
11/1987

→ Rates
USD 300 –
USD 1200

→ Rooms
220

→ **Address**
15 Parliament Street
New Delhi 110 001
India

THE PARK NEW DELHI
Architecture / Interior Design
Sir Terence Conran & Partners

THE PARK
NEW DELHI

→ India
New Delhi

Gently swinging around a design concept involving the elements of earth, water, fire, air and space – and inspired by the ancient Hindu philosophy of constructing buildings ensuring harmony between man and nature – the 220-room The Park New Delhi offers both rich Indian visual tradition and up-to-the-minute minimalism.

Designed by star British designer Sir Terence Conran & Partners, the arched white lobby plays on air and space. White-glass façades allow natural light in and offer an aesthetic shield from the world outside, and a sheer glass-bead curtain winds from the restaurants towards the marble reception and beyond. Breaking the white are sculptural sofas, rugs and lighting in hot pink, a celebratory colour in India. Elements of fire and water are also represented in the restaurants on the ground floor: guests can sample regional Indian cuisine in the leather- and limestone-clad Fire, or move beyond a curved bronze wall to enjoy creative cocktails and fine wines at Agni's glass-beaded 35-foot-long bar. Water makes a cool entrance at Mist, where another glass-bead curtain frames a palette of blues that segues into the hotel's spectacular outdoor pool.

Taking up the elements of air and space again in the private spaces upstairs, the arched corridors lead guests towards their sleek rooms. Dark-timber floors offset by light-coloured décor are accented in bluish-purple and orange as well as by commissioned works by emerging artists. Rooms vary in size according to the curved architecture, and on the two Residence floors, private jacuzzis and a 24-hour butler ensure every traveller the best in Indian service and comfort. Effortlessly vacillating between past majesty and today's sleek simplicity, the hotel's elemental feel might just be a modern mirror of India as a whole.

ALILA MANGGIS   → Indonesia   → Open   → Rates   → Rooms
                   Bali   05/2001   USD 200 –   54
                                              USD 390

→ **Address**
Desa Buitan, Manggis
Karangasem 80871
East Bali
Indonesia

ALILA MANGGIS
Architecture / Interior Design
Kerry Hill Architects

ALILA MANGGIS → Indonesia
Bali

Given its breathtaking location between the sea and Bali's sacred Mount Agung, it is easy to see why the designers at Kerry Hill Architects chose to enhance a free-flowing interaction between buildings and surrounding nature in their hotel concept.

A traditional *alang alang* thatched roof covers the lobby, where blades of grass are lashed around the wooden rafters to create a very neat and attractive finish. This natural feature is beautifully offset with polished ivory and coloured concrete floors. A latticework screen of diagonally laid stones – a Kerry Hill trademark in the Alila group of hotels – is set up on either end of the lobby. Four two-storey buildings of cool white stone, lit up in geometric beams of warm orange tones after dark, hold the hotel's guestrooms.

Each block is set at a 45-degree angle to the beach, allowing all rooms, and the two luxury suites in the building closest to the sea, to face the blue. On the other hand, the golden glow of lights shimmering against the pool's cool turquoise serves as an excellent visual alternative. Each guestroom building is an exercise in contrasting mass and lightness, and a skilful study of traditional and contemporary examples of Balinese architecture. Kerry Hill's interior design concept is deeply influenced by the colours of the Bali Aga villages located in the nearby valleys. Carefully selected details, including hand-woven textiles and local woods such as coconut, imbue each room with a warmth that is further emphasised by comforting shades of cream, sand and chocolate. Clean lines and an understated sense of luxury all reflect the peace and quiet you will enjoy at this Balinese getaway.

ALILA UBUD → Indonesia
Bali

→ Open
04/1996

→ Rates
USD 250 –
USD 450

→ Rooms
64

ALILA UBUD

Architecture / Interior Design
Kerry Hill Architects

Located on a hillside in Bali's picturesque Ayung River Valley and featuring one of the world's greatest infinity pools, Alila Ubud is an easy choice to make for anyone. But it is the hotel's architectural details, effortlessly mixing natural and modern elements, that literally makes up your mind for you.

Straw roofs skirt smooth plaster walls, terracotta tiles blend into gravel and crushed rock, clearly delineating where the modern world ends and traditional Balinese building begins. For ultimate exclusivity, the experienced team from Kerry Hill Architects developed four Balinese villas – perched on stilts and featuring spacious wooden decks – to house the public spaces. Then there is, of course, the pool, which spreads out to form a severely elongated rectangle until its edges seem to disappear down the terraced jungle hillside.

The guestrooms are housed in eight double-storey blocks dotting the landscape in a manner akin to the setting of a Balinese village, complete with a village centre from which mini piazzas blossom. Individual garden terraces and balconies offer sweeping views of the surrounding volcanoes. The beds, always the centrepiece of the rooms, are made of light wood and covered in subtle hues to draw attention to the astoundingly lush views outside, which trump the myriad of colourful impressions inside. And although it is exquisitely secluded, Ubud is by no means a complete secret.

/ 577

→ **Address**
Desa Melinggih Kelod
Payangan, Gianyar 80572
Bali
Indonesia

ALILA UBUD → Indonesia
Bali

ALILA UBUD → Indonesia
Bali

ALILA VILLAS
ULUWATU

→ Indonesia
Bali

→ Open
2008

→ Rates
TBA

→ Villas
87

→ Address
Jl. Belimbing Sari
Banjar / Dusun Tembiyak, Desa Pecatu
Kecamatan Kuta Selatan, Kabupaten Badung
Bali, Indonesia

ALILA VILLAS ULUWATU

Architecture / Interior Design
WOHA Designs Singapore, Richard Hassell, Wong Mum Sum

One hundred metres above the Indian Ocean, on a limestone cliff on Bali's southern coastline, stands the Alila Villas Uluwatu, a cluster of buildings, terraces, pools and gardens on 13.5 hectares of dry savannah. Drawing inspiration from the land on which it is built, the eco-friendly resort blurs the lines between natural and built environment both aesthetically and technically.

Conceived by award-winning, Singapore-based WOHA Designs, the Alila Villas Uluwatu is the first resort in Bali designed from the ground up to achieve Green Globe certification, the highest level of Environmentally Sustainable Design (ESD) certification. Indeed, its leitmotif is harmony with nature, expressed in everything from the local materials to the seamless transitions between indoor and out. Both WOHA and Cicada Landscape Architects of Singapore used the land itself as design inspiration. Ceilings are of local bamboo, walls are constructed with ulin wood recycled from old telephone poles, and garden walls are made from stone cut from the site.

Spacious villas open to the outdoors and offer ocean views from almost every corner. Their contemporary design is softened by traditional Balinese touches such as planes of wood, water, stone and rattan. All are equipped with private pool, cabana, garden and pavilion. Like the villas, the landscaped flora and fauna celebrate the rocky and arid terrain in which they grow. The paper-thin savannah soil of the Bukit Peninsula was, in fact, Cicada's starting point.

Water conservation is achieved with soakaways and rain gardens. Grey water systems are used for recycling, while heat pumps and exchangers save energy. Even the resort's day-to-day operations are designed to reduce its long-term ecological footprint. With a design that evolves from its location and intrudes upon it as little as possible, the Alila Villas Uluwatu embraces and enhances the experience of the dramatic Bukit landscape.

ALILA VILLAS
ULUWATU

→ Indonesia
Bali

THE ELYSIAN

→ Indonesia
Bali

→ Open
10/2005

→ Rates
USD 195 –
USD 400

→ Villas
28

→ **Address**
18 Jalan Sari Dewi
80361 Seminyak
Bali
Indonesia

THE ELYSIAN
Architecture / Interior Design
Brian Quirk

THE ELYSIAN   → Indonesia
                       Bali

While the Elysian offers the ambience and services of a resort, each of the 28 private villas is a cocoon-like getaway with a private living space, pool and walled garden. Its refined blend of traditional Balinese architecture and modern lines was overseen by the multi-disciplinary Kuala Lumpur-based design firm Quirk & Albakri, which has a long-standing interest in local design and materials. Brian Quirk first came to Southeast Asia in 1990 to study indigenous architecture on a travelling fellowship; Zehan Albakri is a founding member of a trust that preserves Malaysian architecture and crafts, and is a ceramicist as well as an architect.

Their expert use of natural materials such as volcanic stones, raw teak, timber and slate pays homage to the location's rich traditions. The architecture creates a sense of openness and instant transformation in the villas, which equally divide their 140-square-metre expanse between indoors and outdoors. Guests can alter the volumes by sliding a door panel or unfolding an oversize window. The living area opens up to become an extension of the private walled garden; the bedroom's three-metre-high, sliding wood-frame glass doors lead to a modern version of the traditional Balinese *bale*, or patio, which is hugged by an L-shaped pool. Shade is an option under the roof overhang or from a frangipani or coral tree.

Materials were chosen also for their ability to age well, ensuring that the longer the property matures, the more it will seem like a small village that has always been there. At the centre of the resort is a clubhouse containing the public areas, including the bar and restaurant, a gym and a spa, and a library for private dining and meetings. It also houses the reception, which is an open pavilion. A 25-metre pool ends at a trellis-covered waterfall, above which is a small Balinese shrine. Even if guests opt for socialising around this shared pool, they can always pull the linens down around one of the four-poster cabana lounges.

UMA UBUD

→ Indonesia
Bali

→ Open
2004

→ Rates
USD 245 –
USD 490

→ Rooms
29

UMA UBUD

Architecture / Interior Design
Koichiro Ikebuchi

A volcanic mountain chain divides Bali into quiet northern coast and bustling southern coast. In between them lies the small but dynamic town Ubud. At its edge, on a three-hectare site overlooking the Tjampuhan Valley, sits Uma Ubud, a resort designed to feel like a luxuriously comfortable rural home in the Balinese hills. With the river Oos running below it, hilly paddy fields rolling around it and banyan trees and coconut palms surrounding it, Uma Ubud is an ideal place for those in search of bucolic bliss.

The resort's 29 double rooms and suites all come with garden terraces or courtyards overflowing with tropical fauna; three Uma Pool Suites also include a private infinity-edge pool, and the Shambhala Suite has its own private spa-treatment area. Japanese designer Koichiro Ikebuchi's interiors are context-appropriate: uncomplicated, deferential to their natural surroundings and culturally authentic. Spaces are simply and succinctly articulated so that the main focus is the location itself. Panels carved from local woods open rooms to the outdoors, allowing easy access for sunlight, forest scents and chirping birds to flood through guestrooms. Pale stone flooring and lime-washed wood provide a pleasant contrast to the usual dark-wood furnishings and floors of most Balinese hotels. At the same time, fine white mosquito nets and soft linens complement the furnishings' cream and light brown tones. In each room or suite, an outdoor area separates the living space from the bathroom, which includes both a bathtub and an open-air shower. Thatched roofs made from indigenous alang-alang blend in beautifully with the trees enclosing the guestrooms, and those rooms pressed right up to the edge of the Tjampuhan Valley provide dramatic views of green vistas and the snaking Oos. To keep the resort's ecological footprint at a minimum, everything here is designed and built in an eco-friendly manner.

The hotel's communal areas share the aesthetic of their private counterparts: clean, understated design interwoven with indigenous touches and informed by local tastes. The lobby, 25-metre jade green pool and bar are all open, providing a pleasant contrast

→ Address
Jalan Raya Sanggingan
Banjar Lungsiakan, Kedewatan Ubud
Gianyar 80571, Bali
Indonesia

UMA UBUD

→ Indonesia
Bali

to the narrow paths leading to the rooms and running between tall, planted walls. Both the yoga pavilion and the resort's main restaurant, Kemiri, are also open-air and afford some of the property's best views. And Trevor Hillier, a Southeast Asian tropical specialist committed to conservationism, refers to the village site-plans that belong to island tradition in his unobtrusive landscaping.

Dining at Uma Ubud, too, is inspired by Balinese custom: Kemiri meals are prepared with seasonal ingredients from local suppliers, and dishes celebrate local gastronomy while adding a modern spin. The special COMO Shambhala cuisine, designed to boost energy and promote health, uses only raw, organic ingredients full of living enzymes, vitamins and sea minerals, with blended nut milk replacing cow's milk and soy alternatives and honey replacing processed sugars.

Four treatment rooms, a reflexology area, meditation bale, steam rooms and sauna provide plenty of places for calm enjoyment of the tranquil atmosphere. And the resort's location is far enough away from traffic and city bustle for secluded relaxation, but close enough to Ubud for spontaneous visits to its many shops, galleries and restaurants – only twenty minutes away by foot or five by car. Nestled amongst hills and paddy fields but within walking distance of a vibrant town, Uma Ubud invites its guests to admire the best of both urban and rural Bali.

ALILA JAKARTA → Indonesia
Jakarta

→ Open
05/2001

→ Rates
USD 104 –
USD 220

→ Rooms
215

→ **Address**
Jl. Pecenongan Kav. 7–17
Central Jakarta 10120
Indonesia

ALILA JAKARTA
Architecture / Interior Design
Denton Cork Marschall Group Indonesia / Budiman Hendropurnomo

ALILA JAKARTA   → **Indonesia**
                    Jakarta

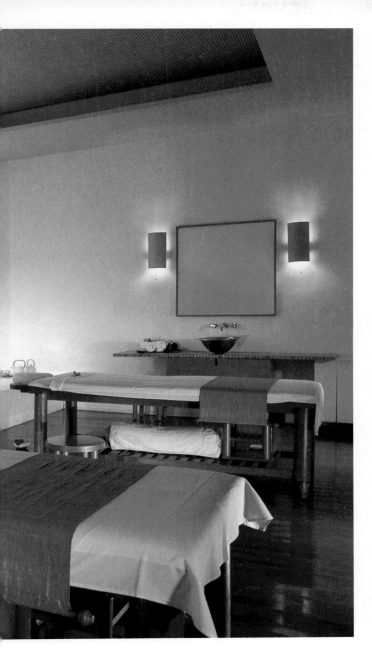

This hotel in the middle of Jakarta's central business district stays true to its name, a Sanskrit word meaning "surprise."

A welcome getaway from the energy of the streets around it, the Alila Jakarta goes for an elegant pared-down look, devoid of any unnecessary ornamentation or excess, throughout its 27 floors. Local architecture firm Denton Cork Marshall chose a minimal feel in design that offers guests a sanctuary from the outside world. The care and attention lavished on its guests are experienced every step of their stay – especially if they are a member of the fairer sex. The concept of the hotel even goes so far as to reserve the entire 15th floor for women only. Steel and local stone, such as Indonesian granite, provide the lobby with a gentle grace that is illuminated by large windows overlooking the garden in the inner courtyard. Chief designer Budiman Hendropurnomo opted to avoid excessive detailing in the lobby, outfitting it with clear-lined geometric furnishings.

An Asian flair is brought to the 215 rooms, which are decorated in a lush palette of dark red tones. Cool heavy cotton is the favoured choice for textiles, contrasting well with the extensive use of local Nyatoh and dark merbau timbers. Offering a pure and abstract design experience, the Alila Jakarta is an exclusive and surprisingly isolated place to replenish your energy reserves.

KEMANG ICON
BY ALILA

→ Indonesia
Jakarta

→ Open
01/2006

→ Rates
USD 150 –
USD 225

→ Rooms
12

→ **Address**
Jalan Kemang Raja 1
Jakarta 12730
Indonesia

KEMANG ICON BY ALILA
Architecture / Interior Design
Sardjono Sani

Kemang is one of Jakarta's chicest neighbourhoods, bursting with art galleries, bookshops, upscale restaurants, luxurious modern buildings and traditional Betawinese residences. At its heart is the Kemang Icon by Alila, an all-suite hotel that combines modern high-tech functionality with innovative design, an urban retreat located in one of the world's busiest cities.

Designed by award-winning Indonesian architect Sardjono Sani, the Icon's lobby is more art gallery than reception area, complete with a thousand-year-old stone sculpture of Ganesh, two French mirrors from the sultan's palace at Surakarta and a painting by Indonesian master Srihadi Soedarsono. Water elements, blue glass walls and numerous artworks are set against a backdrop of cool granite, marble, onyx and metal, imbuing the three-level mezzanine and the hotel's other public areas with a sense of cultural sophistication and visual coherence. A multi-windowed yoga studio provides 360-degree skyline views, as do an elegant rooftop restaurant and a 16-metre infinity pool.

The eight Courtyard and four Edge suites are individually designed and reflect the hotel's primary focus: personalisation. Before arrival, guests choose everything from the type of pillow they would like to sleep on to the aromatherapy scents they prefer. Bathrooms are equipped with personally selected accessories and meals prepared to specific culinary preferences. And in every room, high ceilings, extensive open spaces, large windows and plentiful light provide a peaceful backdrop for flowing silk curtains and modern ivory and teak furniture. The Kemang Icon by Alila presents an effortless convergence of city and sanctuary, bustle and calm.

KEMANG ICON
BY ALILA

→ Indonesia
Jakarta

HOTEL SCREEN KYOTO

HOTEL SCREEN
KYOTO

→ Japan
Kyoto

→ Open
11/2007

→ Rates
YEN 49000 –
YEN 95000

→ Rooms
13

HOTEL SCREEN KYOTO

Architecture / Interior Design
Seki Architect Office / Takuro IGA

Despite its proximity to the ancient Imperial Palace, Hotel Screen Kyoto is a study in modernity. Smooth grey stones and large glass windows fit together in a series of overlapping planes, creating an irregular façade full of balconies, terraces and intersecting rectangles. The reception area inside is clean, straight-lined and unadorned. Natural light floods through the area's floor-to-ceiling windows, providing a pleasant contrast to the all-white walls, sofas and tables, which in turn highlight the lobby's few strategically placed elements of colour – most notably, an elaborate gold and sapphire chandelier and a lacquered red reception desk.

A different artist or designer individually conceived each of Screen's 13 guestrooms and, as such, each has a completely distinctive feel. In his pastel-green Softroom, Sam Liu created a wistful, wool-carpeted dreamland in which all sharp edges are blurred through the use of lavish curtains and discreet filtered lighting. In the Petit Prince Room, Hikaru Kitai decked the ceilings dramatically with a thick layer of bunched-up white spheres that playfully shed light on the white, modern and mirror-filled room below. And in Salvatore Barbiera's room, a low-lying bed rests on a patch carpet that looks like long grass, and dark-wood walls are painted with matt pink and green tree patterns. Most of the rooms feature wood-decked terraces or balconies, which provide stunning views of the rich urban environment below.

Hotel facilities include a restaurant serving Kyoto nouvelle cuisine, a banquet hall, chapel, sky lounge and select shop, where, thanks to a collaboration with local craft artists, traditional Kyoto goods are available for purchase. From one-of-a-kind rooms to handcrafted art pieces, every aspect of the Hotel Screen Kyoto is a celebration of sophisticated and distinctive design.

→ Address
640-1 Shimogoryomaecho,
Nakagyo-Ku, Kyoto, 604-0995
Japan

PARK HOTEL
TOKYO

→ Japan
Tokyo

→ Open
09/2003

→ Rates
JPY 19950 –
JPY 105000

→ Rooms
273

PARK HOTEL TOKYO

Architecture / Interior Design
Frederic Thomas, Dé-SIGNE

In a triangular skyscraper, French interior designer Frederic Thomas has created a sleek hotel concept that connects with the lively milieu of the surrounding business district in downtown Tokyo without succumbing to its fast pace.

The Park Hotel Tokyo features 273 guestrooms spanning the top ten floors of the Shiodome Media Tower. A home to international media organisations and television companies, the tower also offers an oasis of elegant living. Its highlight is an atrium that begins with the hotel on the building's 25th floor and soars all the way up to the 34th. Trees and plants placed on the obsidian and teak lobby floor reflect the Japanese cultural tradition of living in harmony with nature. This soothing haven of trees and greenery, showered in sunlight pouring through the glazed roof, is spun into the atrium as well, which is the tranquil backbone of Thomas' concept.

All the guestrooms face the outside and Thomas' interior design is founded on specially selected off-white furniture, sensuously curvaceous forms and soft fabric covered walls – which creates a softening cushion to the stark backdrop of Tokyo's newer business and cultural centres outside. One of two low-level exits conveniently leads straight to the Waterfront Transit Station, giving guests a quick and easy way to explore the many other facets of fascinating Tokyo.

→ **Address**
Shiodome Media Tower
1-7-1 Higashi-Shimbashi
Minatoku, Tokyo 105-7227
Japan

PARK HOTEL
TOKYO

→ Japan
Tokyo

SONEVA FUSHI &
SIX SENSES SPA

→ **Maldives**
Kunfunadhoo
Island

→ **Open**
10/1995

→ **Rates**
USD 540 –
USD 2885

→ **Villas**
65

→ **Address**
Kunfunadhoo Island
Baa Atoll
Republic of Maldives

SONEVA FUSHI & SIX SENSES SPA

Architecture / Interior Design
Primedaire

SONEVA FUSHI &
SIX SENSES SPA

→ **Maldives**
Kunfunadhoo
Island

In the remote North Baa Atoll region of the Maldives lies a 45-hectare, privately owned island called Kunfunadhoo. It is the home of Soneva Fushi, a luxurious yet laid-back resort fringed by white sand beaches and surrounded by a coral reef lagoon.

Soneva Fushi positions itself as a Robinson Crusoe-style hideaway, and its eco-friendly design supports this claim. Frames, furniture and fittings are all made of indigenous natural materials like wood, bamboo, rope and mulberry bark, while earthy browns, oranges and yellows adorn rustic living spaces decorated in native designs to enhance the "island castaway" effect. But don't let the aesthetic fool you. Offering just 65 accommodations, the resort has spacious rooms fully equipped with the finest modern amenities, though well concealed to preserve the Crusoe ambience. Hairdryers are tucked away in drawers of coconut wood desks, and TVs are hidden beneath water hyacinth baskets. Each villa has an open-air, private garden bathroom, and 32 also feature a private pool. All are located just a few steps from the beach, and dense foliage between them ensures privacy and seclusion. The Jungle Reserve and the Retreats suites even come with a separate tree house, complete with austere bunk bed and wooden balcony. The hotel's timber-framed Organic Garden Restaurant is in itself a tree house: perched four metres above an organic garden, it affords views across the jungle canopy and leads to an observatory tower with telescope, the perfect vantage point for late-night stargazing. Then there is the Six Senses Spa, offering a range of rejuvenating, pampering and holistic wellness treatments to calm mind and body.

In keeping with the theme of "intelligent luxury," the multi-award-winning Soneva Fushi maintains a "no news, no shoes" policy by which mobile phones are checked at the door and guests can feel free to go barefoot through the grounds. Relaxed sophistication is the name of the game at this deliberately down-to-earth resort in the middle of the Indian Ocean.

SONEVA FUSHI &
SIX SENSES SPA

→ **Maldives**
Kunfunadhoo
Island

SONEVA GILI &
SIX SENSES SPA

→ Maldives
Male' Atoll

→ Open
12/2001

→ Rates
USD 985 –
USD 3440

→ Villas
45

SONEVA GILI & SIX SENSES SPA

Architecture / Interior Design
Alysen Construction

SONEVA GILI &
SIX SENSES SPA

→ **Maldives**
Male' Atoll

Scattered around tiny coral islands in the Maldives' North Malé Atoll, Soneva Gili's 45 villas on stilts constitute the first all-water resort in the Maldives. From the island, three jetties stretch across the shallow lagoon waters towards the 29 Villa Suites and 8 Residences, all luxuriously appointed and each located more than 20 metres from the next. Past the jetties, towards the open ocean, there are seven Crusoe Residences as well – enormous bungalows on stilts accessible only by personal boat for those guests seeking the ultimate in privacy.

The villas, restaurant and bar are all built in an environmentally friendly way with renewable forest timber and natural materials. Private rooftops, cantilevered sundecks and carefully placed square "holes" in the oversized villa floors ensure that visitors are constantly reminded of and completely immersed in their watery environs. The interior aesthetic is rustic chic, with creature comforts cleverly hidden in hand-built wooden cabinets and desks. Bathrooms are accessed via an open-air walkway along a private water garden, and a jet bath sits atop the roof of some of the villas. Abundant windows and doors open up to the ocean so that guests can fall asleep to the sound of waves crashing against the coral reef, while thatched, cabana-style daybeds on the private sundecks offer an open-air bedtime alternative.

Even dining here is tightly interwoven with the ocean environment: guests can opt to enjoy a sunny breakfast on their private decks, a pleasant organic garden lunch or a wine degustation dinner in the Gourmet Cellar restaurant. The award-winning Six Senses Spa offers everything one would expect as well as a few features one wouldn't: glass floor-panels beneath the massage tables heighten the sensual aquatic experience. And those wanting to truly dive into some of the world's finest underwater worlds can take advantage of the resort's own PADI diving school. Soneva Gili tops the list of must-do destinations for those in the know.

SONEVA GILI &
SIX SENSES SPA

→ Maldives
Male' Atoll

ALILA VILLAS
HADAHAA

→ Maldives
South Male

→ Open
06/2008

→ Rates
USD 580 –
USD 880

→ Villas
50

ALILA VILLAS HADAHAA

Architecture / Interior Design
SCDA Architects Pte Ltd / Chan Soo Khian

→ **Address**
Ga. Alifu Hadahaa
South Male
Republic of Maldives

ALILA VILLAS
HADAHAA

→ **Maldives**
South Male

Set on a tiny, uninhabited island in the middle of the Indian Ocean, the Alila Villas Hadahaa stands amidst turquoise waters, white-sand beaches and tropical foliage. Designed by architect Chan Soo Khian, the resort features a minimalist modern aesthetic that engages its natural and cultural environment. "My approach responds to the conditions of the context," explains Soo Khian. "My design evokes a sense of place."

This evocation is achieved through fluid transitions between outdoors and indoors and the use of simple local materials throughout. The resort's 14 overwater villas on stilts and 36 beach villas – some with private pools – are understated structures in brown and beige, surrounded on two sides by open-air wood decks. All villas feature two full "walls" of uninterrupted windows that serve to enhance the island's natural beauty by framing panoramic ocean views. In a true reflection of Maldivian spatial sensibilities, the division between living space and ocean – between guest and nature – is obscured by dense indigenous landscaping. This effect is heightened by the natural timber used for the villas' frames, furnishings and finishings, which also serve to imbue the minimalist contemporary design with an indigenous touch. A Maldivian speciality restaurant, cocktail bar, spa (featuring villas with Maldivian thatching, offering a sense of total isolation from the rest of the island), pool, fitness centre, diving centre and library evince a similar fusion of modern and traditional, resort and surroundings.

To ensure that the resort is gentle on the landscape, Soo Khian used environmental impact studies to guide his design. The Alila Villas Hadahaa thus features energy-efficient lighting and heating systems, rainwater harvesting devices and waste treatment plants that minimise pollution of the island and corals around it, which happen to offer some of the best reef snorkelling in the seas.

ALILA VILLAS   → **Maldives**
LONUDHUA   South Male

→ **Open**
06/2008

→ **Rates**
USD 780 –
USD 1180 –

→ **Villas**
50

→ **Address**
Ga. Dhaalu Atoll
South Male
Republic of Maldives

ALILA VILLAS LONUDHUA

Architecture / Interior Design
SCDA Architects Pte Ltd, Chan Soo Khian

ALILA VILLAS
LONUDHUA

→ **Maldives**
South Male

Just north of the equator, in the Maldives' South Huvadhu Atoll, is a flat, 6.6-hectare piece of land known as Lonudhuahutta Island, home to the Alila Villas Lonudhua. Sparkling azure waters, white-sand beaches and tropical greenery serve as the backdrop to this resort, whose architecture literally melds with its surroundings. Here, design pays homage to natural beauty in a blurring of boundaries, an eco-friendly concept and hints of Maldivian aesthetic sensibilities.

In 50 spacious villas – most with private pools – architect and designer Chan Soo Khian created elegant, uncomplicated living spaces meant to immerse guests in the tropical environment. Constructed of natural Maldivian timbers, the villas sport a clean-lined contem-porary design, ornamented with indigenous details that express respect for the local culture. Generous windows frame expansive ocean views, fusing villa with water, guests with nature. Further homage to the natural surroundings is paid in the form of rainwater harvesting mechanisms, pollution-minimising waste treatment plants, energy-saving electrical systems and landscaping that reinforces the existing foliage.

Facilities include two restaurants, a spa, a pool that extends into the ocean, a culinary school and an in-house oceanographic centre where marine biologists can conduct research on the unique un-derwater environment surrounding the resort. In addition to the superb snorkelling and surfing opportunities, the researchers' pres-ence affords guests the opportunity to attend lectures on the effects of global warming and tsunamis on the fragile Maldivian atolls in a truly unique interaction with the stunning environment.

NEW MAJESTIC
HOTEL

→ Singapore
Singapore

→ Open
01/2006

→ Rates
USD 130 –
USD 400

→ Rooms
30

NEW MAJESTIC HOTEL

Architecture / Interior Design
DP Architects Pte Ltd, Ministry of Design Pte Ltd, Colin Seah

Of all the fetching traits of this small Chinatown hotel, a revamp of a historic hotel on a street once known for housing wealthy men's mistresses, the most captivating is its sex appeal. The shop-house façade blends in perfectly with the neighbourhood; inside the hotel, however, juxtaposition of antique and modern, interior and exterior, pushes boundaries.

A balance of exhibitionism and voyeurism pervades the New Majestic, whose 30 guestrooms are individually crafted visions by a diverse group enlisted by designer Colin Seah of Ministry of Design. His core crew of four designers plus nine Singaporean artists came up with four room "typologies" that could conform to varying configurations. The thematic result: Mirror, Hanging Bed, Loft and Aquarium rooms. In the Hanging Bed and Loft rooms, women's faces painted in larger-than-life murals keep an eye on beds and baths beneath them. An antique iron tub is placed centre stage in the Aquarium room. In the hotel's restaurant, swimmers crossing over the ceiling's portholes onto the outdoor pool's floor cast shadows on diners' tables below.

→ **Address**
31–37 Bukit Pasoh Road
Singapore 089845
Singapore

Whereas the cantilevered beds and murals are signs of long-term commitment, DP Architects gave the lobby a transient feel. Sliding glass doors welcome guests into a high-ceiling space with walls, column supports and floors in white terrazzo which emphasise spaciousness. The original ceiling was left with an uneven surface of concrete, wood and peeling plaster, and the vintage chairs – from owner Loh Lik Peng's personal collection – are lightweight and easy to rearrange. But this transience is given a stellar anchor: the hotel's sensuously curved white staircase ensures permanence and pays respect to the surrounding shop houses, many of which have outdoor spiral staircases. In line with the glamour of the time – the 1950s – when the hotel was just The Majestic, Westerners can imagine a line of chorus girls descending the stairs with ostrich feathers and satin gowns, à la Hollywood musical director Busby Berkeley.

NEW MAJESTIC
HOTEL

→ Singapore
Singapore

THE LALU → Taiwan → Open → Rates → Rooms
Nantou County 03/2002 NT 15500 – 98
NT 72800

→ **Address**
142 Jungshing Road
Sun Moon Lake
Nantou County, R.O.C 555
Taiwan

THE LALU
Architecture / Interior Design
Kerry Hill Architects

An idyllic 26,000-square-metre resort located near the aquamarine waters of Taiwan's Sun Moon Lake, The Lalu is a fine example of sensitive cultural design.

Drawing inspiration from both Taiwanese and Japanese tropical building, Kerry Hill, an Australian widely recognised as one of the most innovative architects working in the Asia-Pacific region, has endowed the former summer retreat of Chinese president Chiang Kai Shek with an abstract yet timeless allure. Gorgeous blue-stone villas and elegantly austere wooden terraces channel the calm of nearby Lalu Island, once a holy place for the indigenous Thao people. The sleek designs of teakwood, iron, blue gravel and glass revolve around the Zen principles of serenity and purity. True to the Zen aesthetic, the gentle buildings in no way dominate the wild hillside so lovingly enveloped by lush evergreen broadleaf trees and white frangipanis; instead, all attention is drawn towards the misty lake.

A clever module that employs seven unobtrusive light changes throughout the day, depending on the intensity of the sunlight, subtly combines the area's natural lighting with the hotel's indoor illumination. Created by shadow specialist Nathan Thompson – a lighting professor at the University of Melbourne – it provides magnificent mood lighting in the 98 rooms, suites and lakeside villas.

At The Lalu, paramount emphasis is placed on reflection – in a metaphorical and a literal sense – with every available surface seeming to glint or sparkle, be it large-scale window, lily-pad-speckled pond or canal-length swimming pool. This harmonious balance of modern architecture, soothing luxury and organic splendour illustrates why Taiwan is such a highly desired, and disputed, land.

THE LALU

→ Taiwan
Nantou County

METROPOLITAN
BANGKOK

→ Thailand
Bangkok

→ Open
10/2003

→ Rates
USD 240 –
USD 2000

→ Rooms
171

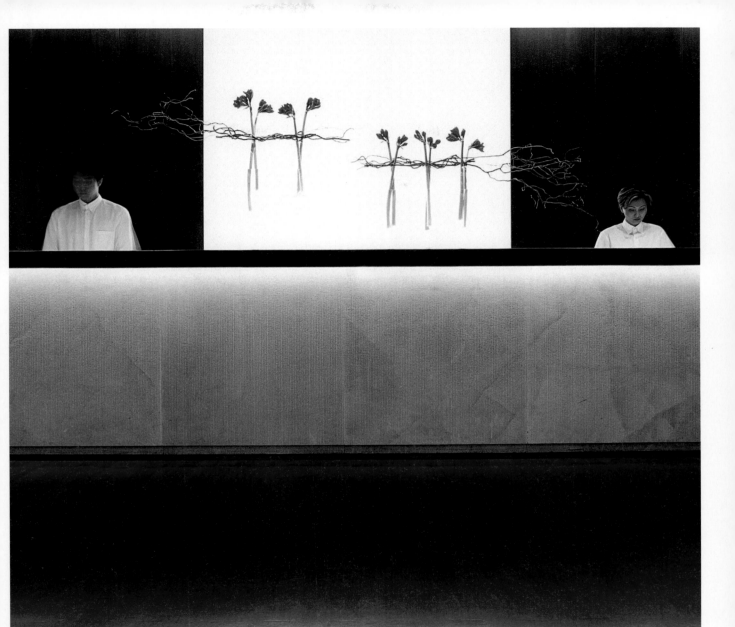

→ Address
27 South Sathorn Road Tungmahamek,
Sathorn, Bangkok 10120
Thailand

METROPOLITAN BANGKOK

Architecture / Interior Design

Kathryn Kng

METROPOLITAN
BANGKOK

→ Thailand
Bangkok

Despite its location in the heart of Bangkok's central business district, minutes away from the city's main shopping and nightlife areas, The Metropolitan Bangkok is set at a remove from the hustle and bustle of the busy Asian metropolis, tucked away on a quiet side street. The hotel's modern design capitalises on this separation, creating an atmosphere of secluded relaxation with its smooth colours and calm spaces, while simultaneously acknowledging its glittering urban environs. Like its sister hotel in London, The Metropolitan Bangkok is original without being aggressively avant-garde, both a haven and a cosmopolitan setting at the same time.

From staff uniforms by Japanese fashion label Comme des Garçons to interiors by prominent Singaporean designer Kathryn Kng, The Metropolitan's aesthetic is a celebration of clean-lined, understated sophistication. In the public spaces as in the 171 guestrooms, Kng draws attention to the inherent beauties of her materials, which range from natural wood to hand-blown glass, and through them expresses a respect for both Eastern and Western design sensibilities. Thus the lobby embraces a surprising combination of rare Thai makha wood and oxidised brass panelling, and the penthouse suites feature both bamboo coffee tables from northern Thailand and highly contemporary Artemide Melampo table lamps.

Throughout the hotel, shapes are minimalist and modern, while detailing includes carefully sourced Asian antiques. On the 11th-floor corridor that leads to the penthouse and presidential suites, for example, Chinese "horseshoe" chairs, an antique teakwood carving and temple bells are on display. Meanwhile, all rooms feature modernism's soft hues and clean lines juxtaposed against wood flooring, natural teak beds, richly pigmented Thai silks and one-of-a-kind artworks by Natee Utarit, an exciting young local artist. Mosaic and limestone bathrooms, floor-to-ceiling windows,

METROPOLITAN
BANGKOK

→ Thailand
Bangkok

METROPOLITAN
BANGKOK

→ Thailand
Bangkok

generous interior spaces and, in some rooms, private terraces complete the picture of luxurious urban retreat. The result is rooms that are international in look, but comfortably local in feel.

The communal areas feature ample and airy volumes flooded with light manipulated by London-based lighting architects Isometrix. The hotel's sleek glass exterior opens onto a vast lobby featuring white leather sofas set upon a scarlet carpet and enormous glass vases holding crimson flowers. In the lobby as in the three event rooms, creams, browns and cool whites are highlighted with dashes of colour – a blue cushion here, a red lacquer finish there.

At the hotel's headline restaurant Cy'an, diners can enjoy seafood-centric Mediterranean meals with Moorish influences either indoors or outside, at tables set on the open-air veranda that flanks the outdoor pool. Like Nobu at The Metropolitan London, Cy'an is not just a place for guests to dine in fashionable privacy, but a gourmet destination in its own right. For an after-dinner drink, there is The Met Bar, open only to guests and members. Like its British counterpart, The Met attracts a dynamic crowd of urbanites with its sleek club chairs, wine-dark walls, moody lighting and London-trained cocktail mixologists.

For those in search of wellness and rejuvenation, the 1,200-square-metre COMO Shambhala Urban Escape spa comes equipped with ten treatment rooms, a hydro pool, steam room, yoga studio and gym. Nearby, the organic restaurant Glow serves fresh foods only, in the form of snacks, light meals and enzyme-rich energy juice drinks. Its intimate soft lighting and lemon-grass-filled steel planters set the perfect backdrop for a healthy, feel-good dining experience. As in the rest of the hotel, a simple, fresh design finds the perfect balance between peaceful serenity and vibrant urban energy.

ALILA CHA-AM → Thailand
Petchaburi

→ Open
12/2007

→ Rates
THB 5600 –
THB 15800

→ Rooms
79

ALILA CHA-AM
Architecture / Interior Design
Duangrit Bunnag

Once a fishing village, the charming coastal town Cha-Am on the sunrise side of the Gulf of Thailand is the tranquil location for Alila Cha-Am, a new and sophisticated beachside resort. Blending seamlessly into the natural environment of white-sand beaches and leafy palm trees, it achieves a balance between privacy and connection that is embodied in every element.

Designed by pre-eminent Thai architect Duangrit Bunnag, the resort redefines the tropical getaway with clean lines and strong geometric forms, softened by a palette of wood, limestone and subtle marble finishes for an understated yet unforgettable impression. Arrival at Alila Cha-Am is designed to evoke an immediate sense of destination, leading up a grand stairway to a large open-air lobby. From here, the breathtaking view unfolds across a rooftop reflection pool and a maze of inter-connected pathways, private terraces and courtyards towards the ocean horizon.

/ 647

→ **Address**
115 Moo 7 Tambol Bangkao
Amphur Cha-Am
Petchaburi 76120
Thailand

Seasonal shrubs and ambient lighting create harmony with nature's seasons and cycles. The studied intertwining of paths with open spaces heightens the sense of strolling through one's own private gardens, while providing an effortless transition between experiences, from casual chic to exquisite elegance.

The resort has two signature restaurants – rooftop and poolside – and a relaxation and wellness zone at the Chill Pool and Red Bar, whose earthy colour scheme is a soothing reflection of the natural surroundings. Guestrooms are intimate hideaways that provide both indoor and outdoor seclusion. Private terraces and hammocks abound, and the ultimate suites – the pool villas – serve as full-scale sanctuaries complete with private garden, pool and terrace. All rooms are spacious and offer unobstructed views, and each features a unique rain shower that brings the outdoors inside and enhances the sense of communion with nature.

ALILA CHA-AM   → Thailand
Petchaburi

650 / ASIA / PACIFIC

KIRIMAYA
GOLF RESORT SPA

→ Thailand
Khao Yai

→ Open
12/2004

→ Rates
USD 260 –
USD 945

→ Rooms
60

→ **Address**
1/3 Moo 6 Thanarat Road
Moo-Si, Pakchong
Nakornratchasima 30130
Thailand

KIRIMAYA GOLF RESORT SPA

Architecture / Interior Design
ISM & Februar Imag

Two hours from Bangkok, on the edge of the mountainous Khao Yai National Park, the Kirimaya is a hotel project by ISM & Februar Image, a Bangkok-based collective of architects, interior designers and landscape designers.

The two-storey property and spa that extends across several outdoor and indoor pavilions is more urban chic than tropical rustic, yet still makes use of local base structures and materials. A thatch-covered walkway and antique door carved in India lead to the central residence with a gently peaked cedar shingle roof and local travertine stone floors. The bamboo daybeds in the guestrooms are just one example of the hotel's successful combination of Asian touches and innovative designs in natural materials such as silks and earthy woods. For a truly unique experience, camp in luxury in one of the four villa-tents made from treated canvas. Floors are covered in bare polished concrete and rugs are created with water hyacinths. Spaces are sensuously separated by sliding panels and flowing curtains. Guests staying in the villa-tents enjoy their own private indoor spa pool and outdoor deck.

Bounty from the resort's organic gardens goes into sumptuous dinners cooked up at the Acala Restaurant, which is modelled on a northern Thai rice barn. Open on three sides, it seems to float on the adjoining lake and provides a breathtaking, panoramic view across a challenging 18-hole golf course exclusively designed by golf legend Jack Nicklaus.

KIRIMAYA
GOLF RESORT SPA

→ Thailand
Khao Yai

MUANG
KULAYPAN
HOTEL

→ Thailand
Koh Samui

→ Open
12/1996

→ Rates
THB 5600 –
THB 21870

→ Rooms
42

MUANG KULAYPAN HOTEL

Architecture / Interior Design
M.L. Archava Varavana

Architect M.L. Archava Varavan has given this Samui island retreat a design blending Zen form and southern Siam style, creating a setting where the décor bathes the senses in serenity.

The unassuming, two-storey hotel has no lobby, but an intriguing sunken meeting area that faces North Chaweng Beach. Through hallways suffused with light, staff members dressed in black chiffon and silk glide by, serving morsels on dishes edged with ancient Thai numerals. The beachfront hotel is named after an ancient Javanese city in which a royal love story unfolded and became the legend of Prince Inao. Mother Nature is echoed in the architectural layout, carefully blending in with the rise and fall of the surrounding landscape and providing a sometimes not-so-gentle lesson in humility with Thai roofs so low you must lower your head to enter the rooms. But a look higher up the roof is rewarded by sculptures of seven children holding sacred objects in their hands – the perfect symbols of innocence, simplicity and joy. The hotel's atmosphere tenderly reminds us of these elements without aspiring to excess.

All rooms feature balconies and batik-covered beds, some of them on raised platforms, Japanese style. Interiors are exquisitely simple, with the bathroom's glossy black tiles perhaps the most extravagant touch. All furnishings of raw materials were also designed by Varavan and made on-site, except for the bed in the VIP Inao room, which once belonged to King Rama IV of Thailand, the architect's great-great-grandfather.

→ **Address**
100 Moo 2, Bophut
North Chaweng Beach, Koh Samui
Suratthani 84320
Thailand

THE LIBRARY

→ Thailand
Koh Samui

→ Open
01/2007

→ Rates
THB 12000 –
THB 15000

→ Rooms
26

THE LIBRARY   / 657
Architecture / Interior Design
Tirawan Songsawat

THE LIBRARY

→ **Thailand**
Koh Samui

Noble intentions and high-end execution come together at the Library, which is located on Thailand's Chaweng Beach in Koh Samui. Architect and designer Tirawan Songsawat has designed an elegantly minimalist structure around a lush environment, preserving a heritage property on the beach while only minimally intruding on its ecology and aesthetics.

The hotel's 26 suite-studio complexes are distributed over an expansive 6,400 square metres of beachfront. These complexes consist of a suite space on the ground floor and a studio upstairs, which comes complete with an ocean view and a special bonus – a view of the old-growth trees that have been spared from the developer's bulldozer. The vegetation includes skilfully interspersed artwork and sculpture to provide a balance of nature and art, offsetting a bold colour scheme in which white, red, black and grey predominate: the Library's exterior and bookshelf-lined library is white, the swimming pool red, the restaurant grey.

Interiors feature the same ultraminimalist colour palette and some of the lowest-slung, most rectilinear furnishings and layouts around. In fact, "How low can you go?" serves as a design mission: rooms are organised around descending levels of furnishings, from wall fittings to beds, down to sofas and, finally, tables that sit mere inches above the ground, making the floor the centre of attraction. Vivid red settees contrast with plain walls; flat-screen televisions are for once a design element and complement living quarters that come close to creating a two-dimensional ideal. But this is not cold minimalism, as exotic touches, wood shutters and golden Buddhas provide a balance. It all makes for a minimally distracting context in which to enjoy the panorama.

THE CHEDI
PHUKET

→ Thailand
Phuket

→ Open
1995

→ Rates
THB 8700 –
THB 54300

→ Rooms
108

THE CHEDI PHUKET

Architecture / Interior Design
Edward Tuttle

Amid coconut palms and gently rolling slopes, The Chedi Phuket elegantly sashays down a varied landscape to rest along the island's finest white sandy beach at Pansea Bay.

Paris-based architect and designer Edward Tuttle not only specialises in tropical destinations but also actually lives part-time in Thailand. Tuttle transformed this retreat rather than build it from scratch, as it had been created from the floor plan of a previous resort. In collaboration with Bangkok-based designer Jon Vorapot Somton, Tuttle combined local materials and traditional Thai designs with modern functionality. All roofs are thatched, and the resulting geometric forms are contrasted with the naturally irregular shapes of the surrounding palms, shrubs and rocks. A Western design approach is apparent in the choice of a herringbone floor pattern for the library and the restaurant's dramatic lighting. The latter's umbrella-shaped ceiling is in wood, but floors and walls are in grey granite, as are the steps that lead to the hexagonal pool. Lustrous black anthracite, the hardest of all coals, makes up the pool's tiling and creates dramatic reflections at night.

To permit views of the ocean as much as possible, pavilions and public buildings are linked by elevated walkways. Upon entering the private areas, which consist of pavilions and cottages, guests find that all furnishings have been tailor-made and especially designed to underscore The Chedi Phuket's unique style. Cottages literally invite the surrounding nature inside through their shuttered doors and are likewise covered in teak floors and filled with earth-coloured fabrics. A private veranda and secluded sun deck nestle each cottage beautifully into its own patch of paradise.

→ Address
Pansea Bay, 118 Moo 3
Choengtalay, Talang District
83110 Phuket
Thailand

X2 KUI BURI

→ Thailand
Prachuab
Khirikhan

→ Open
12/2007

→ Rates
THB 7000 –
THB 42000

→ Rooms
23

→ **Address**
Moo 13, Ao Noi
Muang District
Prachuab Khirikhan 77210
Thailand

X2 KUI BURI

Architecture / Interior Design
Duaungrit Bunnag Architect Limited

Drawing inspiration from local materials such as mountain rock, sea pebbles and even the ocean's liberating openness, X2 Kui Buri, Thailand, is a veritable love letter to the purest aspects of design. Located on 3.2 hectares of beachfront on the Gulf of Thailand, the resort's design focuses on the interplay of natural light and soft indoor illumination, uninterrupted sea views and the combination of indigenous materials with smart lines.

Designed by Duangrit Bunnag, the visionary behind Costa Lanta, the aesthetic at X2 Kui Buri is feng shui meets utopian community. In Bunnag's world, simplicity does not mean minimalism – he uses the word to mean uncomplicated and spatially economical. The 23 villas are largely identical, yet a certain individuality lies in their proximity to the bordering terrace, adjacent pool and neighbouring garden areas. The resort makes use of invisible wall design – what is a craggy structural stone wall to one villa appears as a fence partition to another. This novel approach to spatial perspective comes from Bunnag's belief that ease, comfort and nature are the only things needed to create a stylish atmosphere that is both visually stunning and impossibly relaxing.

The purity extends to the surrounding property, where the landscape displays unique flora and fauna native to Thailand and the tranquil white-sand beach is untouched by development. A smooth wooden boardwalk modelled after a maze runs throughout the resort, the idea being that each turn will reveal a different stunning panorama. In a land better known for its bright lights and fast-paced instant gratification, X2 Kui Buri provides the perfect environment to regain serenity and equilibrium.

X2 KUI BURI

→ Thailand
Prachuab
Khirikhan

666 / ASIA / PACIFIC

EVASON
ANA MANDARA &
SIX SENSES SPA
AT NHA TRANG

→ Vietnam
Nha Trang

→ Open
09/1997

→ Rates
USD 252 –
USD 535

→ Villas
74

EVASON ANA MANDARA & SIX SENSES SPA AT NHA TRANG

Architecture / Interior Design
Eva Shivdasani, Bernhard Bohnenberger

Set in 26,000 square metres of private tropical gardens leading to a stunning white-sand beachfront in Nha Trang, Evason Ana Mandara Hideaway – "ana mandara" is a Vietnamese phrase that means "beautiful home for guests" – was created to reflect the feel of an authentic Vietnamese village.

Interior designers Eva Shivdasani and Bernhard Bohnenberger have embellished the entire resort with artefacts collected from around the country. The Pavilion Restaurant is adjoined by an indoor bar that extends into a bamboo courtyard sheltered by a majestic banyan tree.

Here, a kind of local simplicity creates an utterly peaceful, serene atmosphere. Guestrooms are 74 gracefully designed, low-rise cottages with red tile roofs, and each room offers a magnificent view of the sea or gardens from individual verandas. The floors are tiled and furniture is made of native woods, such as ironwood, pyrinka and nyatoh as well as rattan. Beds are given that familiar tropical look by being softly draped in essentially useful mosquito nets. Even bath toiletries have a distinctly local flavour, with salves made from Vietnamese herbs. The unique experience of the infinity pool overlooking the ocean is enriched by its idyllic setting in the tropical gardens, and the Six Senses Spa offers sublime relaxation with a slightly more international flavour. Enjoy this total immersion experience in Vietnamese style.

→ **Address**
Beachside
Tran Phu Boulevard
Nha Trang
Vietnam

EXPERIENCE
DESIGN HOTELS™
CALL TO MAKE
YOUR RESERVATION

GENERAL CONTACT DETAILS
RESERVATIONS ------ → +49 30 420 940 21
WEBSITE ------------ → WWW.DESIGNHOTELS.COM
E-MAIL ------------- → RES@DESIGNHOTELS.COM
GDS CODE ----------- → DS

SHOULD YOUR COUNTRY NOT BE LISTED PLEASE USE
THE GENERAL RESERVATION NUMBER, BUT BE AWARE THAT
INTERNATIONAL CALL CHARGES WILL APPLY.

PLEASE NOTE:
THE TELEPHONE NUMBERS FOR THE COUNTRIES LISTED
ARE FOR CALLS MADE FROM WITHIN THAT COUNTRY ONLY.

FOR GENERAL ENQUIRIES
ABOUT DESIGN HOTELS™
DESIGN HOTELS AG
CORPORATE HEADQUARTERS
STRALAUER ALLEE 2C
10245 BERLIN
GERMANY

PHONE ------------- → +49 30 420 940 40
FAX --------------- → +49 30 257 698 96
E-MAIL ------------ → RECEPTION@DESIGNHOTELS.COM

INTERNATIONAL TOLL FREE
RESERVATION NUMBERS

→

AMERICAS
USA -------------------------- 1 800 337 46 85
CANADA -------------------- 1 800 337 46 85
BRAZIL --------------- 0021 800 37 46 83 57
ARGENTINA -------------00 800 37 46 83 57

→

EUROPE
AUSTRIA ---------------- 00 800 37 46 83 57
BELGIUM --------------- 000 800 37 46 83 57
DENMARK -------------- 00 800 37 46 83 57
FINLAND ------------- 990 800 37 46 83 57
FRANCE --------------- 00 800 37 46 83 57
GERMANY -------------- 00 800 37 46 83 57
GREECE -------------- 00 800 49 12 90 54
HUNGARY ------------------- 06 800 1 22 36
IRELAND -------------- 00 800 37 46 83 57
ITALY ---------------------00 800 37 46 83 57
NETHERLANDS -------- 00 800 37 46 83 57
NORWAY --------------- 00 800 37 46 83 57
PORTUGAL ------------- 00 800 37 46 83 57
RUSSIA --------------- 810 800 20 74 10 49
SPAIN ----------------- 00 800 37 46 83 57
SWEDEN --------------- 00 800 37 46 83 57
SWITZERLAND ----------00 800 37 46 83 57
UNITED KINGDOM ------- 00 800 37 46 83 57

→

AFRICA
SOUTH AFRICA ---------- 09 800 37 46 83 57

→

ASIA/PACIFIC
AUSTRALIA ---------- 0011 800 37 46 83 57
CHINA ------------------ 00 800 37 46 83 57
HONG KONG ----------- 001 800 37 46 83 57
JAPAN ---------------- 0041 800 37 46 83 57
NEW ZEALAND --------- 00 800 37 46 83 57
SINGAPORE ----------- 001 800 37 46 83 57
THAILAND ------------- 001 800 37 46 83 57

→

TERMS AND CONDITIONS APPLY

→

PUBLISHED BY
DESIGN HOTELS AG
STRALAUER ALLEE 2C
10245 BERLIN
GERMANY

PRINTED IN GERMANY BY
GRAFISCHES CENTRUM CUNO
GMBH & CO. KG
GEWERBERING WEST 27
39240 CALBE (SAALE)

DISTRIBUTION
DGV – DIE GESTALTEN VERLAG
WWW.DIE-GESTALTEN.DE

CREATIVE DIRECTION
MICHAEL SCHICKINGER

ART DIRECTION
JOHANNES SCHWARK

ILLUSTRATION
NIMH / WWW.NIMH-LAB.COM

PRODUCTION
PATRYCJA PAPPELBAUM
BERND NEFF

EDITOR IN CHIEF
KIMBERLY BRADLEY

LAYOUT
MICHAEL SCHICKINGER
JOHANNES SCHWARK
EVA RÖHRIG

PREPRESS
GREGOR ORLOWSKI

AUTHORS
KIMBERLY BRADLEY
RACHEL B. DOYLE
GEOFFREY GARRISON
CHRISTINA KNIGHT
JENNA KRUMMINGA
TOBY ALLEYNE-GEE
STEPHAN HOTTINGER-BEHMER
RALPH MARTIN
ANDREAS TZORTZIS
ANJA VOPARIL

COPY EDITOR
GINGER A. DIEKMANN

GLOBAL MEMBERSHIP SERVICES
ASTRID BACHMANN

PRODUCTION ASSISTANTS
MAUREEEN GENNER
SVANTJE WERNER
PETER BARTON

THANKS TO
ALL OUR MEMBER HOTELS
AND ALL THEIR PHOTOGRAPHERS
WORLDWIDE
ESPECIALLY UNDINE PRÖHL

ISBN 978-3-89955-204-1